Raising
ROVER

Raising ROVER

Breed-by-Breed Training from Afghans to Yorkies

JUDITH HALLIBURTON

ST. MARTIN'S PRESS NEW YORK

In the "Breeds" section I speak of using a breed of dog for what he was bred to do. I wanted you to know that I am not an advocate of hunting for sport. It's just that some of the sporting breed skills are so keen that these animals aren't happy just as pets.

A THOMAS DUNNE BOOK.
An imprint of St. Martin's Press.

Design by Bonni Leon-Berman

Library of Congress Cataloging-in-Publication Data

Halliburton, Judith.
    Raising rover / by Judith Halliburton.
        p.   cm.
    "A Thomas Dunne book."
    ISBN 0-312-14399-0
    1. Dogs—Training.   2. Dog breeds.   I. Title.
SF431.H2155   1996
636.7'0887—dc20   96-6091
                                            CIP

First Edition: June 1996

10 9 8 7 6 5 4 3 2 1

To Douglas G. Krous, my teacher then and now.

Special thanks to Jeanne Newlin, my mother, and Bobbie Leach, my sister, for all of their love and support.

Thank you to Carl Koski, of Easykind Behavioral Training.

Contents

Introduction

To judge by the number of books on my shelf and the number in the bookstores, there are as many methods of training a dog as there are breeds. These methods have obviously worked for the authors, or they wouldn't have written their books. What makes mine different? Read on, Human, and the difference will become clear very quickly. With this book, you're not going to just train your dog, you're actually going to *raise* Rover. (From this point I will refer to you as "Human" and your dog as "Rover.") You're going to be working at your dog's level of understanding. I'm going to teach you how to think the way Rover might, instead of applying human emotion and thought. Most people underestimate their dog's ability to understand, so Rover's potential is never tapped. I'm not going to let you do that.

Rover can develop a vocabulary of 300 to 350 words (some say up to 500). Most people don't realize that their dog understands words they use all the time. If I'm in the kitchen cooking and I say "Oops!" my dogs, Larri and Fido, are there in seconds. The same goes if I'm in the kitchen cooking and I say "Dammit!" (I didn't realize how often I say "Dammit" in the kitchen until my parakeet picked it up.) Have you ever had a dog that you had to spell around? Some dogs understand not only the word but its spelling, so the word has to be changed altogether.

It never ceases to amaze me how often and in how many ways we make fools of ourselves in front of our dogs. For example, knowing that Rover understands a word like "walk" or "ride," some people, not wanting Rover to think he's going out, will whisper. Rover, somewhere in the room, is thinking: "They're whispering again, which usually means I'm not really going to go for a ride or walk. Oh well, I'll get to go as soon as they say it out loud."

The acuteness of Rover's hearing is beyond our imagination. In Scotland, Border Collies are used for herding sheep. It appears as if the dog's doing everything by himself, but he's taking whistle commands from the shepherd—and the shepherd is a mile away. (While I'm on the subject, if Rover is wearing more than one tag on his collar, please tape them together so they don't jingle. We get used to that sound. Rover does not. It's a constant low-level source of irritation. I've seen something as simple as taping the tags calm a dog down. I had one client who roughened up the backs of the tags and then glued them together, face out, using epoxy.)

To help you work with Rover at Rover's level of understanding, I'm going to give you information about both dogs in general and particular breeds of dog. Some traits and behaviors are basic to all dogs, while others are specific to a breed of dog. For example, Shelties are barkers, Basenjis are not; Dobermans have natural protective tendencies, Poodles do not. You'll be amazed at how much easier it will be to socialize, train, and understand Rover when you know why he does or doesn't do this, that, or the next thing. I'm not going to cover every breed, but I will discuss the popular ones. If you have one of the more uncommon breeds, you'll still find the general information helpful, and you'll be able to use the "breed type" (Terriers, Sporting Dogs, Hounds, and so on) to understand your dog. If you have a Mixed Breed dog and you know what the cross or crosses are, read the information on those breeds and you'll be able to recognize definite breed personality traits.

If you're reading this book before getting Rover, let me take a moment to tell you a few things that might help. If you're undecided about what kind of dog to get, call a veterinarian, *not a breeder.* (Sorry, breeders, but most people need a disinterested opinion.) Veterinarians don't see just the health of a dog; they see personality traits, what happens when a breed of dog gets too popular, what a breed is like under stress, and much more. I was a veterinary technician for twelve years, and in that time I learned more about the different breeds than I ever have in formal study. The Rottweiler is a good example. This breed is what I call a macho dog or a manly man's dog. When we first started seeing Rottweilers they were mellow, sure of themselves, and easily able to handle stress. Rottweilers were bred to herd; when all the other herding dogs went off duty, Rottweilers stayed on to guard. They have natural alpha tendencies, which means leadership qualities, which means Rottweilers are naturally aggressive. Unfortunately, Rottweilers became very popular. When that happens, breeding is taken out of the hands of good conscientious breeders and taken over by "backyard breeders," who raise dogs for money and pay absolutely no attention to disposition. Within two years of the breed's becoming popular we started seeing three-month-old Rottweiler puppies that wanted to bite our hands off. I'm not saying you can't get a good Rottweiler anymore; you can. But pay attention to breeding. A veterinarian can give you invaluable advice on almost any breed of dog you're thinking about getting.

I'd like to make one other point. If you're reading this before getting a dog for your child, *please don't get one when the child is very young.* Perhaps you're thinking, "They can grow up together." But if you get a dog when your child is two, Rover will be middle-aged to old by the time the child is old enough to want a dog as a companion. Over the years I've come to the conclusion that most children are seven to ten years old before they can enjoy a dog.

Okay, Human: Let's raise Rover.

Raising
ROVER

HOUSETRAINING

Here you are with Puppy Rover, and already confused about housetraining methods. There is no such thing as a foolproof method, nor is there any guarantee that Rover will be housetrained in a certain period of time. I don't understand how authors can get away with saying their method will have your puppy housetrained in seven days, or ten days, or whatever the promise is. There are too many variables—breed, age, where the puppy came from, your environment . . . What works with one breed or personality may not work with another.

I've found that most people become impatient and frustrated when a puppy isn't housetrained within a certain period of time. To avoid this trap yourself, don't even consider a time frame. I've known puppies that were completely housetrained in three days, while others took sixteen to twenty-two weeks. If housetraining takes longer than you expected, don't blame it on Rover. Believe me, your dog isn't being stupid or naughty, he's just confused.

The housetraining method I'm about to describe is based on young-canine behavior and designed to help you have a better understanding of Rover's needs and behavior. I'm hoping that with this better understanding, the housetraining process will be easier for you and the new life in your house. As you're reading, please refer to the breed list. Find your breed and read about housetraining it.

The first thing you need to do is make a commitment to concentrate on housetraining. Be prepared to keep a watchful eye on Rover. Keep in mind that he has just left an environment in which all his needs, including cleanup, were taken care of.

Begin by confining Rover to one room, as close to the family as possible. Dogs are very social animals. A puppy that's confined in an area away from you will make every effort to get your attention or try to get to where you are. Don't give Rover complete run of the house too soon.

He will be overwhelmed by the vastness of it all, and housetraining will take much longer.

If you have a Doggy Door, lock it. You may be thinking that if the puppy can go in and out at will he'll housetrain faster. Exactly the opposite occurs. You can't expect Rover to know the difference between "inside" and "outside" when all that separates the two is a Doggy Door flap or a door frame.

The area where you want Rover to eliminate should be off-limits except when he needs to be there. That way he'll more quickly associate the area with its function. (Playtime and exploring there can come after Rover is trustworthy in the house.) It will also help Rover learn more quickly to let you know in some way that he needs to be let out. If, after a while, you find him sitting at the door crossing his legs and waiting for you to read his mind, you might want to help him by hanging something from the door that will make a noise—bells, for instance. Show him that if he hits the bells with his paw or bumps them with his nose, they'll ring and you'll open the door. You can also stand with him at the door and say, "Do you want to go out?" in an excited voice, and as soon as he paws at the door or barks, quickly open the door.

During the training period don't think of eliminations in the house as setbacks; use them to teach. Rover has to learn what "wrong" is before he can begin to understand what "right" is. *Do not overpraise or overdiscipline.* If too much emphasis is placed on either praise or discipline, the whole training process can become traumatic and frustrating for both of you. You want to communicate your pleasure or displeasure to Puppy Rover as quickly and simply as possible.

Begin to establish the difference between "good Rover" and "bad Rover." When Rover has an elimination in the correct area, *point* to it and *verbally* praise him. When you find an elimination in the house, *gently* take him to it, *point,* and *verbally* discipline. Don't worry if he doesn't appear to be interested in what you're pointing to. He knows the smell of his own urine or stool, and his peripheral vision is 70 percent better than humans'. If you point to the elimination rather than dispense a lot of hands-on praise or discipline, Rover will begin to understand what he is being praised or disciplined for. *This is the only time you will ever discipline Rover for something after the fact.* (I'll explain this in

Chapter 3.) If the elimination is obviously recent, there is no point in immediately rushing the puppy outside. Having already eliminated, he won't understand why he's suddenly outside. If you catch him in the act, though, don't hesitate to scoop him up and rush him out. And you should certainly remove him from the area before you clean it up. This is essential to housetraining. You don't want Rover to see you clean up his messes! The mother dog cleans up for the litter until they're weaned, as well as teaches general cleanliness. If she doesn't continue, the previous owner, pet shop, or kennel takes over. Rover won't be the least bit bothered by having eliminations in the house if he knows you'll clean up after him.

In beginning the housetraining process, take advantage of the first couple of times Rover urinates indoors by taking a clean rag and soaking up as much of the urine as possible. Take the rag outside and stake it in the ground in the area where you want Rover to use. Every time you take him out, take him to that spot. The smell of his own urine will help to establish the reason for being there.

Indoors, the converse applies. To keep Rover from having a favorite spot to eliminate in the house, you need to neutralize the odor. The best and least expensive way to do this is with white vinegar and water. Use it on all indoor surfaces. Don't underestimate Rover's ability to smell his own urine; nor should you assume that because a surface is hard it isn't porous.

When to Be on the Alert

AFTER MEALS. Put Rover on a set feeding schedule as quickly as possible. Putting food in his bowl and letting him have access to it all day can create physical and behavioral problems later on and will make it impossible for you to watch for after-mealtime patterns. After meals is a particularly tough time for puppy and Human. The tendency is to rush Rover out as soon as he's finished eating, but you'll spend ten to fifteen minutes waiting for him to eliminate. You become impatient and decide he doesn't need to go, so you bring him back in the house and within minutes he has an "accident." To avoid this situation, watch Rover closely after meals to learn his patterns. You've probably noticed that he spends some time looking for a place to urinate, but very little time looking for a place to defecate. Ask your veterinarian about the best foods for puppies and avoid any foods described as "all natural" or containing no preservatives *while you're housetraining.* Also, stay away from the "semi-moist" foods. All these foods are high in salt, which will make Rover drink more water.

AFTER PLAY. Whether Rover has been entertaining himself or playing with his Human, he will begin to look for a spot to eliminate as soon as play stops.

AFTER SLEEP. Even if it's just a nap, when Rover wakes up, he'll stretch, he'll more than likely yawn, and then that little nose will begin to search for a place to go.

AFTER CHEWING. Watch Rover after he's been chewing (rawhide chews, toys, you . . .) for any length of time. The digestive system is stimulated by chewing, just as it is in us when we chew gum or suck on hard candy. (Veterinarians have told me there can be problems with the small rawhide chew sticks, especially in large puppies. When the rawhide softens, the dog may swallow it whole and choke.)

I realize that people have busy schedules and keeping such a close eye on Rover may be almost impossible. But you've committed yourself to this new life, and he requires your time and attention. Since my method is based on young-canine behavior and Rover's ability to understand, you will be able to get him housetrained even with a busy schedule. It will just take a little longer. I hope you're going to have Rover for a very long time. When you think of the years of enjoyment ahead, the time spent housetraining is very short. (It just *seems* like forever.) Most dogs want to please their Humans, so if you let Rover know what pleases you, he will try very hard to do just that. When housetraining seems to draw out way too long, it isn't because Rover is stupid and it isn't because he is "mad at you." Nor is he being naughty or willful. He's very simply confused. If you can't find the area of confusion, you may have to start over from scratch. Just hang in there, Human; you'll get him housetrained.

Don't rub Rover's nose in his urine or stool!

Refer to your Rover's breed for special instructions on housetraining.

2

AS ROVER GROWS

A lot of growing and changing and learning is going to happen over what, in human terms, is a short period of time. For instance, I've found that humans often become discouraged with a pup when they find that he wants nothing to do with this petting and affection stuff. As soon as a hand begins to pet, he starts chewing on the hand to play. Not to worry: Rover will learn to love affection when he's about four months old. Before that, he'll just eat, sleep, and play. Tell your kids to be patient; Rover will sit on their lap when he's a little older.

At six months old Rover is the equivalent of about ten human years old. At eight months old he's going to start going through his teens. I heard you groan. We can be thankful that this period lasts only a few months.

DOG'S AGE	HUMAN'S AGE
6 months	10 years
8 months	13 years
10 months	14 years
12 months	15 years
18 months	20 years
2 years	24 years
4 years	32 years
6 years	40 years
8 years	48 years
10 years	56 years
12 years	64 years
14 years	72 years
16 years	80 years
18 years	88 years
20 years	96 years
21 years	100 years

All kinds of decisions have to be made as soon as you bring Rover home. Read on, Human, and I will walk you through them.

One of your very first concerns will be "Where is Rover going to sleep?" I want you to put serious thought into this decision. If at all possible, the spot you choose should be wherever you want Rover to sleep for the rest of his life. There are a few general things you need to take into consideration. I'm a believer in Rover having his own corner of the world, and you can create that for him easily. First of all, be aware that Rover will very quickly begin to understand everything about your scent as positive. So take a small blanket or towel that you don't mind giving up, rub yourself down completely with it before bathing or showering, and put it where you've chosen for him to sleep. It will become his very own "blankie." Where this corner of the world is depends on a number of things: whether he's an indoor or outdoor dog; what other animals live with you; whether you have an apartment or a house with a yard. Rover's potential size is an important consideration as well. If he's a Great Dane, you might not want to get him started in your bed. If he's a Toy Poodle, you don't want to put him outside. Also consider the weight of his coat. If Rover has a heavy coat, he'll want to sleep someplace cool. If he has a light coat, he'll prefer someplace warm.

I've found over the years that people are embarrassed to admit their dog sleeps with them. Don't be embarrassed. Rover is a loving member of your family. But if you are a very restless sleeper and Rover is really small, it might be safer for him to sleep in his own bed in your room. If he does sleep in your bed, I recommend he sleep below your knees, as close to the foot of the bed as possible. This will avoid behavior problems later. (See Chapter 6.)

A paragraph back, I mentioned Rover's coat. I want to tell you about the importance of respecting it. A lot of people think that because Rover is "just a dog" he should be able to get along okay outside. Wrong! Another assumption people make that I cannot understand is that if Rover is a big dog he can be outside: "He'll grow a winter coat." Wrong again! A Great Dane doesn't have a "winter coat" to develop any more than a Chihuahua does.

Pay attention to what Rover is all about. If you find, after a while, that he doesn't like the spot where his bed is, notice where he prefers to sleep. As long as this spot is not out of the question, respect his wishes. If your Rover meets the criteria for being an outdoor dog, make sure his corner of the world is close to the house, and preferably close to the room where most of the human activity takes place. If you have a doghouse for him and you set it some distance from the house, it's very unlikely he'll use it even in bad weather.

Who's Going to Feed Rover?

I bring this up just in case you got Rover for your children with the agreement, "If we get you a puppy, you have to take care of him. He's going to be your responsibility. Understand?" The kids are nodding their heads eagerly, bright-eyed with anticipation at having a puppy of their very own. As a parent, I learned over many looonng years that those bright excited eyes meant the kids weren't hearing a word I said. They just knew when to nod. Parent, was that you who fed Rover this morning? When asked "Did you feed Rover this morning?" your child may have answered in one of many ways: "I was going to, but I didn't have time before school"; or "I will in a minute, as soon as I get off the phone"; or "I can't feed Rover and do my homework too, jeez." Dear, dear Parent, life will be so much easier if you accept the possibility that within a month, maybe less, *you* will be the one feeding Rover.

By the way, if for any reason you want Rover to bond strongly to one person in the household, that person should not only be the one to feed Rover but should be the primary caretaker for the first few months. This goes for playtime and training as well.

DOS AND DON'TS OF DISCIPLINE

From now on, use "No" only when Rover is doing something you don't ever want him to do again. Under all other circumstances you will use a command.

This applies whether Rover is a puppy or an adult. Remember his vocabulary potential; "No" is a very serious command, and if it's not used correctly he will become desensitized to it. Then it will no longer be of any use to you. If Rover is chewing on your hands, you don't want to tell him "No," because there will be times when you play with him with your hands. If he gets into the garbage, it's a "No." But if he barks, don't tell him "No," because there will be times when it's okay for him to do so. If he growls, and it's not in play, that's an absolute "No." When you use "No" correctly, you don't put Rover in the position of being a constant repeat offender.

Many uses of "No" are idiosyncratic. Some people can't stand being licked by a dog (with my social life I take it where I can get it), so for their dog licking would be a "No." Rover can learn that something is okay to do with you, but not with your spouse.

Whenever you use a command, it puts you in control. Let's say, for example, that Rover is sniffing something on the coffee table that is none of his business. Tell him, "Rover, leave it alone." Hearing his name will make him look at you. Consequently he leaves whatever it is alone, so you say, "That's a good boy." After you've established this command, you'll be able to put something on the coffee table and tell Rover "Leave it alone" before he thinks about sniffing it.

If he gets hold of something you don't want him to have, *don't chase.* Stay low-key, and as you take the object from him say, "Rover, give it," or maybe "Rover, drop it." Then say, "Thank you. Good boy." (You don't have to say "Thank you." I find I say it automatically, because I was raised to say it if anybody gave me anything. I even said "Thank you" once when a police officer gave me a traffic ticket.)

You'll notice I don't limit commands to just one word. If you do that you limit the vocabulary you can use with Rover. With my dog Larri I can say, "Lar, let's go to work," "Lar, that's none of your business," "Lar, trust me on this one." To her each of these sounds like one long word.

From now on, the command to stop jumping will be "Off." "Off" will mean that all four feet are to be on the floor. If Rover's jumping on you, gently push him down and say, "Rover, off." If he's on furniture and you don't want him there, push him off and say, "Rover, off." If he's jumping on the door—"Off"; on the counter—"Off"; on company—"Off."

Please don't do the knee-in-the-chest bit. Dogs aren't stupid. They figure out quickly that if they come at you face to face, you're going to put your knee up. So Rover won't jump up at you face to face; he'll jump at your side or your back. You can't stick your knee in a small dog's chest anyway. Another popular method to stop jumping is to step on the dog's toes. I've never been able to figure out how to do that without turning it into a dance, which Rover will love. Besides, this method can't work on small dogs either.

The reason I'm going into such detail on this one command is that often we actually train our dogs to jump, although we're not aware of it. When you first brought Rover home, he was a cute little puppy; he put his paws on your leg and you gave him some petting. Even when he got a little older and his paws came up higher, you still gave him affection. Now you have a seventy-five-pound dog hitting you in the chest and you're saying, "Judi, I did not train him to do that!" If Rover is no longer a small puppy and you're just beginning to introduce "Off," he will let go of the jumping behavior slowly. That's why you'll want it to mean "All four feet on the floor."

Here is an example of a command putting you in control. If company comes over and you know Rover is going to get excited and may jump, you can say, "Rover, stay off" before those front feet ever leave the ground. If you *don't* mind Rover jumping on you, use a second command that means it's okay to jump, like "Rover, jump" or "Rover, up here."

I must repeat: If Rover is grown-up when you start training him not to jump, it's going to be a hard task. It is going to take patience and time.

When your dog's barking becomes irritating, you go to the door or window and yell, "Rover! *Stop that!* Rover, *no!* Rover, *be quiet!*" Watch Rover the next time you do that. You'll notice his barking will become more rapid, his tail will wag faster, and he'll turn to look at you, saying, "Boy, did you see/hear that, too?"—because you're out there barking right along with him. Don't yell. Use a command that means "Stop barking." I use "Quiet"; my sister says, "Hush"; parents with a lot of kids say, "Shut up." The command is entirely up to you.

There can be as many commands as there are situations. Commands can cover things you want Rover to do as well as things you don't want him to do.

There is only one proper way to discipline a dog physically. That is the way a bitch does it with her litter: She grabs a pup by the scruff of the neck, gets at least the front paws up, and gives it a firm shake. When you physically discipline Rover, get him by the scruff of the neck, give him a firm shake, and say, "Rover, *no!*" Don't lecture, saying, "Rover, how many times have we talked about this? I keep telling you not to do this, and you ignore me. Shame on you, Rover."

Don't be surprised if Rover screams and cries like you're killing him. You haven't hurt him physically. He knows he's being disciplined, and that's why he's crying. If he fights you, *by all means hang on to him until the fighting stops or he attempts to show submission.* If he fights you when you discipline him and you don't remain in control, you're going to have serious behavior problems from that point on.

The best way to physically discipline and introduce the seriousness of "No" is to actually set Rover up to misbehave. If there's something you know he's going to do and you don't want him to do it, set the stage. That way, you're prepared to make the correction, and there's no doubt in Rover's mind about why he's being disciplined.

To introduce Rover to commands that are replacing "No," you're going to use an aluminum can (a soda or beer can, or the like) with a few pennies in it. Don't use tin cans, and don't use pebbles. You may have heard about "penny cans" before, but I'm going to tell you how to use one so it works. Perhaps you were told to shake the can. Shaking the can is going to get you nowhere. If all you do is shake the can, it amounts to making a threat, and you can't threaten a dog; he'll take advantage of you every time. (In the same boat are people who discipline their dog with a newspaper. The dog does something wrong, so the owner says, "You're in trouble now. I'm going to get the newspaper. You've really had it as soon as I find the newspaper. . . . Honey! Have you seen the newspaper?" The dog sighs and thinks, "Oh well, it usually takes her about forty-five seconds.")

You're going to put five to ten pennies in the can and actually throw it. Not to worry—you're not going to throw the can at Rover, just in his direction. With just a few pennies in it, even if it does hit him it's not going to hurt him. By throwing the can you're going to create what's called an orienting response, which means you're going to get his attention *suddenly!*

To apply this to Rover: Let's say, for example, that he's barking. You throw the can and immediately say, "Rover, quiet." The barking will stop, and you will say, "That's a good boy." Teaching "Quiet" is the same as teaching "Sit"; you have to hang in there with the command. For example, if Rover starts barking again right away, clap or throw another can and say, "Rover, I said *quiet.*"

You're going to notice that Rover has a good healthy respect for the can, because when you first start throwing it he's not going to have a clue where it came from. He's going to think Chicken Little threw it. After you've thrown the can a few times, you'll notice that just the sound of the can will stop him in his tracks, but either drop it or throw it anyway.

You're going to want more than one can. We don't want a fear response, we just want a startle effect, so you'll notice there are going to be times you'll throw the can and Rover will turn to look at it like, "Hmm. What was that?" He may even pick it up and run off with it. You don't want to have to say, "Excuse me, Rover, I need to pick up my can so I can throw it at you again." Have another can handy. You're going to use the can only long enough to introduce a command. Once Rover understands "Quiet" or "Back off" or "Settle down" or whatever, you no longer have to use the can. You'll be able to say "Rover, quiet" and the barking will stop on command.

Puppies become desensitized to the can very quickly, so be sure to use it correctly, and don't overuse it. And please don't let children use the can. A penny can in the hands of kids from two to twenty becomes a lethal weapon. They seem to go through a power surge as soon as the can is in their hands.

POSITIVE REINFORCEMENT FOR NEGATIVE BEHAVIOR. This one's a biggie. I really want you to understand this one. The best example I can give arises when you visit someone who has a large dog. You walk in and Rover's nose goes straight for your crotch. That's embarrassing, so you put your hands on the dog's head in a loving manner and say to your host: "You have a lovely dog. I didn't realize he was so big." The whole time your eyes are pleading, "Please do something with your dog." This is also embarrassing for the owner, so he gets hold of Rover gently and says, "Now, Rover, you stop that." Then he really makes you feel wonderful by saying, "I'm so sorry, I've never seen him do that before." (Oh, sure.) Anyway, what it comes down to is that Rover is getting affectionate handling. So he's thinking, "I just love it when company comes, because they always pat me on my head." What should the owner do? The owner should tell Rover, "No!" and pull him away immediately. Believe me, the guests will appreciate the owner taking control. We may find it unpleasant and embarrassing, but sniffing the crotch is to Rover what a handshake is to us.

Another example: Chasing and being chased are a natural part of what a dog is all about, so if Rover gets hold of something you don't want him to have, *don't* chase him saying, "Rover, what do you have in your mouth? Rover, give me that. Rover, drop it. Honey, Rover has my shoe and he won't drop it. See if you can catch him when he comes around the corner." The instant you begin to chase, Rover looks around and thinks, "Wheeeee! Yeeeeeaaaah, you can't catch me, you can't catch me! Boy, I love this chase stuff." From the day you bring Rover home, if he gets something you don't want him to have, approach him slowly, and casually take whatever he has while saying "Rover, drop it" or "Rover, give." If you refuse to chase from the very beginning, taking something from him will be relatively easy.

I had a client whose Cocker Spaniel, Mischief, loved nothing more than to grab Carol's reading glasses for the sheer pleasure of being chased. I don't know how many times I said, "Carol! Don't chase her! As soon as she knows you're not going to chase her, she'll get bored with the game and leave your glasses alone." Carol had to have her reading glasses replaced seven times. The store gave her her eighth pair free. For some reason that embarrassed her, and she stopped chasing Mischief. She hasn't had to get new glasses since.

Yet another good example of positive reinforcement for negative behavior arises when you're in your yard landscaping. Before I explain what happens, I first have to tell you that all dogs are completely and totally narcissistic; they're sure the entire world revolves around them. Now, with that in mind, consider a scenario that goes something like this: You're on your knees planting a rosebush. Rover runs over to play, because he can't imagine any other reason you'd be down on your knees. He licks your ear, jumps on you, tries to bite your hands, and in general makes a nuisance of himself. You push him away, he comes right back; you push him away again, he comes right back; you pick something up to throw for him so he'll leave you alone, but he comes right back. After the rosebush is safely in the ground Rover thinks, "Gosh, we had fun putting that thing in the ground. It would really be neat if I dug it up so we can put it back in again." My advice is to leave Rover out of the landscaping plans until he's an adult. Keep him inside while you're planting. Otherwise you may encourage digging and chewing.

As you can see, it's easy to give positive reinforcement for negative behavior in many different ways without being aware of it. Try to see things from Rover's point of view and you'll have a better idea of how to avoid some of these problems.

Dogs can also create their own positive reinforcement—for example, when they go through what I call a power surge. Take dogs who chase cars, for example. Rover chases the car, and the driver of the car becomes concerned, so he slows down. Rover has absolutely no idea that the person in the car slowed the car down. No—he's thinking, "Am I bad, or what? I can slow that sucker down, and I can make those red things in the back go on and off."

PUPPY CHEWING AND DESTRUCTIVE CHEWING

The difference between puppy chewing and destructive chewing is the item chewed! There are a few things about "puppy chewing" that I'm going to scream at you until there is absolutely no doubt in my mind that you understand their importance. Far too many dogs are abandoned, left at dog pounds, or banished to a chain outside because of chewing.

I've found that most people are surprised to find that Rover is chewing well beyond six months of age. Actually, chewing is a very important part of a dog's daily routine. Instinct tells him to chew for teething and to strengthen jaw muscles, but he also chews to relieve tension, frustration, boredom, and loneliness. Chewing is a source of entertainment, too. Keep in mind that Rover can't take in a movie, color in a coloring book, watch a favorite show on TV, or play with the kids down the street. Sooner or later, he is going to chew things you don't want him to. I can't give you a surefire way to avoid this, but I can give you some good constructive advice on how to avoid serious destructive chewing, and I can help you understand its causes.

A myth I'm going to dispel right away is "Don't give Rover a shoe to play with, because it'll teach him to like shoes." That's nonsense! If you give Rover a shoe to play with and he gets another shoe it isn't because you taught him to like shoes, it's because he had access to shoes. You put shoes at the foot of the bed, or you left the closet door open. The reason puppies like shoes in the first place is because shoes have a very strong scent of you. You'll notice that if you give Rover a shoe he'll immediately go for the inside. Remember, everything about your scent is positive. Your scent becomes Mom's apple pie, a favorite old song on the radio, and Grandma's violet perfume. Other items Rover will go for are toilet paper, tissues in the bathroom wastebasket, today's newspaper, your underwear, and sometimes the remote control—all for your scent. Avoiding this kind of problem chewing is easy. Just don't give Rover access until he's more mature and the chewing is under control. If you have a small child, you child-proof. Do the same for Rover.

If you're reading the newspaper and Rover is driving you crazy trying to get a piece of it, occasionally take a page you don't mind giving up, wad it into a ball, and throw it for him. He'll have a terrific time pretending he's a wolf and shredding the fruit of his hunt. I know, he's going to get shredded paper all over the floor. But it'll take you only minutes to clean it up, and the important thing is that you were in control every step of the way. I can assure you that you won't be teaching Rover to expect his own section of the newspaper.

When Rover is about five to six months old he's going to go through a phase of what's called Displacement Behavior. This is the time when there can be serious and expensive destruction. During Displacement, Rover becomes very anxious about where you are when you're not with him. The closest human attribute that I can compare it to is separation anxiety, but that really doesn't come close. A human can pick up a phone, a human can watch TV, a human, in short, can relieve the anxiety. Rover cannot. Even though he's seen you leave and come home again for months, when he goes through Displacement he has no idea that you're coming back again. He's trying to figure out how he's going to take care of himself, and he's really worried because he can't remember where you keep his food. Within a short period of time after you leave he will begin to "stress-pace." He will pace in a circle or back and forth. Slowly his heart rate will speed up, his blood pressure will rise, his eyes will dilate and *he will not be in control.* When dogs become confused or frustrated they don't go out and throw themselves in front of a car and end it all. The anxiety must be released somehow, and when Rover is going through Displacement it will be released on the handiest thing around. I'm hoping that if you have some idea of what Rover is going through, you'll be understanding and patient. I'm going to give you tips on how to make displacement a little easier for both of you, and you can start most of them right now.

You're going to begin to establish a security base. From now on I want you to tell Rover good-bye every time you leave, whether it's for ten minutes or a whole day. With my dogs I say, "I'll see you later." I have one client who says, "Guard the house and kill the burglars," and another who says, "May the Force be with you." It doesn't matter. Just decide what you're going to say and have everybody in the household say it every time. If only one member of the household is leaving, that person should say good-bye. This will have the same effect on Rover that it does on young kids. We have a tendency to say the same thing every time we tuck them into bed or send them off to school. This gives them a sense of security. Larri accompanies me quite often and she knows if she doesn't hear me say, "I'll see you later," she's going with me.

Something else that can trigger destructive chewing is anticipating your homecoming. Dogs are creatures of habit to the point of being compulsive. If they were humans, they would all be smokers, alcoholics, drug addicts, compulsive hand-washers, etc. If every time you come home you have an excited reunion with Rover, he will lock in to a pattern and it will become compulsive. If you could videotape Rover when he knows you're about to enter the house, you'd notice that he moves as if he's memorized a dance. If you have a set daily schedule, Rover knows to the minute when you come home, and he begins to anticipate the reunion. Now, let's say you're five minutes late, or you stop to talk to the neighbor, or when you walk in the phone is ringing. Rover is at fever pitch by now, and all of that has to be released. It's usually released on the first thing around—the pillows on the couch, for example, or the doorframe, or the miniblinds. The anticipation of that reunion can cause destructive chewing. When you come home, either ignore Rover altogether or just acknowledge his presence. You can get him as excited as you want five minutes later. By that time he's in control. I recommend this low-key homecoming for two reasons. The first is the one I just explained. The second is that because of Rover's compulsive personality, he'll carry out his end of excitement whether you participate or not. But there are going to be many times in his life when you come home with groceries in your hands. Or the phone will be ringing. Or you'll be in your Sunday best. I can go on and on. The point is that you can't explain this to Rover, yet for some reason we humans expect him to understand. I realize that keeping the homecoming lowkey is going to be difficult. I know it's wonderful that Rover's so happy to see you, but try to put your ego aside and think of Rover.

When you notice destructive chewing beginning, pay attention to what Rover likes to chew on. He may have a favorite thing or type of thing—for example, paper, wood, pillows or cushions, or maybe the garden hose. If he does, I want you to give him a version of that material when you know he's going to be alone. Even though I've explained that you won't be "teaching him to like it," I can still hear that little voice in your head disagreeing with me. Think of it this way: Rover already likes "it," so you might as well make an effort to be in charge of what "it" is. If he likes paper, give him a book or magazine of his own. Be prepared to come home and pick up paper from one end of the house to the other—at least your books will be intact. If Rover loves wood, go to the lumberyard and get him a piece of a dense wood, like teak or oak. The wood will eventually begin to splinter, so throw it away and give him another one. Maybe you're trying to protect the cushions on the couch. Give him a child-safe stuffed animal, or a pillow of his own. The stuffing will fall out of it, but your couch will be untouched. Many people don't learn that Rover's favorite thing to chew on is the garden hose until they turn it on. You're going to have to buy a new hose anyway, so give him a piece of the old one. Yes, Human, you should even give Rover an extension cord of his very own.

When you're home, put away whatever you gave him to destroy, and give it back to him when you leave. If your Rover has shown a tendency to swallow everything he gets in his mouth, make sure whatever you give him can't be swallowed. Very few dogs are swallowers, though, so it's not usually a problem.

Unfortunately, there will still be Rovers out there doing some serious destructive chewing. Your dog is not being willful; he is not trying to tell you not to leave him. He doesn't "know better," and he's not "mad at you." I can't begin to tell you the number of times I've heard, "Judi, he knows he's done something wrong, because as soon as I come home he looks guilty." I cannot stress it strongly enough: *He does not know he's done something wrong!* Rover can know he's done something wrong only if you've caught him in the act. For Rover to understand he's done something wrong, he first has to say to himself, "I know I'm not supposed to chew this, I know I'm going to get in trouble, I know I'm going to be yelled at and disciplined, but I don't care, I'm going to do it anyway." This dog wants to please you, not displease you intentionally! "Then why does he look guilty as soon as I walk in the door?" Calm yourself, sit back down, and I'll explain it to you.

The scenario goes something like this. You walk in the door, see destruction, and start yelling. You only have to come home and do that three or four times before Rover learns that you come home in a really bad mood, so he goes into a submissive or cowering posture automatically. Remember when I said, "Don't discipline Rover after the fact"? The reason you don't want to do that is because of the way Rover interprets your actions. You walk in the door, go immediately to the object that's destroyed, *point to it,* and yell in a very angry voice, "Rover! Look at this! Look what you did! This is a no! *Don't ever do this again!"* If you can picture yourself, you'll notice that you're yelling at the object. You are also reemphasizing the object. It now becomes a greater point of interest to Rover. What goes through Rover's mind is, "Boy, that pillow sure got in trouble. That hole in the ground is really getting yelled at. That's a bad rug! I wonder if it's gonna get grounded?" And he doesn't have the vaguest idea why you're sharing this with him. *The more emphasis you put on the destruction, the more confusion is created, and the longer the destruction will go on.*

Having a puppy is like suddenly having a two-year-old child. Be prepared for the bad times because there will be some, and if handled correctly they will be temporary. Keep an eye on the future and what you pictured life with Rover would be like. It'll happen; just be patient.

PLAYTIME WITH ROVER

Playing ball with Rover seems to be the only game Humans know. I want you to stop and rethink this fetch stuff. You can play ball all day with a Lab, Golden, Cocker, Springer, and so on, because they're Retrievers. Fetching is a part of who they are. Now let's take one of the herding breeds and see what they think of playing fetch. When Rover is a puppy you roll the ball out for him. He goes to it, sniffs it, and asks, "You don't want this?" There you are, Human, saying, in an excited voice, "Bring me the ball. Get the ball, Rover. Bring it here." Rover looks at you in confusion and says, "That's kind of pointless, isn't it? You just threw it away." As he gets a little older he'll say, "Okay, Human, let me see if I've got this straight. You're going to throw the ball, I'm going to go get it, bring it back, and drop it, and then you're going to throw it again. Right? No. That's okay, you play amongst yourselves." At some point Rover may bring you the ball but as soon as you put your hand out he dodges, you put your hand out and he dodges again. To get the ball you either have to play tug-of-war or chase. Pay attention! This is the way Rover wants to play.

All breeds were developed for a purpose. The vast majority have become strictly pets. They are rarely used for what they were bred to do. If we can exercise Rover's natural abilities through play, he'll be happier for it and he'll make a better companion for you.

If you have a herding dog, his favorite game is going to be to chase or be chased. You'll notice that when Rover is young, he'll see the birds in the trees, frown, and think, "You should all be in one tree, not scattered willy-nilly." He'll then run around, probably bark, and try to get all the birds into one tree. Instead of throwing out one ball for Rover, throw three or four. He'll herd them together, pick the one he wants, and either bring it to you or lie down and chew on it. If he lies down and chews on it, you'll notice he keeps looking at you to see if you're going to try to get it from him. The minute you start walking toward him, he'll pick up the ball, and the chase is on. At that point he's in seventh heaven. The breeds that chase for a living, such as hounds, are going to love this game too.

Mastiffs, St. Bernards, Newfoundlands, Great Pyrenees, some Dobermans, and other similar breeds love to get something and hold it on the ground. Get a soccer ball or basketball and let most of the air out. Roll it for Rover; he'll run after it, hold it on the ground, and wait for you to kick it out from under him. Mastiffs, especially, can play this game all day.

Any of the breeds with a good nose will love any game that has anything to do with hide-and-seek. You can play with humans or objects. As soon as Rover knows the names of humans or toys, hide one or the other and say, "Rover, go find Dad," or "Rover, go find your ball." His nose will go down and he'll locate whatever it is in minutes.

If you have one of the breeds thought of as aggressive, I'm sure you've been told not to wrestle or play tug-of-war, because it will teach aggression. There are trainers and training kennels that teach a dog aggression, and it's quite a time-consuming project. It can take as long as six months. If you've ever seen two dogs play, you'll notice that it is impossible to tell which one's the dominant dog. The dominant dog will go down and over on his back as often as the subordinate dog. The subordinate dog will stand on the dominant dog's back, which is something he would never do except in play. When you wrestle with your Rottweiler, he's going to love it—and I promise, in play you are not going to teach aggression.

There are a few things I recommend to teach Rover to entertain himself. As long as he's not a swallower, give him an empty plastic milk container with the residue of the milk still in it. He'll be attracted to it by the smell of the milk. Then he'll find out that when he hits it with his paw it makes a really neat noise. Then he'll discover it has a handle—and suddenly he becomes king of the mountain. When you find bits of plastic around, throw the jug away and give him another one. Another toy I recommend is a string bone. It's a lot of twine twisted and tied in knots. Most pet shops have them. There is something about the texture that dogs like for chewing. Plus string bones are cloth, so if you get your scent on Rover's he'll be attracted to it even more. String bones make great tug toys, and dogs like to throw them around. If you find string in Rover's stool or in his teeth, take the toy away and replace it. Finally, squeaky toys are always good to teach him to entertain himself.

A client gave me this next idea and I've recommended it for latchkey dogs ever since. (But if you hang your clothes on a clothesline, don't set up this toy.) Tie a clothesline between two trees, from tree to porch post, or however you can rig it up. From this line hang anything you can think of that Rover might enjoy: old socks, a tug toy, a ball inside a sock, an empty milk container . . . Use your imagination. Set the line low enough that he can get hold of anything on it, but high enough so that he can't jump and bring the whole line down. I had one client who had no porch and no trees so he got several lines, tied things to the ends of the lines, and hung them from the roof. Leo, his Yellow Lab, loved it.

The only sense I can make of the proverb "You can't teach an old dog new tricks" is this: If dogs don't know how to play when they're young, they never learn. Play with your Rover! Please, Human, think in terms of what your Rover is all about and *respect* it. Let Rover determine how play is going to go. If you insist that he play your way, his will be a trained response, not a play response.

6

THE PECK ORDER FACTOR

When I think of the peck order, I imagine it as a ladder with each rung being the place occupied by a member of the pack. If you can imagine it in the same way, this chapter will be easier to understand.

Dogs relate to humans exactly the way they relate to other dogs. That's their only frame of reference. We relate to everything in the same way we relate to humans. We even do it to plants. We apply our knowledge of human thought and emotions. If you have a basic understanding of this fact, it will help you interpret Rover's body language and reactions.

Always remember: You are Rover's pack. Within every pack there is a peck order. When this is not understood we put into effect what I call the Rover Peter Principle, which means we promote Rover to his human level of incompetence. When he's promoted to that level, there is constant flux in the peck order and Rover reacts to it by taking on more responsibility than he knows how to handle—taking care of you, your house, and himself. When a dog believes he's his own master, serious behavior problems begin.

Rover knows the peck order in the human relationships in your home. He knows who is dominant and on down the line. We want him to understand where *he* is on that ladder. He should be on the bottom rung. Nine dogs out of ten don't care where they stand in the peck order, just as long as they know where it is and it's consistent. There are exceptions. Read the chapter on breeds to see if you have one of these.

The two major areas of confusion in a dog's relationship with humans are body language and tone of voice. I'm going to give you an analogy that will help to explain the way Rover interprets body language. Let's say that Rover is an established pet and you bring home a baby. Ninety-five percent of the time Rover sees the baby belly up and obviously very weak. Rover is totally dominant and the baby is totally submissive. I have to pause here and explain the significance of "weakness." If you've ever been around two dogs, you noticed that if you stepped on the toe of one and he cried, the other dog was on the spot immediately. That wasn't because he was concerned. He was determining whether there was a weakness that could cause restructuring of the peck order.

The baby is a very weak human. When babies begin to crawl, their hind ends are up in the air a little bit, their backs arch, and their heads are down somewhat. Rover sees that as play posture. A dog sometimes uses play posture to throw off what he believes to be a stronger opponent. If Rover doesn't want to play, he just moves away. Rover is dominant, the baby subordinate.

When babies begin to support themselves on things before they start walking freely, two factors are involved. One, that Rover knows Humans walk upright freely. Two, the baby falls and cries a lot. So Rover sees continued weakness. He is dominant, the baby subordinate.

Now, when babies begin to walk freely, their chests stick out a bit and their arms are out to help them balance. Rover has been dominant over this child for anywhere from ten to fourteen months—and suddenly the child approaches, upright. As Rover sees it, this is a challenge for dominance. It's during this period that children are bitten in the face or upper arm. But most dogs won't bite; instead, they wait for their opportunity to casually brush by the child and knock him down. Or maybe Rover will bump the child with his nose to make him fall down. Then he will stand either very close to the child or right over him. You may still be dominant over Rover, but now the peck order is you, Rover, and then the baby.

When Rover becomes dominant he has all the responsibilities that go along with that: grooming (licking), teaching, discipline. (In Rover's view, the young child should obey his rules.) Of course, along with all these responsibilities comes protection of the child.

Back to Rover's interpretation of body language. When you are lying on the floor, if Rover is standing or sitting he's dominant. If he lies down with you, you're in the position of a litter mate. If Rover is large and he sits next to you on the floor or on the couch, he is physically equal. If Rover is a small dog and allowed on the furniture, you'll notice that he sits on the back of the couch or the chair, which makes him dominant or equal. If there's flux in the peck order, equality amounts to dominance. Confusion comes in when you stand up: Suddenly you're back on the top rung of the ladder. Rover has to depend on you for his food, and you are in control in other ways, which makes you dominant. Throughout a normal day, the peck order could shift several times. This confuses Rover. And remember: When a dog becomes confused or frustrated, he releases the emotion in some way, such as growling, snapping, destruction, or barking.

A special point has to be made about the toy breeds. They have a reputation as barkers, snappy, unfriendly, and terrible with young children. Unfortunately, that reputation is grounded in truth. But the toys don't start out this way. Rather, through body language we inadvertently insist that they be dominant. From day one we hold them above our heads, the way we do infants. We carry them very close to our faces. We let them share our bed pillow and equal space on the furniture. Over time, Toy Rover accepts the role of dominant individual and takes on all the responsibilities that go along with that role. Pay attention to your body language with Toy Rover. He really doesn't want to be dominant; he just wants to be your special companion.

If you have a hard time getting Rover to come to you, pay attention to the way you're standing. If you're bending from the waist, you're doing what is a "stand-over." I'm sure at some point you've seen a dog put his head over the neck of another dog. That's a stand-over. The dog being stood over is going to show submission or accept the gesture as a challenge for dominance. If Rover has a submissive personality, he will show submission as soon as you bend from the waist, and that will make it hard for him to come to you. On the other hand, if Rover is feeling threatened, as soon as you bend from the waist you pose a threat or he has to challenge you for dominance. Stand straight or squat, and you'll notice Rover comes to you easily.

I want you to put this information in the back of your mind so you can recall it if necessary. It's true that with certain breeds you're going to have to make a conscious effort to keep yourself on the top rung of the peck order ladder. (In Chapter 12, "Problem Solving," I'll tell you how to use body language to your advantage to put yourself into an undeniable lead position.) For the most part, though, you can wrestle with Rover on the floor and let him sit on the back of the couch. Please, relax and enjoy your dog. Remember: Of two children raised in the same environment by the same parents, one can grow up to be a secure, productive member of society, while the other grows up insecure, with all kinds of problems. The same holds true of dogs. You can do all the wrong things with one dog and have absolutely no problems. Do those same wrong things with another dog—and that's when I'm called in.

IT'S OKAY, IT'S OKAY

You, Human, can actually train Rover to become aggressive, shy, suspicious, nervous, anxious, frightened, and even panicked, just with your *tone of voice*. I'm going to give you several examples of the way Rover interprets your tone of voice. This way there won't be any doubt in my mind that you understand "It's okay, it's okay."

Let's say Rover sees the mailman or meter reader; he barks, growls, and lunges. You go to him immediately and in a soothing and comforting voice you say, "It's okay, it's okay. That's just the mailman, he's not going to hurt you. Calm down, it's okay." Rover doesn't understand the words. He understood your tone of voice, which is telling him, "That's a good boy, Rover. Attack the mailman." *His aggressive behavior has just been reinforced.*

Suppose it's the Fourth of July or there's a thunderstorm. Rover is startled by the noise; he begins to tremble and attempts to get under or behind something. You go to him, and in a soothing, comforting tone of voice you say, "It's okay, it's okay. Did you get scared?" You crawl behind or under the something with him, because at this point there's no way he's going to come to you. You continue to say, in a soothing and comforting voice, "It's okay, Rover. It's going to be all right. It's okay, it's okay." Rover's a basket case by now, because *you just reinforced his fear.* Rover knows it's not okay, so don't tell him it is.

Maybe you take Rover to the animal clinic for shots. I know: You feel sorry for him because he has to get shots. As soon as you walk through the clinic door you say, in a soothing, comforting tone, "It's okay, it's okay, it'll be all right." You're in the exam room and the first shot is given. Rover jumps, cries, turns and snaps or growls—and you say, "It's okay. Did that hurt you? Just one more and we'll go home." The second shot is given—and Rover's reaction is twice as strong, because *you just praised his behavior.* Rover knows it's not okay, so don't tell him it is.

Let's say Rover is, for whatever reason, shy, and Friend John comes for a visit. You invite Friend John in; Rover begins to back up, maybe he barks and cowers a little. You hold him immediately and say, "It's okay, it's okay, that's John, he loves dogs." As Rover is struggling to release himself from the hold you have on him, you say to Friend John: "John, come on over and pet Rover." To Rover you say, "See? John just wants to pet you." At this point Rover is a nervous wreck. He will have a problem with Friend John for the rest of his life because *you reinforced his shy behavior* and convinced him that he had good reason to be leery of John.

Suppose you find a lost dog or a street dog and you want to help him. He won't have anything to do with you, so you begin to coax with food. You offer the food and say, "Look what I have here." Street Rover shows interest in the food, but backs away. You continue to offer the food and in a coaxing voice say, "It's okay, boy, this is good food." Street Rover continues to back away. After several unsuccessful attempts to get him to take the food, you put it on the ground and back away. Street Rover, with his eye on you every second, grabs the food and continues to back away. *This dog was rewarded with food and "It's okay, it's okay" for backing away* and not taking the food from your hand.

With a good understanding of how your tone of voice can affect Rover, you'll avoid all kinds of behavior problems, now and in the future.

Rover can interpret "It's okay, it's okay" in three ways. First, he can assume you're praising whatever behavior he's showing at the time. Second, because he knows the situation doesn't call for praise, he can conclude that you've proven you can't take care of him under the circumstances. So he has to take care of himself. (When I was working in the animal clinic and a dog came in believing he had to take care of himself, everything and everyone was a threat to him, so he came in swinging and serious. The owner would be saying, "It's okay, it's okay," the whole time. As the dog was snarling, growling, and trying very hard to bite one of us, the owner would say, "I'm really sorry, Doc. I don't understand it—he's not this way at home.") Third, Rover can learn to manipulate you. If that were the only result of "It's okay," we'd have no problems. Starting around the Fourth of July and on through our monsoon season, I get numerous calls from people whose dogs are going off the deep end. The summer before last we had one thunderstorm after another. I had three separate clients whose dogs had been startled by the thunder, producing a lot of "It's okay, it's okay." The three dogs thought this stroking and "It's okay, it's okay" stuff were really neat, so whenever thunderclouds came over the mountains they'd go into their "I'm so scared" act. One of the three had a pond in her backyard. Whenever Goldie was out in the rain, her Human would bring her in and rub her down with nice warm towels. Well, Goldie got to the point where, if the clouds didn't produce rain, she threw herself in the pond and came to the back door wet. A very irate but humble client called me. She'd dried Goldie off three times before she realized it hadn't rained. When you step on Rover's toe and apologize, then the next time he wants attention he holds his paw up, you're being manipulated. As I said, if this were the only result of "It's okay," it would be no problem.

Listen up, ladies. It'll be harder for you to stop saying "It's okay" than it will be for men. Women are naturally more nurturing, more sympathetic, and more affectionate. God did that on purpose so that we could be mothers. I even catch myself "It's okay"ing, especially with frightened puppies. If you find yourself doing it, whether you be man or woman, simply stop. It's that easy, just stop. Remember, you can comfort a human; you *cannot* comfort a dog. I have been in this world of animals for nineteen years and I have never seen "It's okay, it's okay" calm a dog down. Clients ask, "Judi, what do I say?" Whenever Rover is under stress, keep your voice matter-of-fact, or don't say anything at all. Once Rover sees that you have the situation under control, he'll relax. You can also put him through some commands. That will get his mind off the stress long enough to calm him down.

8

THE HEAD HONCHO HUMAN

That's you I'm talking about. This chapter is all about putting you into an undeniable lead position with Rover. (You may have heard it called the alpha position or dominant dog position.) Everything I'm going to have you do is at Rover's level of understanding.

First, let's make sure you're not putting Rover in the dominant position without being aware of it. No matter what you've read or heard, *don't hold Rover up at eye level in front of your face.* When you do this you're putting him into a physically dominant position and you're encouraging eye contact. *Do not get into eye-contact situations with Rover.* Using eye contact to gain dominance or to intimidate is a fad now. This fad could be dangerous for you. When it comes to eye contact, Rover knows what he's doing 100 percent of the time, you don't. In using eye contact you are entering Rover's world. It doesn't make any difference how hard you concentrate; if you're holding serious eye contact with Rover and the phone rings, you're going to avert your eyes. Whether Rover is an eight-week-old puppy or a two-year-old adult, the instant you avert your eyes it's Round One for Rover.

Anybody who works with dogs can tell you about "that look." It's scary. When a dog gives you "that look," he means to intimidate you or challenge you for dominance. The dog knows exactly what he's doing. If you've ever seen "that look," you'll remember that your heart went into your throat and instinct told you not to get involved. I hope you followed your instinct.

Another thing I don't want you to do is suddenly throw Rover down and hold him on his back. As I said, you're going to be doing everything at Rover's level of understanding and "throwing down" can become confusing. To gain physical dominance you don't have to manhandle Rover. Read the discussion of Rover's body language in Chapter 6, "The Peck Order Factor." Okay, Human, let's begin to make you Head Honcho.

The first thing I want you to do is see to it that you go through every doorway before Rover does. That means living room to kitchen, hallway to bedroom, inside to outside: *every door.* If you're going to open the door to let Rover out and you're not going out yourself, give him permission to go: "Rover, go ahead." All this will remind Rover of what he once knew to be correct behavior. When you first started to housetrain him, and you opened the door for him to go out, you either had to give him a little shove, or you had to pick him up and carry him out, or you had to go out yourself and then he would come out. The reason was that Puppy Rover knew instinctively that it was incorrect to pass you and walk in front of you. Whenever two dogs walk down the street, one will be in front and the other a little behind. The one in front is the lead dog. That's the position I'm putting you in. The one a little behind would let himself be hurt before he passed that lead dog without permission. That's how strong pack etiquette is.

To enforce your precedence, you can push Rover back with your foot or say, "Rover, stay back," and give him the hand signal for "Stay." If you have to, turn around and back through the door. Whatever you do, just see to it that you get through first. I use doorways to emphasize your leadership because there's a definite passage, so a definite point is being made. If you have small children you may have to carry them to get them through the door ahead of Rover. If you have stairs, take advantage of them: Insist that Rover go up and down behind you. As you become the Head Honcho you'll notice that Rover will pause and let you go first.

I also want you to pay close attention to your body position. Make sure the upper part of your body is higher than Rover's at all times for at least three weeks. If you are lying down and Rover is higher than you on account of his size, stand up immediately. If Rover is a small dog, don't let him lie on top of you or on the back of the furniture. When you play with him, make sure the upper part of your body is higher than his.

For ten days to two weeks, I want you to do a "straddle" and a "down" twice a day. To do the straddle, put Rover in the "Sit" position and put one leg on each side of him. You can bring your hands down to his chest, stroke him, and talk to him in a positive voice. *Make sure you release him. Don't let him release himself.* If he becomes tense, hold on until he relaxes. To do the down, gently lay Rover down and get him on his side or all the way over on his back. Kneel over him so that the upper part of your body is over the upper part of his. You can rub his tummy and talk to him in a positive tone. If you have small children, you can pick them up and hold them over Rover. When you do this, you're telling Rover that you insist that the child be dominant. Again, *make sure you release him. Don't let him release himself.* If Rover fights your straddle or down, it means he believes himself to dominant.

POWER PLAYS. Even though Rover doesn't want the dominant role he's been put in, he's familiar with it and may not let it go easily. Consequently, you may see some power plays. I'm going to give you a list of what you may see and how to handle it. You may see only one power play or you may see them all.

1. You may see an intentional attempt at getting through a doorway before you. If Rover does this, there should be no doubt in your mind that when he pushed you aside or suddenly ran ahead, it was a power play. Call him back through the door and insist that you go first.
2. He may attempt to get his face level with or higher than yours. If he's medium-sized to large, he will put his paws on your legs when you're sitting. If he's small, he will stand on your lap or get on the back of the chair or couch. If he does this, don't get into any kind of struggle with him. Just stand up.
3. He may try to initiate significant eye contact. I'm not talking about the kind of eye contact you see when you're talking to him. I can't describe the eye contact I'm talking about. You'll know it when you see it. If you do see it, simply push his face away. Don't get into a staring contest with him and don't make a big deal of it. Read Chapter 3, "Dos and Don'ts of Discipline."
4. He may do some humping. There is nothing sexual about it. It will be a power play. He may hump the air, or he may try some kind of contact with you. If he humps the air, ignore it or leave the room. If he tries contact with you, stand up and move away.
5. If he's never been allowed on the furniture or your bed, he may give it a try. Tell him "Off."

6. He may get pushy at mealtimes. I can't tell you exactly what he'll do, because it varies. But you'll know it when you see it. Don't put his bowl down until you're in control. Get him to sit or stay.

7. He may do something totally out of character for him. This is another variable power play. I had one client whose Dalmatian raced him to the phone and then tried to take it away from him. A Shih Tzu took her food bowl under the bed so that her Human would have to get down into play posture to get it out. A Springer started catching birds and setting them loose in the house. I had a woman client whose Chow jumped on her boyfriend's car and spent a serious amount of time scratching the hell out of the hood. Whatever you see along these lines, don't put any emphasis on it.

You'll notice I've advised you to put little or no emphasis on any of the power plays, except for the doorway situation. The more you emphasize a power play the more you involve yourself in a true power struggle with your dog. I know it will be hard, but try not to react at all. Usually Rover will give a power play one good shot. If it doesn't work he'll let it go.

If you persevere, and make practical use of your knowledge of body language, "It's okay, it's okay," and Head Honcho, you'll clear up any possibility of confusion—and you, Human, will once again, be on the top rung of the peck order ladder.

9

NATURAL PROTECTIVENESS

Certain traits are part of particular breeds' identity. A German Short-haired Pointer will produce a perfect point without any training. A Collie will herd small livestock when he's very young and without any training. A Coon Hound will chase and tree an animal without any training. What dogs were bred to do goes so far back that it's in their genes. This is also true of dogs with natural protectiveness. That's why I call it natural. And many humans adopt a dog for just that quality. They choose the dog for its size and reputation. It's when the dog becomes an adult that I get called in: Rover won't let anybody in the house (or the yard). Or I hear, "Rover is protecting me and won't let anyone near me." I get calls when Rover is protecting the children and he doesn't like any of their friends. At the other end of the scale I hear, "We got Rover for protection and he loves everybody. He won't even bark when the doorbell rings."

I'm going to tell you how to recognize natural protectiveness, how to tap into it, and how to be in control of it. If you don't want to take Rover through formal protection training but you still want to tap into his natural ability, then this chapter is for you. The more control you have over a dog that has natural protectiveness, the better. Let's say you have total control over Doberman Rover and you're taking him for a walk. On this walk, you believe you're being followed. If you feel that, your pace is going to alter. You're going to speed up or slow down. Your heart rate will speed up, which means your breathing will, too. As soon as these things happen to you, Rover is going to notice the difference and will immediately be alert to everything around you. If there is an attack he'll know you're not in control and he will take over.

When I hear, "Rover won't bark when somebody comes to the door," I cringe. Humans, listen up!: An intruder is not going to knock on your door or ring your doorbell! You want Rover to be alert to *agitated* sounds, such as fingers on a screen, odd sounds by the doorknob, sounds around a window, things that go bump in the night. A good Doberman, German Shepherd, Rottweiler, Mastiff, or the like may not bark even then. He'll listen silently, become very alert, and move around to filter scents. He'll bark only when he perceives a threat. Believe me, if there is an intruder, Rover will do his thing. If Rover barks at every sound around the house, he will no longer be any use to you as protection or watch, because you'll cease to pay any attention to his barking.

When you have a dog with natural protectiveness, you'll notice, even when he's a pup, that when you let him outside he'll pause, throw his chest out, put his ears up and forward, and stand like that for a few seconds. He's telling the world that he's in charge. (Just between you and me, the rest of the world doesn't know. Don't tell Rover that; he'd be ever so disappointed.) With some you'll see this behavior at eight weeks; with others you won't see it until he's six to eight months old.

I want you to make sure you're not encouraging protectiveness the wrong way. Don't say, "What is it, Rover? What do you hear?" every time he alerts to a sound or barks at something. If you do that, you're not training him to be alert to unusual or threatening sounds, you're training him to be alert to any sound. You're not training him to bark when there's a threat, you're training him to bark at anything. Don't play fight among yourselves to see if he'll protect you. If you do that, you're not training him to protect you, you're training him to join in with play fighting. Now that we've got that straight, I can trust that you're going to have control over your Rover and tap into his natural protectiveness in a responsible manner.

Because of his size and reputation, Rover is already a deterrent to intruders. Now we want to make him a serious threat to intruders. What I'm going to have you do is play mind games with people at your door and teach Rover at the same time. You can begin this at whatever age you like. In other words, don't think he's too old to start.

To begin, you'll practice going to the door with Rover at a stand-stay beside you. If you need to, put a leash on Rover and say, "Rover, let's go to the door." At the door, get him at a stand-stay and open the door as if there were someone there. With the door open, look at Rover and give him a code word. Among my clients' code words have been "airwolf," "brava," "fruitfarm," "storytime," "domino," and my all-time favorite, "peanut butter and jelly." You will look at Rover and say, "Rover, [code word]." Take a minute to get this picture in your mind. Meanwhile I'll explain the psychology behind what we're doing. If your Rover is a large dog, no matter what breed, when you open the door to someone who doesn't know you, the sight of Rover will make them step back. They won't even realize they've done so. When you look at Rover and give him the code word, that person is going to think, "If there's a word that means 'Everything's okay,' there must be a word that means 'Attack.' "

Remember the compulsive habitual personality? We're tapping into that, as well as taking advantage of Rover's natural protectiveness. After you've gone to the door and given Rover the code word a number of times, he's going to get used to hearing it. In fact, if he doesn't hear the word he'll alert to a problem, become very aware of the difference in you, and, if necessary, take over. Do you see what I mean by playing mind games? Everyone is going to know that you have a large dog and they're going to suspect that you've had him protection-trained.

I've done this with a variety of breeds, for clients with a variety of reasons: for example, women who live alone, women whose husbands travel, and latchkey kids. There was one gentleman who made jewelry in his home, and an elderly woman who took care of young children. I've worked on it with outdoor dogs at a gate, an Airedale in an art gallery, and a Collie in a horse stable.

If you have a dog with natural protectiveness, I strongly recommend that you teach obedience. You must have total control of Rover so he won't turn that protectiveness to his own advantage. He has to understand that you are the Head Honcho. You don't want him believing he needs to protect you all the time, and you definitely don't want him believing he needs to protect himself.

LIVING WITH
MULTIPLE DOGS

Far too often, by the time I'm called in on a "fighting dogs" case, there have been serious injuries, and I have to recommend that the client purchase spike collars. You know the collars that you see with the spikes on the outside? The kind they put on cartoon dogs? Those collars have a purpose and that is to protect the jugular vein. Please, Human, if you have more than one dog, read this chapter carefully.

Memorize! Their relationship has to be established. There is no equality, there is no democracy. *There has to be a dominant dog; there has to be a subordinate dog.*

Memorize! There is no such thing as jealousy. There is no such thing as hurt feelings.

Dogs are pack animals; even though they are domesticated, pack etiquette is part of who they are. Canines in a pack will not injure, maim, or kill each other, because all members are needed for hunting. If one is injured or killed, it weakens the pack. They will not weaken the pack intentionally. I'm sure you have some idea of Rover's power and the strength of his jaw and teeth (even if he's a Chihuahua). If he wanted to injure, maim, or kill, he could.

Now that that's understood, Human, we can go on.

I'm going to dispel the jealousy myth first. Jealousy is a very complicated emotion, with a lot of thought going into it. Dogs don't have the ability for that. What you see in dogs and call jealousy is one of two things: competition (which is the equivalent of sibling rivalry) or a straightening out of the peck order.

Let's say, for example, we have Rover One and Rover Two. Rover One is dominant. You're petting Rover Two, and Rover One approaches. His ears are up and forward, his tail is wagging, and his body is animated. That's competition. You can pet both dogs at the same time.

Straightening out the peck order works like this: You're petting Rover Two, and Rover One approaches. His ears are up and forward and his chest is out. If his tail is wagging at all, it's moving very slowly. There's no liveliness in his body, and there's purpose to his walk. He will attempt to get between you and Rover Two. He's saying that he doesn't want Rover Two that close to you. You'll notice that Rover Two attempts to back away. Let Rover Two go. He knows what he's doing.

When dogs fight over and over again, it's usually on account of incorrect human interference. For example, when Rover One is straightening out the peck order, the human tendency is to say, "Rover Two, honey, you come back here." To Rover One you say, "Go on, I was petting Rover Two first," and you push him away. Rover Two is thinking, "Please oh please oh please don't do this. I don't mind, I'll just go over here." Rover Two knows Rover One will have to punish him later. Don't forget, they can't explain it to you. With your tone of voice, you praised Rover Two and you disciplined Rover One. You compromised Rover One's position as the dominant dog, and you did it in front of Rover Two.

When Rover One and Rover Two actually have a fight, our human tendency is to go immediately to the underdog, the one showing submission. You go to Rover Two and begin to check him for injuries, saying, "Are you all right, did Rover One hurt you?" All this is said in a soothing, comforting tone. To Rover Two you say, "Rover Two, shame on you! You get out of here and leave Rover One alone! Bad dog! Bad dog!" All this is said in a stern tone. You praised Rover Two in front of Rover One and you disciplined Rover One in front of Rover Two. Again you've seriously compromised Rover One's position as the dominant dog. Both dogs now believe you want Rover Two to be dominant, and they're thinking, "Oh, jeez, now we have to fight all over again," because their relationship has to be reestablished as it applies to you and your position in the peck order. After a short period of time you have two dogs that get along beautifully when no one's around and fight as soon as someone's with them.

There's serious danger when this kind of fighting starts: The slightest provocation can start a fight. I call those stimulus fights. For example, the doorbell rings and both dogs run for the door. That can start a fight. They're in the yard and they both bark at something. That can start a fight. You walk into the room. That can start a fight. Company can start a fight. When stimulus fighting begins, there is no longer any "fight posturing" and absolutely no pack etiquette. With the loss of pack etiquette and fight posturing, the dogs fight with the intent to hurt each other. They don't know why they're fighting. As I said, this is when I have to recommend the spike collars. When you see Rovers One and Two stiffen and form a broken S or you see Rover One place his head over Rover Two's neck, there is still fight posturing.

It's very simple to prevent serious fighting. Simply *don't interfere.* Now, Human, I know that's not easy to do because when they start fighting it sounds unbelievably vicious and you think they're killing each other. They are not hurting each other. A fight seldom lasts longer than three minutes. It only seems like an hour. Any injuries are usually accidental—a scratch on the face (usually done by a toenail) or a nick in the ear. Occasionally there's a bleeding tongue. If you just can't help it, and you must get involved, do so without saying anything to either dog. If you believe you need to check for injuries, do it silently and check Rover One first. Do not separate the dogs after a fight. By that I mean, don't put them in separate areas. If you do, you take the chance that they'll fight again as soon as they see each other. Don't attempt to break up a fight alone. You can get seriously bitten and the dogs won't even know they did it. If you honestly believe they're getting hurt, and you have a helper, each of you should get hold of one dog's tail or hind legs and pull. In my business I learn constantly. I've just learned that hairspray can stop a fight quickly. All you have to do is spray around the nose and mouth. It's best to get the aerosol type; if you use the pump type, you could cramp before the fight stops.

If you have dogs that are fighting or beginning to fight you can ward off serious problems by putting a few rules into effect. If you absolutely, positively know for sure that Rover One is dominant, give him preferential treatment. You don't have to make a big deal of it. Put his food down first. Pet him first when you come home or the dogs come in the house or you go out to them. When you give Rover One preferential treatment you are letting both dogs know that you respect Rover One as the dominant dog.

If you're not sure who is dominant, notice which one goes through a door first. Who's in front when they walk across the yard or the living room? Don't base your opinion on food. Dogs have food available to them on a daily basis. Sometimes the dog that guards food or fights over it is a heavy eater, and food means more to him. For example, Dachshunds can be real chow hounds, so when you see your Doxie standing over his food and growling, it's just because the food is important to him; it's not a show of dominance. Dogs *can* show dominance over food. Just don't pin your opinion on that one thing. Pay attention when you see one dog walk across the room and hesitate in front of the other dog. The subordinate dog will turn his head a little and look away. Once he does that, the dominant dog will continue to walk.

If there's been a lot of fighting, it's sometimes very difficult to tell which dog is dominant, because the subordinate dog is constantly on the defensive. I liken him to a child who has been beaten up and pushed around by the school bully. This child's always on guard, looking over his shoulder and ready to defend himself at any moment. It could be the subordinate dog who's starting fights. If one of your dogs is that defensive, you'll have to watch for subtle signs of who's dominant. Watch them closely and objectively. Objectivity is sometimes hard to achieve. You may have a favorite dog, and you want that one to be dominant. Or one dog is of a breed that you think should be dominant, and you refuse to believe that he's not. Whatever your circumstances are, you can't deny the dominant dog. You must respect the dogs' relationship. You can't decide which one is going to be dominant.

If you have dogs that are fighting no matter what you do, take them to your veterinarian. It's possible the dog that doesn't seem to want to give up has a weakness of some kind; this could make him overdefend himself. I had one case where the dogs reached the point of intentionally injuring each other. It turned out that one of them had serious hip dysplasia. In another similar case, one dog had a serious uterine infection.

There is one situation where I recommend interference. If you have an elderly dog with geriatric problems like cataracts and arthritis, or one that is weakened for some reason, put yourself in the Head Honcho position and protect that dog. Under most circumstances the stronger dog will leave the weaker one alone as long as it's understood that he is dominant. But every now and then I run into a dog that is a bully or has poor social skills. Also, there are dogs that will fight any other dog at any time for no apparent reason. These dogs are few and far between, and usually they do fine if they remain in a home with no other dogs.

If you already have a dog and you want to bring a new dog in, it's best to introduce them off your property. That way you avoid territorial fighting. You'll want to do this even if the new dog is a tiny puppy. Once you've introduced them, you can bring them home together. You don't have to go too far. Down the street will be fine.

I hope that after reading this, you have a better understanding of the dynamics of the peck order and how important it is in your dogs' lives.

OBEDIENCE

I'm going to walk you through obedience commands and how to teach them. But before you read this chapter, check to see what I have to say about training your breed. For some there will be special instructions.

First, there's a very important canine reflex that you must understand. This reflex is called counterpressure or natural resistance. If you pull on Rover's leg, you'll notice that he tries to pull it back. That's counterpressure. I hear, "My dog doesn't like to have his feet messed with. Giving a pedicure is a nightmare." Counterpressure has nothing to do with Rover "not liking his feet messed with." He can't help resisting. The reason the counterpressure reflex arose in dogs is that it's a survival mechanism. If a wild animal were to get hold of a dog's hind leg, the dog wouldn't lie down and try to talk him out of it. He'd resist! If you put slight pressure on Rover's side, you'll notice that he pushes back against your hand: counterpressure. If you put a leash on Rover, it doesn't make any difference who starts the tension. Once it's started, you're in a counterpressure fight with Rover that he can't help. When a dog is being taught aggression, the trainer pulls back on the leash, the dog pulls forward, and that is praised. The trainer is taking advantage of counterpressure. To teach sled dogs to pull, again the trainer pulls back on the leash, the dog pulls forward, and that is praised. I get so frustrated by the number of professionals who work with dogs and don't know about counterpressure. Well, now you'll know something they don't.

Equipment

You'll need a training collar. I hate to call it a choke chain, but I'm afraid that's what they're called, and that's what you need. If you put Rover's leash on his "everyday" collar there is counterpressure all the way around his neck and it's constant. I'm very picky about collars, because they pass on almost all the messages you send. They have such a variety out in the pet supply world, and I'd say the majority of them are useless or downright ridiculous. When the collar is on and you tighten it a little, there should be no more than two to four inches of slack. Whether Rover is a 125-pound Rottweiler or a five-pound Poodle, get the heaviest, smoothest chain you can find. Pay close attention to Rover's coat and skin. If Rover is a Collie and you get a narrow chain, it will catch in his coat and tighten down. If Rover is a Bloodhound or Shar-Pei and you get a narrow chain, it will pinch him. If Rover is a Cocker and you get a wide-link collar, the combination of the weight of the collar and the clasp on the leash will tighten the collar down and it won't relax. If you get a collar that is too light, it will hang up on itself and it won't relax. If you get a collar that is too long, it will wrap around on itself and it won't relax. Remember counterpressure. We want that collar to stay relaxed unless we're trying to send a message. Once the message is sent, that collar should relax immediately. If the collar goes on easily but is hard to get off over the ears, it's too tight. Get one two inches longer.

You need a six-foot leash. I prefer the nylon because it's cheaper, it's cleanable, and in the long run it's easier on the hands. Leather absorbs your scent and won't let go of it. Then the leash becomes a toy instead of a tool, because Rover is so attracted to it. Also, leather expands and contracts with the weather, which causes cracking. If Rover is a large dog, that can get uncomfortable on the hands.

About Commands

There are a couple of things I want you to know about commands before we begin the teaching process.

NUMBER ONE:

When you know for a fact that Rover understands a command, then the first time you give it to him, it's a command, the second time it's a request, and the third time you're begging him. I'm sure at some point you've seen someone saying to their dog: "Rover, sit. Rover, sit. Sit. Sit. You know how to sit, now sit." Rover is pointing and saying, "Watch this. She does this every time, and I don't have to sit if I don't want to." I know it's hard not to say the command that second time, but try hard not to beg. I have a client whose dog thinks the "sit" command is said four times. He'll sit on the fourth "Sit," every time. When you give Rover the command, pause to let him follow through. If he doesn't, physically reinforce it.

✓NUMBER TWO:

When you're talking to Rover, always respect him enough to give him his name first. There are two reasons for this. First, there are words in your vocabulary that are going to be a part of Rover's vocabulary. For example, let's say Rover understands "Sit," and you say to me, "Judi. You can sit over there." Rover thinks, "I know that word," but nobody has looked at him and made him do it. The next time you say, "Rover, sit," he's going to think, "I didn't have to last time." Second, Rover's name gets what's called a sympathetic response. For example, you can be in a crowded restaurant, waiting for your name to be called for dinner. They can call fifty names; you don't hear those. You hear your own. That's a sympathetic response.

"ROVER, SIT." As you say, "Rover sit," pull back slightly on the leash or his collar, and with your other hand at the base of his tail, apply gentle pressure until he sits. *Praise.* If you place your hand too far up on his back, and you notice he resists, counterpressure has reared its ugly head. Just put your hand closer to his tail.

You're not going to teach Rover to sit and then never use the command. There are very definite reasons why I teach a dog to sit. This is a command I want you to work hard on. You're going to get more contempt and back talk for the "Sit" command than for any other command. Books and obedience classes always tell you the dog resists "Down" more than any other command. They don't resist "Down," they resist the way "Down" is taught. People try to teach Rover "Down" by pulling down on his collar. Remember counterpressure. Rover has no choice but to resist. Very rarely do you see a dog just sit. They're standing, moving around, or lying down. When you can get an immediate sit out of Rover you've got control. Dogs get out of control of themselves very easily. You can use "Sit" to help Rover out. A dog can't do two things at the same time. So if Rover is under stress, you can say, "Rover, sit." He'll say, "Whew, thank you, I can do that." That one command can right his world for him. You may know how, when children are close to hysteria or panic, you can give them something familiar to calm them down. "Sit" can work that way for Rover. I tell mailmen, meter readers, and cable installers that if it looks like they're going to have a problem with a dog they should just yell "Sit!" Most dogs have been taught to sit at some point. Whether the dog sits or not, I guarantee you it'll stop him in his tracks.

There are going to be times when you say, "Rover, sit," and he'll go down very slowly as if to say, "I was going to sit anyway." Other times you'll say, "Rover, sit," and when you see the look on his face there will be no doubt in your mind that he just said, "*&%$#@*." Don't put up with that kind of back talk. Make him sit. There's no point in teaching Rover to sit if you're not going to use the command. He should sit before eating; that's basic manners. He should sit before going in or out of a door; that's basic manners. Call him to you, tell him to sit, and pet him.

"ROVER, STAY." To teach Rover to stay, you're going to take advantage of counterpressure. Hold the leash straight up above his neck and put a little tension in it. Because of counterpressure, he has no choice but to stay pretty much right where he is. Keep tension in the leash, put the palm of your hand in front of him as a hand signal, and move around him, saying, "Rover, stay." Circle him, but if he tries to spin when you go around behind him, it just means he's a little insecure when he can't see you, so stay where he can see you. (If you notice Rover has a hard time swallowing, you have too much tension on the leash.) Slowly begin to loosen the collar as you move around, saying, "Rover, stay." When you can loosen the collar and move away you know he's got it. Needless to say, you're *praising* this whole time.

I know, I know, this isn't the way they taught you to do it in obedience class, and this isn't the way the other book said to do it. What you were told to do was to put Rover at a sit by your side, use the hand signal, say, "Stay," and walk away. Rover walked away with you, so you told him no, put him back into the sit, and told him to stay. Listen up, Humans. There was a very good reason why Rover walked off after you. He was instinctively exhibiting "allelomimetic behavior," which is a fancy way of saying "following," "copying," or "mimicking." In other words, he had no choice but to follow you. And then he was told no. In his view we're a very confusing species. You can't really blame him for thinking that, can you? You'll notice when you're walking him and he is on the street side he will speed up his pace when a car, bike, or jogger passes. That's allelomimetic behavior. Once whatever it is has passed by, Rover will check his pace.

I see absolutely no point in teaching a dog to "stay" so that you can walk backward for fifteen feet. Use this command! "Rover off. Stay off." "Rover quiet. Stay quiet." He can stay down, he can stay with someone, he can stand-stay, stay back, stay out. You can use this command to extend his vocabulary. I know it's hard to believe, but Rover can understand the two commands put together. If Rover jumps when he gets excited, you can anticipate the jumping and say, "Rover, stay off" before the front paws leave the ground.

"ROVER, GO LIE DOWN." Here again, I see no point in teaching Rover to go down with a hand signal given from twenty feet away. One of the things I'm trying to do in this book is to apply everything to your environment. I want him to be a good companion in your home. So, we're going to teach Rover "Go lie down."

As I've said, the classes and the books tell you that Rover resists "Down" more than any other command. But now that you know about counterpressure, you can understand why he resists it so. To introduce the "Down" command, you're going to do all the work for him. This way we're going to avoid any resistance. Oh, I almost forget to tell you. The books and the classes say the dog resists "Down," because it puts him in a submissive position. Wrong. When a dog goes straight down on his stomach and chest, it is not submission. Take my word for it.

Get Rover in the "Sit" position and kneel at his side. With your left hand lightly on his shoulders, bring your right arm under his right leg, pick up the left leg, and bring him to the "Down" position while saying "Rover, down." *Praise.* Keep your praise low-key on this command, because we don't want him to think it's a game every time you kneel next to him. You're going to throw a hand signal in here. Just before you put him in the down, pass your hand in front of his eyes down past the end of his nose, with one or two fingers extended. Just after you put him in the down, use the hand signal again, maybe two or three times, while you're saying: "That's a good *down*, Rover [emphasize the word "down"], good boy, good *down*, Rover." When Rover begins to anticipate the down, and you believe he's beginning to understand the hand signal, it's time to go to the next step.

Pick a spot in which Rover is already comfortable. There can be as many spots as there are rooms available. Make sure that the spot is not isolated from you, or he'll never stay there. You can use the leash or his collar. Make your hand signal in front of his face, and as you lead him to the spot say, "Rover—go—lie—down." When you say "Down," your hand should be pointing to the spot and Rover should go down. This part is all brand-new, so be prepared to physically put him in the down. Your goal is to be able to use your hand signal and, staying in one place, make Rover go lie down. I've had clients tell me they got their money's worth using that one command. They were finally able to eat in peace.

So that you're not surprised when it happens, be ready to see Rover in a down position but crawling toward you. He'll crawl on his belly until he's right next to your feet. This is a natural and common response. *Don't try to correct it!* It is so natural that the military and police canine units take advantage of it to teach their dogs to crawl under barbed wire and vehicles. You can respond in one of two ways. You can ignore it, and the novelty will wear off. Or you can turn it into a command: As Rover is crawling say, "Crawl, Rover, crawl." If you turn it into a command, he'll do it only when you tell him to. If you ignore it, he'll stop doing it as soon as he's secure in the fact that you're not going to leave him wherever you sent him down. After a short while you'll be able to say, "Rover, go lie down, and stay down." Won't that be neat? Yes, Human, I know it's a long sentence, but I assure you that Rover will understand. Let's take it apart so you can see what I mean. Rover knows his name. "Go lie down" has become a command. He understands "Stay," and he knows "Down." "And" is the only word in that sentence that he won't understand.

"ROVER, LET'S GO." Now that you have a good understanding of counterpressure and you've actually seen it in action, we're going to start walking Rover on a leash.

A famous trainer by the name of William Koehler developed a wonderful method of teaching a dog to walk on a leash at your side. As you may have figured out, I don't train for show. Too many things that Rover does naturally have to be trained out of him for show. For example, when you put Rover at a sit at your side, you'll notice he turns in toward your leg. That has to be corrected for show. Koehler trained for show, so I won't take the heeling process as far as he does. We're going to be doing Judi's version of William Koehler's method.

The hardest part of telling you how to walk with Rover on a leash is going to be describing how to put the collar on correctly. Put the collar on your left wrist, pretending that it's Rover's neck. Put your right index finger through the top ring on the collar, and pull out. If the collar is on correctly, the ring is sliding *over* the links. When it tightens it will relax immediately. If it's on wrong, you'll notice the links riding over the inside of the ring. When it tightens it will stay tight. Got it? I didn't think so. Okay, let's try this. When the collar's on right, it looks like a "P." If it's on wrong it looks like a "9." Once you have it on Rover's neck, pull the ring out with your finger. If, when you let it go, it relaxes immediately, it's on correctly. If, when you pull it tight, it stays tight, it's on wrong.

Whether you walk Rover on your right or your left is entirely up to you. Rover's ambidextrous, he doesn't care. The reason the left side is the common side is that most people are right-handed. In the long run you'll be holding the leash exclusively with your right hand. If you're left-handed, just reverse everything. With Rover on your left, the leash will come across your body and be held in your right hand. If Rover is on your left and you hold the leash in your left hand, you will have a tendency to put tension on the collar and keep Rover at your side by pulling. The goal is to have Rover at your side, leg in sight and the collar nice and loose.

I don't use "Heel," and rarely will I let my clients use it. "Heel" is too easily abused. The command "Heel" means "Begin walking"—period. I'm sure you've seen someone walking his dog. The dog gets up to the end of the leash and you hear "Heel!" and the dog is yanked back. This only has to happen three or four times before that poor dog begins to connect the word "heel" with being yanked back to the owner's side. The original meaning of the command is lost.

Use whatever is comfortable for you. "Let's go," "Let's walk," "Walk with me." If you use a command that obviously implies forward motion, you won't use it when you yank him back.

Now that you have the collar on correctly, and the leash is attached, and you've chosen your command, you're ready to go. What you're going to do now is convince Rover that you've gone two sandwiches short of a picnic and you don't have the vaguest idea how to walk on a leash, so the best thing for him to do is keep an eye on you.

With Rover at your side, the leash in both hands, and your arms relaxed at your sides, say, "Rover, let's go," and start walking. Rover is going to head straight out in front of you at a gallop. Fix this picture in your mind for a moment. Rover is at leash length in front of you, and the collar is tight. Play this scene in slow motion in your mind. If you continue walking in the same direction as Rover, his collar will stay tight, and the leash will stay tense. What's happening? Right! Counterpressure. We want the collar to be loose, the leash relaxed, and Rover at your side. With Rover over six feet in front of you, make a right about-face and walk, *with purpose,* in the other direction. Rover is on the other end of the leash, so if you turn with purpose, he has no choice but to go where you go. Make sure you don't *pull* him around, and don't wait for him to catch up. At the same gallop, he'll turn when you do and run right past you. Pause for another moment and picture this. We're not actually "teaching" Rover anything. We're letting him figure out that the best place to be is at your side, keeping a close eye on your left leg, and the collar loose. *He has to understand what's wrong before he can understand what's right.* Let *him* make the mistake. Let *him* hit the end of the leash. Let *him* tighten the collar. Concentrate! If he's out in front of you, he can't see your left leg, so he can't anticipate your direction. About-face, right turn. If he's ranging out to one side, he can't see your left leg. Turn right. If he's lagging behind, turn around and walk right by him. Don't pace yourself to him.

I want you to use some common sense. It never ceases to amaze me how many Humans are terrifically proud that "Rover walks on a leash as if he was born to it." When I see Rover it turns out he's a small dog and, bless his heart, it takes everything he has just to keep up. It's like watching a three-year-old who has to run like crazy to keep up with the parent holding his hand.

As you see Rover galloping past, slow your pace and get ready to make your turn. When he hits the end of the leash and comes around he sees your back. Take advantage of the loose collar as he comes around and bring him to you as he catches up. He may only be at your side for a split second, but when he is there praise, quickly. The only words he's going to hear from you will be positive, and he'll hear them only when he's at your side with your leg in sight. The rest of the time we want him to concentrate on the fact that you forgot how to walk on a leash. He'd better stay close to you because when he's not looking you're wandering off in one direction or the other.

You're not going to limit yourself to right turns for the rest of Rover's life, so let's make a left. As you're walking with Rover at your side, place your left hand down close to the collar, pull back *slightly* on the leash, and make your turn. Don't shove your leg into him; don't nudge him with your leg to keep him back with you. Getting your left leg involved with the turn is simply not necessary. One of the advantages of making a left turn right now is that Rover has no choice but to pay attention to you.

Two things will tell you that Rover's catching on. One, he'll start to anticipate your turns. Two, he'll begin to look up at you and ask, "How much longer do you figure we'll be going in circles?" When you see that look, you'll know he's figuring it out.

There are several advantages in my method of walking with Rover on a leash. One of them is that dogs go toward a sound, rather than away from it. If you're walking along and you hear a bike coming up behind you, Rover heard that bike long before you did. I want Rover to hear that bike and think, "My Human is going to do something stupid, so I better keep my eye on that leg." When you back up to let that bike go by he's going to back up, too. Your environment is Rover's environment, and your environment is a hostile environment for him. It includes cars, other dogs, kids, bikers, in-line skaters, and so on. We can't let him get hit by a car to teach him he could get hurt. Do not—I repeat, *do not*—"socialize" Rover with other dogs on a walk. When two dogs meet, their relationship has to be established immediately, with the possibility of a fight. There is absolutely no point in putting Rover through this. These two dogs aren't going to sit down and say, "Whattaya think of those Cowboys?" Kids are sometimes hard on dogs. Until they're about twelve or thirteen years old their movements are erratic. They can be at a standstill, then suddenly at a dead run, screaming the whole time.

When you can walk with Rover from one end of your block to the other without having to about-face too often, it's time to take him out into that larger environment. This is a high-stress situation. High stress is anywhere around you that's active. As you're walking him in a high-stress situation, be prepared to make some about-face turns. When you're walking along and Rover starts to go toward another dog, turn and walk in the opposite direction. If he wants to say hi to some people, turn. I want Rover to begin to think of everything "out there" as just so many reasons to keep an eye on you. He's going to begin to understand that you don't like any of that neat stuff on a walk, so he'd better just keep an eye on you.

When Rover is starting to pay close attention to you, offer him some challenges. As you're walking, break into a jog and then come to a dead stop. Take a few steps very slowly, one slow step at a time. Make sudden hard rights and lefts. Use your imagination. Rover will enjoy this, and you will have his undivided attention.

It's time to pocket your left hand. From now on, the only time you're going to use your left is to make a left turn. I want you to put all of the leash in your right hand. The leash will be across your body in front of you. Bring in enough slack to get Rover close to your leg, but make sure the collar remains loose. It may take a couple of minutes to get this right. Take as long as you need. Watch the collar. It should remain loose all the time. Put your right arm down to your side, relax, and walk as you do without a leash in your hand. Instead of turning, you're going to do what I call "putting the power in your right." As you're walking, if you notice Rover beginning to drift, give a quick pop on the leash. Your arm is down at your side, right? Good. The leash should go straight across your body, and you should hear the links going through the ring of the collar. If you don't hear that sound it means you're pulling. It is totally unnecessary to jerk! All you're doing with that "pop" is telling Rover, "Hey, kiddo, I'm still in control here." If you find yourself using your left hand too much, put it in your pocket. If you don't have a pocket, put your hand behind your back.

Have you ever seen a good cutting horse do his thing? That's what it should look like when you're walking Rover. If you haven't seen a cutting horse, then picture a dance. There's not a move you can make that Rover can't anticipate, and there's not a move Rover can make that you can't anticipate.

I firmly believe that the dog should enjoy the walk as much as the person does. When you're walking along and Rover indicates that there's something that he really wants to check out, give him permission to do so: "Go ahead, Rover." Let him do his sniff thing for a minute, then say, "Rover, let's go." You're in control of releasing him and you're in control of starting up again. Make sure you're not releasing him to lift his leg and mark. This insures that Rover does not walk you.

YOU COME TO A STOP AND ROVER SITS AUTOMATICALLY. This command allows for more attentiveness and gives you added control.

We know ahead of time that we're coming to a stop. Our brain sends the appropriate message to our muscles, and we begin the process of stopping. Rover has to pay attention to that and then go through the same thing himself. Remember, a dog cannot do two things at the same time. He can't go through this automatic "sit" process and lunge into the street or after a dog at the same time. The goal is to have Rover sit automatically without a command every time you come to a stop.

As you're walking, decide where you're going to stop. Come to your stop, tell Rover to sit, and physically sit him. *Praise* and say, "Rover, let's go." Whatever you're saying for walking forward is now going to become a command. You're going to tell Rover to sit and physically sit him at least thirty to forty times. (You don't have to do this all in one lesson.) When he begins to anticipate, continue to tell him to sit, and physically sit him (and praise) about a dozen more times. When he's sat automatically without being told to ten to fifteen times, you know he's got it. Expect it of him every time.

By the way, if you stop to talk to a neighbor, don't correct him if he lies down while you're talking. Remember, sitting isn't one of a dog's favorite things to do, especially for any length of time.

"ROVER, HALT." This command is easy but can be important. As you're walking, stop, quickly say, "Rover, halt!" and just as quickly start your walk again. This command is handy if Rover is off leash and you want him to stop forward motion. If he's on a run the command will immediately get his attention. Even if he doesn't come to a complete stop, he will slow his pace and come to you when you call him. The main reason I teach this command is that there are times when you're afraid Rover is going to run into the street, or he's making an excited mad dash toward someone.

"ROVER, COME." Work hard on this command: It can save a life.

Getting Rover to come will take more time and effort than all the other commands put together. This is one of the only commands that you can't reinforce physically. It has to be reinforced vocally.

You don't have to say "Come." You may find you say "Come here" or "Come on." I have a client who says, "Daisy, come here, come on." Notice what you say naturally, and make that the command. Whatever word or words you choose, say them in a positive tone. Coming when called is always going to be a positive thing to do. *Never call Rover to you to discipline him.*

The introduction to "Come." Put Rover at a sit in front of you, tell him to stay, and back up to the end of the leash. (You may have to say "Stay" a few times.) When you're at the end of the leash, say "Rover, come." Bring him to you with a hand over hand on the leash. (Counterpressure can become a problem if the dog is considerably larger and more powerful than the human. If this is the case, give a few gentle tugs on the leash and Rover will understand what you want.) As you praise him like crazy, bring him to a sit in front of you without actually saying "Sit."

Bringing him to a sit allows for a pause. If you don't establish it, then when you say, "Rover, come," he'll come to you, say, "Hi, Human," and run right on by. I don't care if, in the long run, he sits when he comes to you; I just want him to do a mental and physical pause. Don't get cocky about the stay—that is, don't try dropping the leash when you get to the end. If Rover breaks the stay you've compromised yourself. I want him to understand that you are in complete control of bringing him to you.

The casual "Come." The reason for the casual "Come" is to imprint on Rover's mind that when he hears his name and the word "come" he's in front of you immediately. Relax the leash and let Rover check things out. When he's not paying any attention to you at all, suddenly say, "Rover, come," and bring him to you.

When you've done the introduction a few times you'll notice Rover will give a bored sigh and say, "We're going to sit, stay, come." Sigh. "Sit, stay, come." When you notice this attitude go on to the casual "Come." After you've done the casual "Come" a few times he's going to say, "Hey, my mother didn't raise no fool, I'll just stay close to you." When you notice that attitude, go on to something else entirely.

The round robin "Come." I teach this one for two reasons. First, it's another way to work on the "come." Second, it allows all family members to get involved in Rover's training. It's never a good idea to have only one member of the family who can call the dog.

Put an extension of some kind on the end of Rover's leash. Another leash or rope will do. With everybody in a circle, the first Human says, "Rover, come," and brings him in. While praising him, throw the leash to the next Human. They say, "Rover, come," and so on around the circle. Do the round robin "Come" even if there are only two of you. Rover will enjoy this one because of all the attention and praise on each end.

Work on coming when called *on leash* for at least two weeks.

If Rover doesn't sit, you can sit him; if he doesn't go into a "down" you can put him in one. While you're working on coming when called on leash do not—I repeat, *do not*—call Rover to the command "Come" when he's off leash. If he's in the yard and you want him to come in, use a whistle, or call out just his name and pat your leg. Use anything but the word "Come." Right now, if Rover is off leash and you call,

"Rover, come," and he doesn't, there is absolutely nothing you can do about it. You are the one compromised, not Rover. We don't want to give him too many choices too soon. We'll give him choices soon enough. For right now, hang on to that leash.

"Rover, come," off leash. Do this lesson in a confined area.

Take Rover's collar and leash off. Do this casually, so that he doesn't suddenly realize he's off the leash and bolt. Release him. Just say: "Okay, Rover. Take off. Go ahead"—something along those lines. When he gets a few feet away, say, "Rover, come." When he comes to you, *praise* as you never have before. Release him again. When he gets a little farther away this time, say, "Rover, come." As before, *praise like crazy*.

At some point when you release him, he's going to make the choice not to come to you. This is when you begin to reinforce the "Come" command vocally.

If he has come to you off leash, even if only from a short distance, you know he knows his name and understands "Come." So you also know that when he doesn't follow that command he is *choosing* not to. He is saying, "No. I don't want to." He turns his head and says, "I'll be there in a minute." He is insulting you. Are you starting to feel a little insulted, Human? Do you feel as if you're dealing with a naughty dog? Good. Let those feelings come out in your voice. Here we go. Give Rover the "Come" command. When he doesn't come you're going to rain on his parade, big-time. Start moving toward him *slowly* while saying things like: "Rover! You heard me. I am so disappointed in you. Shame on you for ignoring me like that. Rover! Mary had a little lamb, and I'm going to have you for breakfast. Little Bo-Peep lost her sheep, and I'm losing my mind. When I tell you to do something I want it done now!" The whole time you're doing this you're moving toward him *slowly*. When you get very close, say, "Rover, come." If he comes to you from six inches, it's the equivalent of ten feet. Praise him as if he'd won an Academy Award. Remember, "Come" should always be said in a positive tone. Don't say "Come" while you're stalking him. You're going to give him that first opportunity to come, and then another at the end. Your yelling and carrying on is not downtime. It's training time! You're teaching Rover that coming to you when called is very positive, while not coming when called is no fun at all. You're going to become impatient. Don't let that worry you. I had to stalk a dog in his own backyard for fifteen minutes. Every time I got close to him he would go down into play posture and run off.

In working on "Come" at increasing distances, release and call, release and call. Sometimes, when he comes to you, stop the lesson altogether and play. At other times put the collar and leash back on him and go for a walk, or work on other commands. Vary your pattern enough to keep Rover from expecting to be released as soon as he comes to you. The first time you give Rover the "Come" command off leash and he ignores you, try getting into a squat position to make "Come" more inviting. If he doesn't respond, you need to start over with the leash. Don't fret, we'll get him where we want him. Take him back out into high-stress situations a few times. High stress always puts you in control.

If you need to reinforce the "Come" command some more physically, purchase clothesline rope. Cut a thirty- or forty-foot length and tie one end to Rover's collar. Work with him on the "Sit, stay, come" and the casual "come." The casual "Come" really makes a point this way. Using the rope you can get Rover to come from quite a distance. As important as "Come" is, the more ways we can work on it, the better.

When working with Rover on any command, remember counterpressure and bear in mind the canine tendency to allelomimetic behavior. When Rover sits at your side he will have a tendency to lean in; that's natural. Don't try to correct it; he'll stop when he becomes more secure.

Pay attention to what your Rover is all about and respect it. If you work against his breed and personality, everything will turn into a struggle for both of you.

PROBLEM SOLVING

No matter what problem you're having with Rover, part of the solution is going to be putting yourself into an undeniable lead position. This is going to be true whether the problem is biting or chronic barking. You are going to become the Head Honcho. Read Chapter 8, "The Head Honcho Human."

Barking

Before telling you how to correct a barking problem, I want you to understand a little about why Rover barks. Almost all dogs bark to a certain extent, and they bark for numerous reasons. I want you to understand those reasons, so that when you begin to correct the barking you'll go at it with some knowledge of why Rover is doing it in the first place.

What Humans usually do when Rover's barking becomes a nuisance is go to the door or window and *yell*, "Rover, no! Rover, stop that! Rover, quiet! Rover, no!" As I mentioned in Chapter 3, this response amounts to barking right along with him. Don't do that anymore, Human: You're training Rover to bark. Not to mention what you're doing to your image.

In Chapter 3, "Dos and Don'ts of Discipline," I explain how to use an aluminum can to introduce commands. This is the time to use it and introduce Rover to "Quiet." Throw the can; the instant Rover's barking stops, say, "Rover, quiet." Just as with any other command, repeat if necessary. In other words, if Rover starts barking again right away, stay with it and say, "Rover, I said quiet." Soon you'll be able to go to the door or window and say, "Rover, quiet," and his barking will stop. Remember, anytime you use a command it puts you in control. The goal is to be able to say, "Rover, stay quiet."

Barking Causes and Corrections

CAUSE: SURVIVAL MECHANISM. You see this kind of barking when a dog is feeling threatened in some way. What Rover will do is start barking and begin to back up. What he's attempting to get across is, "Don't come any closer! I'm really scared right now. I don't want you to pet me! Don't come any closer!"

CORRECTION. Put yourself in the Head Honcho position, so that Rover won't feel as if he needs to take care of himself. When he begins to bark under stress, simply get his attention and give him the command you've chosen that means "barking stops." As you begin to take over as Head Honcho, you'll notice Rover's barking will lessen considerably.

CAUSE: BREED. Some breeds of dogs are natural barkers. Barking is a part of who they are, and must be respected. Shelties, Beagles, and Lhasa Apsos are good examples.

CORRECTION. You can't really correct breed barking, but you can control it. Start when Rover is a puppy, introducing the command that means "barking stops." The hardest part of controlling breed barking is not laughing. When a six-week-old Sheltie sits back and barks, it's cute and funny. The tendency, for me anyway, is to encourage the barking by talking to the puppy. Yes, I know, Human: I, of all people should know better. What can I say? Of course, I'm quick to tell my client not to do the same.

CAUSE: TO ALERT. This kind of barking arises if Rover sees or hears something he thinks you should know about. It's the kind of barking most Humans want from their dog.

CORRECTION. This kind of barking usually doesn't need to be corrected. Rover will bark a few times to alert you, and then will stop. Make sure you don't encourage him to keep barking by asking him what he hears, and it shouldn't be a problem.

CAUSE: COMMUNICATION. Wild dogs bark to stay in touch with each other on a hunt. Even though our domestic dogs don't need to do that, they still do. This is what's happening when you hear one dog bark and the rest of the neighborhood chimes in, or when you hear howling in response to a siren.

CORRECTION. Be a responsible dog owner and get your Rover to stop. Use the can to introduce "Quiet." Just between you and me, if Rover stops barking but the rest of the neighborhood continues, go outside and yell *"Sit!"* You'll be amazed at the results.

CAUSE: FRUSTRATION. All kinds of factors can come into play here. Maybe Rover hears a sound but can't identify it. Maybe he's been left alone too long. Maybe he's trying to get attention. Maybe he's tied up. Et cetera, et cetera.

CORRECTION. Use the can to introduce Rover to the "Quiet" command. The command will work a lot better if you can pinpoint the source of frustration and, if possible, eliminate it.

CAUSE: TERRITORIALITY. This barking arises when Rover wants to get another dog or person off his territory. It can become nuisance barking. Rover goes through what I call a power surge. He sees someone walking at the corner of his property; he begins to bark; he follows the "intruder" with his bark until the person has walked on by. Rover has absolutely no idea that that person had every intention of walking from Point A to Point B. He thinks he got the guy off his territory. So the barking reinforces itself.

CORRECTION. The first thing to do is to put yourself in the Head Honcho position. If your dog is becoming overly aggressive in taking care of his territory, the stronger your lead position is the more he can go off duty. Don't hesitate to use the can to introduce the "Quiet" command.

CAUSE: PROTECTION. You have to know what you're seeing (or hearing) with protection barking. (I'm not talking about trained protection dogs.) Is Rover protecting you, the house, himself, or all of the above? This kind of barking gets out of hand easily. To avoid this make sure you aren't encouraging Rover to bark at every sound he alerts to. In other words, don't say, "Rover, what is it? What do you hear?"

CORRECTION. Put yourself in the Head Honcho position. Rover needs to learn the difference between barking at people on the street, and barking at a possible intruder. He learns it if he feels the need to protect everything, including himself.

CAUSE: COMPULSIVITY. The best example of compulsive barking: The doorbell rings and Rover rushes to the door barking.

CORRECTION. All you have to do to stop a negative compulsive pattern is alter it. But correcting this problem is going to take time. Given Rover's compulsive habitual personality, he is now locked into everything that happens the instant the doorbell rings. The first thing you need to do is desensitize Rover to the sound of the doorbell. Ring it over and over until he doesn't react. Next, desensitize him to the opening and closing of the door. With Rover beside you, open the door just a crack; if he makes any movement, shut the door. Shut the door at *any movement,* even if it's just a slight extension of the neck. As you're able to open the door wider without getting a reaction, tell Rover, "Stay back." If he makes even the slightest movement toward the door, shut it. Eventually you will be able to open the door all the way with Rover at a stay back.

The second aspect of this training goes like this: No matter where you are within the household, when the doorbell rings you make *the exact same moves every time.* This will convince Rover that you need help getting to the door. If you're in the kitchen when the doorbell rings, open the refrigerator and talk to the vegetables, turn the water on and off, walk to the door backward. If you're in the living room, turn the TV or stereo on and off; pick up a book and drop it. Use your imagination. Rover will eventually start to check to see if you're coming to the door. When that happens, you'll be able to tell him to "stay back"—and then you, Human, are in charge of your very own front door.

CAUSE: ISOLATION. Dogs don't handle solitude well. Rover will do anything to get you to him, or himself to you.

CORRECTION. The only way to correct this kind of barking is to get Rover out of isolation.

CAUSE: ENCOURAGEMENT. This kind of barking develops because you have said: "What is it, Rover? What do you hear?" Encouraged barking can become nuisance barking very quickly. Once it's nuisance barking, Rover is no use to you as a watchdog. Car alarms are an example of the problem. It doesn't take much to set off a car alarm, so by now hardly anyone pays any attention to them. You will reach that point with Rover.

CORRECTION. Use the can and introduce Rover to the "Quiet" command.

CAUSE: NONE. The barking's mindless. I have a client with a Border Collie Cross. He jumps in the bathtub every now and then and barks for a while. He likes the sound of his own voice. Obviously, if he were human, he'd be a bathroom singer. Mindless barking also arises when Rover is startled. He will give a few high-pitched barks and then settle down. My Fido always seems to do this when she's right next to my ear.

CORRECTION. There's really no need to correct this kind of barking.

Fence Jumping

I always groan when I get a call about a fence jumper. There are almost as many variables as there are jumpers. When Rover jumps the fence, everything becomes incredibly positive. The second Rover gets over the fence he goes through a "freedom reflex": His heart races, his blood pressure is way up, and his pupils are dilated. He is not in control. This is when you see dogs get hit by cars. It makes no difference how car smart or street smart a dog is; when they're in the grip of a freedom reflex they are not in control. Depending on breed and circumstances, the "high" can last anywhere from ten seconds to close to thirty seconds. Once Rover comes down, he finds himself in a new area with wonderful new smells and sounds, plus friendly people and dogs.

When they realize Rover is gone, most Humans immediately jump in the car and start looking for him. If Rover likes riding in the car, he's going to think this new jumping stuff is really neat. A Human who sees Rover leave immediately runs outside, starts calling him, and gives chase. Rover looks around, sees his Human chasing, and yells, "Yeah! I love this game!" What we have here, Human, is positive reinforcement for negative behavior. The hardest thing to overcome with jumping is that everything about jumping is positive.

Because I don't know what kind of fence you have, I'm going to give you several methods to choose from.

Nine times out of ten, Rover will jump over in the same place every time. He trusts that spot. So if you know where it is, there are a few things you can do. If possible, put something on the other side of the wall that will make the jump unpleasant or appear hazardous. You can position a wading pool so that he'll jump into it. Use your imagination, as long as what you choose is not harmful. If the time of his jumping is predictable, you can station yourself on the other side of the wall; the instant he jumps, you leap up like a crazy person, yelling, "Rover! No!" and push him back into your yard.

If you have to do everything from your side of the fence, we need to work on deterrents. If you have a cinder block wall, get plastic gallon containers (such as distilled-water jugs) and set them on the wall about three to four feet apart. I don't know who figured this out, and I can't tell you why it works. Have you ever noticed gallon containers on the corners of someone's lawn? That's to keep loose dogs out of their yard. My only guess is that the jugs create an optical illusion of some kind. As for the containers on the wall, we're hoping Rover won't jump through them. Another deterrent that I've found to work is balloons. Blow up three or four balloons, approach Rover, and pop the balloon right at him. Approach him again and pop another balloon. Do this three or four times.

Put him where he can't see you, blow up however many balloons you think you need, and set them along the fence. When Rover goes out he'll see those balloons and, we hope, stay away from the fence. Unless something pops them, balloons deflate slowly, so the deterrent lasts a while.

If Rover is a climber instead of a jumper, you can use mousetraps. I hear you, I hear you! I promise you, Rover is not going to get trapped in the mousetrap. Set some mousetraps and turn them upside down. Put them on the fence, and cover them with a light layer of cloth, leaves, or whatever you have. When Climbing Rover goes over the top, those mousetraps are going to pop, and he's going to think the wall did it.

I'll warn you now, I've known dogs that found popping balloons was wonderful fun. I've also known dogs to snap all the mousetraps and collect them.

Sometimes chicken wire works wonders. Buy a roll of chicken wire (it's cheap!). Tack it to the top of the fence, then bring it out at an angle and tack it to the ground. This one keeps Rover away from the fence altogether.

If your Rover is fence-jumping no matter what you do, or if for some reason deterrents aren't practical for you, there's still another method up my sleeve. Remember, I told you any time you use a command it puts you in control. You're now going to put that fact into practice. I want you to open the door or the gate and give Rover a command to take off. "Go ahead" or "Go on" works. Now, calm down and hear me out. You know that no matter what you do Rover is going to get out, right? Okay, this puts you in control of it. You're going to get one of two reactions from Rover. He's either going to look up at you in bewilderment, or he'll say, "I'm outa here" and take off. It's going to take a few weeks, but if you consistently do this Rover will learn not to leave your home area without permission. I know this is hard to do and hard to believe. Keep telling yourself that he'd be getting out anyway. Not only does this put you in control, but this way you prevent Rover from having the dreaded freedom reflex.

Finally, tap into Rover's compulsive habitual personality and walk him around your block the exact same way every time. If you do this enough, when he does get out he'll very likely run the same route. And end up home.

Terrible Walking on a Leash

I've found that usually when I'm presented with this problem, the dog has been through obedience training of some kind. If Rover has been terrible walking on a leash for quite some time you're going to have to make some drastic changes, because he now believes that the way he's supposed to walk on a leash includes jerking, tugging, lunging, and pulling. Hear me on this one, Human: Rover doesn't know any other way of walking on a leash.

The first thing you need to do is read the section in Chapter 11, "Obedience," that covers the command "Rover, let's go." You're going to start from scratch. I want you to change the side you walk Rover on. If he's been on your left in the past, put him on your right. As soon as you change sides it's a whole different story. Remember the compulsive habitual personality; whenever you see a negative pattern, to stop it all you have to do is alter it. That's what you're doing when you change sides and start teaching from scratch.

Jumping on People

First of all, read Chapter 3, "Dos and Don'ts of Discipline," where I explain why you shouldn't put your knee in his chest or step on his toes. I also discuss what command to choose and how to put it into action.

If you're starting this with Rover when he's six months old or older, he's going to let go of jumping slowly. That's why it's important to make the command mean that all four feet must be on the floor. One of the hardest times to get Rover to stop jumping on people is when company comes. As soon as they're through the door, Rover's jumping. You try to stop him and company says, "Oh, that's okay, Human, I don't mind." They don't mind for less then a minute. Once Rover begins to understand "Off" you can prevent jumping completely, cut it off before those front feet leave the floor. Remember, whenever you use a command it puts you in control. When company comes over and you know Rover is going to get excited and jump on them, you can say, "Rover, stay off," before those front feet ever leave the ground.

Humping

If Male Rover or Female Rover does this as a puppy it's masturbation. If Rover continues to hump a favorite pillow, blanket, or stuffed animal, it's still masturbation. Embarrassing, I know, but totally natural. The more emphasis you give it the more and longer it will go on. Ignore it, if possible, and he will grow out of it.

If Male Rover or Female Rover attempts to hump your torso, your arm, or your leg, it is a power play and must be dealt with. Males do it to males, females to females, females to males, and males to females. There is nothing sexual about it. It is nothing more or less than a dominance play. If Rover starts this behavior with a member of the household it means there is a disturbance in the peck order and he's trying to gain dominance. So it's not unusual for dogs to hump children, especially young ones. Pay close attention, and you'll probably notice other power plays—making a point of getting through doorways first, intentionally putting himself in a physically dominant position, attempting significant eye contact, and maybe growling and snapping when the situation doesn't call for it. Read Chapter 8, "The Head Honcho Human," and put yourself in the lead position with Rover immediately.

Digging

The first thing we need to do is figure out why Rover's digging. If we don't know why, there's really not much I can do to help. Here is a list of possibilities; choose the one that fits and follow that correction.

BREED. Almost any of the water breeds are going to dig around a sprinkler, a soaker hose, or a drainpipe. Almost all the northern and cold-weather breeds are diggers, too. You must understand and respect it. Instinct tells Rover to dig in the dirt to get cool, and in the snow to get warm. We know he doesn't need to do it, and eventually he'll figure that out himself and stop digging. Until that time my advice is to shrug and decide you'll have a nice lawn next year. If you attempt to correct this kind of digging, you will only confuse the issue, and the digging will get worse. If he's digging someplace where it cannot be tolerated, barricade that area so that he can't get to it.

I can hear you saying, "Judi, I am not giving up my yard for a dog. He'll just have to learn not to dig—that's all there is to it!" You're going to have to trust me on this one, Human. The more you try to stop the digging, the longer it will go on. If you cover the hole up, Rover will dig it again within a day or two.

BURYING STUFF. Again, my advice is to ignore the digging, because it's natural. Not all dogs bury things, but the ones that do are doing so out of instinct. This kind of digging is easier to ignore because the spot or spots are small and usually hidden, and once Rover buries whatever it is he covers the hole up himself.

GROUNDING. Rover sees a small rodent, chases it into its hole, and begins to dig to catch his prey. Rover sees a beetle, follows it until it goes under something or behind something, and begins to dig to catch his prey. The situation will develop in one of two ways: Rover will stop because his prey got away, or he'll realize this digging stuff is fun. But the novelty will wear off.

BOREDOM AND ENTERTAINMENT. This kind of digging starts when Rover isn't getting enough attention and/or exercise. You know your situation, and you know deep down if you're being fair to Rover.

FRUSTRATION. Frustration digging can start if there's confusion in the peck order, if a dog is isolated, if he's being presented with totally new and different sounds and/or smells, if there's a major disruption such as arguing in the household or the loss of a family member, dog or human. Frustration digging can get seriously out of hand.

DIGGING OUT. This is self-explanatory. The method of correction depends on the type of fence you have. If you have wood or chain link, buy a roll of chicken wire. It's cheap and easy to use. Tack the wire two to four feet up on the fence. Dig out a flat surface next to the fence, about an inch or two deep. Bring the wire straight down and out. Lay it flat on the surface you've created. You can use large construction staples to tack the wire into the ground. Use the dirt or grass you dug up and bury the wire. When Rover starts to dig, his paws will hit the wire, which will be very uncomfortable. If you have cinder block, and Rover is digging out you must admire his tenacity. Buy a bundle of the stakes used to mark off lots. Dig deep holes and put the stakes in point up. Make sure only the points show, so that Rover can't pull up the stakes with his teeth. He's going to have a tough time digging around them.

CORRECTION FOR MOST TYPES OF DIGGING. Read Chapter 3, "Dos and Don'ts of Discipline," and remember, *don't yell at the hole.* Nine times out of ten Rover will go back and redig any hole you fill in. Leave him one or two holes and booby-trap the rest. Get however many mousetraps you need. Fill in the holes, set the mousetraps (turn them upside down so that Rover won't be hurt), put them in the hole, cover them with a light layer of dirt or grass, and wait. Make sure Rover doesn't see you do this. As soon as he starts to dig, that mousetrap will pop and he'll think the hole did it. (As I mentioned in the section on fence jumping, I've known dogs that love nothing more than popping mousetraps.)

Being in Charge of the Front Door

About 90 percent of the time I visit a house with a dog in it, I'm greeted by a Rover barking and being totally in charge of the front door. For tips on how to deal with this problem, see the section on compulsive barking, p. 68.

Begging

Almost all dogs are beggars to a certain extent. Just watch Rover the next time you cook anything with garlic, or fry bacon. To keep Rover from watching every spoonful travel from your plate to your mouth, don't give him Human food. I had a Poodle/Pomeranian named Buster that concentrated so hard, levitation would not have surprised me. His favorite taste in the world was peanut butter; I thought he was going to have a nervous breakdown one night when I entertained and served peanut butter and celery. You can imagine what this poor dog went through trying to keep track of who in the crowd was having peanut butter.

I hear, "Judi, all he ever thinks about is food. I can't eat anything in peace without him begging." Let's look at this from another angle. As soon as you get up in the morning, you're thinking of breakfast and/or coffee. Around eleven you begin to think about lunch, until you've eaten, sometime around noon or one. Between four and five P.M. your mind is on dinner. Rover isn't the only one, now, is he? You can't eat anything in peace without him staring at you? All he thinks about is food? No. The only time Rover thinks about food is when you're eating, or when you feed him.

The correction is simple. From this point on don't give Rover anything to eat other than his dog food. Having a habitual personality, he's going to watch you eat for quite some time. You're going to have to be strong, and avoid those big brown eyes. Read Chapter 11, "Obedience," and work on "Rover, go lie down."

Marking Territory in the House

This can be a problem with females as well as males. And there's a big difference between "breaking housetraining" and "marking." When Rover breaks housetraining the urine is copious and light in color. When Rover marks, there's a small amount of urine, it's darker in color, and the odor is strong. Dogs will mark with stool as well.

Pay attention to where Rover is marking. The most common places are the corner of your bed, the chair or couch you sit in most, clothes on the floor, in the bathroom, and in front of doors and some windows. He knows what will hold his scent for a while, so newspapers, cardboard boxes, and your knitting are not unusual choices. A Longhaired Chihuahua marked in front of a floor fan so the odor would disperse all over the house. Unfortunately, the middle of your bed is also not an uncommon spot.

I'm going to list the main reasons for marking territory in the house; you pick the one that fits your situation.

1. He believes he needs to take care of the house when you're gone. Along with putting yourself in the Head Honcho position, create a security base for him. Start telling him good-bye *every time* you leave the house. Say the same thing every time. Take a T-shirt, a towel, or a small blanket and rub yourself down with it completely. Give it to him when you're going to be gone. Your scent on something that you give him will relax him.

2. He believes he needs to take care of you, and he can't do that when you're gone. Along with putting yourself in the Head Honcho position, you're going to let him know you're perfectly capable of taking care of yourself. If he's good on a leash, take him into a high-stress situation. As soon as you get him into high stress, he has to give you any control he feels he has. While you're in high stress, take the opportunity to put him in a "sit" at your side, and put your leg in front of him. This will let him know that you are taking care of him, you're guarding him. Tell him good-bye every time you leave him, and give him something with your scent on it.

3. If he believes he needs to take care of you it stands to reason that he has to take care of himself. Solve the problem the same way.

4. Suppose he marks only during school hours. He believes he has to take care of the kids, and he can't do that when they're in school. Usually this marking is done in the kids' bedrooms or in front of the bedroom doors. Put the kids in the Head Honcho position and make sure Rover understands that *you* take care of the children.

5. There have been changes in Rover's life. You moved; you had company staying with you; there's been a lot of arguing or a serious schedule change; you went on vacation and had a house-sitter; he was boarded for a long period of time; there was a death in the family, human or animal. This kind of marking usually stops when things get back to normal, if they do get back to normal. Put yourself in the Head Honcho position and get Rover into high stress.

You'll notice that when Rover marks, the urine is in small amounts and concentrated. In the intact male there is also testosterone. A neutered male will mark territory as well. He has no idea that he no longer has a source of testosterone. When you take Rover out for a walk, whether it be in your neighborhood or in a high-stress situation, *do not* let him lift his leg! If he's allowed to mark territory, that then becomes territory he has to take care of. We don't want to extend his territory beyond his home.

Playful Biting

Usually this is a problem when Rover is a puppy and his teeth are like needles. The correction is the same if he's a pup or an adult. When the puppies want to play with the bitch and she doesn't want to, she freezes. As long as there is no movement there's no attraction. When Rover starts to bite, our reflex is to pull the hand away, which immediately begins the follow-the-hand game. Fortunately, certain things cross the lines between humans and animals. One of those is "Ouch." Next time Rover starts chewing on your hand or foot, say "Ouch!" He'll stop immediately, as long as your hand is not continuing to move. This also works if your Rover is an adult.

Playful biting is not a "no." There are going to be times when you play with Rover using your hands. If you tell him "No," you'll be creating a repeat offender each time he plays with your hands.

Eating Feces (Pica)

Humans find this incredibly disgusting. To Rover, it's an okay thing to do. Wild dogs recycle their food this way when the hunting season is lean. But if Rover is doing this constantly he may end up having teeth, gum, and throat problems.

There are products on the market now that you can put on Rover's food, the cat's food, or other dog's food to make their feces smell bad.

I've seen this work beautifully and I've seen it fail miserably. If Rover's getting into the cat litter I know it's almost impossible to clean it fast enough. The only sure way I've found of stopping Rover from snacking out of the litter box is to make it inaccessible.

Usually, by the time you realize Rover is eating his own stool, it's a pattern he's locked into. To stop him you're going to have to go back to housetraining days, when you stayed with him while he had his eliminations. As soon as he has a bowel movement, get his attention somehow to distract him from his stool. Don't make a big deal about cleaning up after him. If he's really set on eating his feces he'll eat it immediately or he'll guard it so that you can't take it from him.

Lunging, Barking, Growling, or Cowering at other Dogs

In other words, he has problems with dogs not your own. Unless you plan on showing Rover, there is absolutely no point in having him socialize with other dogs. It's not like he can meet other dogs in the neighborhood and have them over for a slumber party or to watch the Super Bowl. For how to stop a negative reaction to other dogs, read Chapter 11, "Obedience." Pay attention to "Rover, let's go." When you're walking him and he starts to react to another dog, do an about-face and head off in the other direction. Every time he sees a dog, you're suddenly doing something crazy, so the best thing for him to do is keep an eye on you instead of other dogs.

Squirming or Fighting When Handled

Almost all dogs will fight handling if it's confining or too tight. Instinct is going to take over to fight the restriction. Usually the only time we have to hold on to Rover this way is at the veterinarian's or during grooming. If he is held in a relaxed manner and you're not saying "It's okay, it's okay," he probably won't squirm too much.

There are a few breeds that do not tolerate restrictive handling, among them the Chow Chow, Shar-Pei, Chesapeake Bay Retriever, Boxer, and Pekingese. If you have one, you'll have to practice holding him in a manner that he will tolerate.

Car Chasing

Car chasing is such a wonderful, positive thing for Rover to do, it may take some work to get him to stop. Chasing is a part of what Rover is all about as a canine, and if he's a member of a herding breed you've got a combination that has to be recognized and respected. When Rover starts chasing a car, the person in the car becomes concerned so they slow down. Rover has absolutely no idea that the person in the car slowed it down. He thinks he did. Power surge.

Pay attention to whether the car chasing has become compulsive, and whether he does it with your car as well. If he's chasing cars in general, ask a friend to help you work with Rover. Arm Friend with aluminum cans and maybe a couple of water balloons. As soon as Rover starts to chase, have Friend throw the cans and balloons at Rover while he drives by. Friend can also stop the car, get out, and chase Rover off. If possible, use two or three different cars.

If Rover is chasing your car when you leave and come home, alter the pattern. Remember, if a pattern is compulsive and negative, to stop it all you have to do is alter it. So as the chase begins, stop the car and open and close the door a couple of times. Put the car in reverse and back up a few feet. Get out of the car and walk around it. Come to a stop and sing with the radio. You can throw a can or balloon. Use your imagination. You're trying to alter the pattern and make Rover stop and think.

Introducing New Human

When you introduce a new person to the household, *don't think in terms of jealousy!* Jealousy is a complicated, very human emotion. Rover doesn't have the ability for that.

NEW BABY. If possible, introduce Rover to baby smells—baby powder on a blanket, formula or breast milk, and a diaper—before the baby comes home. Let Rover check out the nursery, crib, and toys. When you come home with the baby, try to remember that Rover is not going to know you have a baby in your arms when you walk through the door. He's going to do his normal, excited glad-to-see-you-home moves. If possible, leave the baby in the car for a few minutes and go in and say hi to Rover to give him a few minutes of excitement. Then, when you bring the baby in, Rover will be in control and ready to see the new member of the family. Read the section on body language in Chapter 6, "The Peck Order Factor," so that you have a good understanding of the way Rover will interpret the baby's body language. Occasionally pass the baby over Rover. This is a show of physical dominance by you and the baby.

BOYFRIEND/GIRLFRIEND. If you and your new Human sit side by side on the sofa and Rover approaches with tail wagging and a lot of animation to his body, that's competition. Pet him and let him be included. If he tries to get between you, with obvious purpose, that's a straightening out of the peck order. You are the accepted leader in his life, and you've been dominant. This new Human has not established himself or herself as dominant to Rover, who doesn't think it's right for the new Human to be that close to the Head Honcho. So the new Human should take the time to read Chapter 8 and put himself in a lead position as well. You may notice that if you're sitting and the new Human comes to bend over and hug or kiss you, Rover will get as close to you as possible. In terms of body language, the new Human took a dominant position over you and you did not object or challenge for dominance. Rover is going to become confused. If you pay attention to the peck order factor he'll relax and learn to accept and love your new Human.

Guarding Food

If Rover is standing over his food, tense and growling, you have a situation that needs to be handled immediately. *Read Chapter 8 and get started on becoming Head Honcho right away.* I don't want you to be bitten, so don't try to take Rover's bowl away from him right away.

Start by standing quietly a couple of feet away. That's all you're going to do, just stand there. Rover will continue to tense over his bowl, but if he wants to eat, he's going to have to relax and put up with you standing there. Stay there until he finishes eating or walks away. Don't worry if he doesn't eat. He will, when he gets hungry. Follow this procedure for two or three days. The next step is to walk by and drop a dish towel, or something along those lines. Squat down from the knees, pick it up, and walk away. *Absolutely do not bend over from the waist.* (This is explained in the section on body language, in Chapter 6.) Do this two or three times. Make sure you're far enough away from Rover so he can't reach you if he snaps. These two procedures should take you two or three days.

For the next step I want you to sit down, quietly, on the floor. Make sure you're just beyond snapping range. Do this two or three times as well. By this time Rover should be eating while you're around. If he's growling and eating at the same time, don't worry; we're getting there.

Now you're really going to throw him for a loop. Turn the bowl upside down, and place the food on it any way you can, depending on the type of bowl you have. As soon as he sees his food that way, he's going to look at you and realize you're in control of this situation. Next time put his food on a dinner plate. From this point, use your imagination. If he starts to guard his food as soon as things go back to normal, replace his bowl altogether, and for a short time give him a different kind of food. If there are young children in the house, introduce them to this situation slowly, and wait until Rover is no longer guarding from you.

Snarling and Growling

These are a "No!" They are not tolerated. If possible, get hold of Rover quickly and physically discipline him. Give him a firm shake and say: "Rover! No!" Right now, read Chapter 3, "Dos and Don'ts of Discipline," and Chapter 8, "The Head Honcho Human." Now that Rover realizes you are not a happy camper, let's figure out why he snarled and growled in the first place. Here are some possibilities.

TRUE AGGRESSION. This kind of growling is due to breeding. If Rover is a puppy and showing serious aggression, the breeder was neglectful. No attention was paid to the disposition of the bitch, or the stud, or both. If Rover is a member of one of the breeds commonly used for guard, watch, or attack, don't make the mistake of being pleased that he's already showing aggression. If it is allowed to continue you will have on your hands a dog that nobody can handle or get near, including you. Get yourself into the Head Honcho position immediately, before Rover can become dangerous.

If Rover is an adult when growling starts, something has happened to make him think he needs to take care of himself. Here again, you must get yourself back on the top rung of the peck order ladder. If Rover is fairly good on a leash, and you know you have control of him on a leash, I want you to get him out into a high-stress situation—any situation around you that is active. Here in Albuquerque, we have a walk path that I wish I could rent. It is always active, with bikers, joggers, kids, and people with their dogs. There's not an overload of stress, but just enough to make Rover feel he has no choice but to turn all control over to you. If you can get Rover into high stress two or three times a week for the next two weeks, you'll notice a marked difference in his attitude. There will be a calming effect, because he can relax and know that you're going to take care of him.

FEAR. "They" call this fear aggression, which can turn a dog into a fear biter. I have a problem putting "fear" and "aggression" in the same sentence. When a dog is growling out of fear, it isn't aggression I see, it's self-defense. An aggressive dog is not going to back himself into a corner. When you begin to think in terms of defense it changes your attitude toward what's going on with Rover. Many people know what it's like to have an anxiety attack. Imagine that for a minute. That's what Rover is going through every time he growls. Correcting this is not a disciplinary matter, it's an understanding matter. *Do not, under any circumstances, say, "It's okay, it's okay."* (See Chapter 7.)

Get yourself into the Head Honcho position right away. I strongly recommend working with some obedience commands, especially "Sit," "Stay," and walking on a leash. Even if he's only slightly proficient at these commands, it may be enough to stop an anxiety attack.

Biting

If Rover is biting, it means he's become dominant. It means he believes he has to take care of himself. It means he believes he has to take care of you, your home, your family, your yard, and everything in his environment. (Or it means he corners himself out of fear and biting is the only way out. It is definitely one or another combination of the above.) Needless to say, if Rover is at the point of biting we've got serious behavior problems. I say "problems" because rarely is there only one cause for biting. There are only two circumstances under which biting can be excused. The first is that a dog is in pain. The second is that a bitch is protecting her litter.

Whatever the reason, you must get yourself in the Head Honcho position immediately. If Rover hasn't been taught any obedience it's time to start. If he has been, it's time to use it. You must in every way possible put yourself in the lead position, and commands will help. If Rover is at all walkable on a leash, get him out into high stress (see Chapter 11) so he has no choice but to turn control over to you. You're the one controlling the leash, the walk, and his reactions to the stress you encounter. Every now and then take the opportunity to sit Rover at your side and place your leg in front of him. With this posture you're telling Rover that you're the protector. Also take an opportunity to sit him at your side, tell him to stay, then hold him with your voice. "That's a good *sit*, Rover. I'm impressed with your *stay*. I like your *sit* and *stay*." In other words, talk to him in commands. If you don't see marked improvement within a week. Talk to your veterinarian or seek out a behaviorist. If you don't have one in your area, talk to a trainer with experience in handling problem dogs. You don't want a dog you have to guard all the time. You also don't want one about which you have to say, "Leave Rover alone when he's eating. Leave Rover alone when he's sleeping. Don't let the children play with Rover." And on and on and on.

With the majority of dogs this problem is correctable, so give yourself and Rover a chance to see if you can make it work.

MYTHS, OLD WIVES' TALES, AND OTHER NOTIONS THAT ARE JUST PLAIN WRONG

You should wait until your bitch has a heat before you have her spayed.

Wrong. Letting her go through a heat will not make her a better female. The heat period in the female dog is strictly physical; there are no psychological aspects.

You should let your bitch have a litter before you have her spayed.

Wrong. Having a litter is not going to calm her down. It's not going to make her gentle around kids, and it's not going to make her a better sporting or working dog. There's no doubt in my mind that this one was started by a male chauvinist.

If you have your bitch spayed, she'll get fat.

Nope. The female is under the influence of estrogen only twice a year. The loss of it has no effect on her weight. Here's another one that perhaps was started by a male chauvinist whose wife or mother had a hysterectomy and gained weight.

If a purebred female is impregnated by a mixed-breed dog, she'll have mixed-breed dogs forever. Or she won't be able to get pregnant by a purebred dog in the future.

Nonsense. In most myths I can find a smidgen of a factual origin. This one is beyond me. It doesn't make biological sense. It doesn't make common sense. It just puredee-downright don't make any kind of sense.

If you neuter a male, he will gain weight.

True. When the male is neutered the loss of testosterone causes the metabolic rate to slow down, so consequently he won't burn off calories as before.

If you neuter a male, he will stop fence jumping, marking territory, fighting, and any aggressive behavior.

Maybe he will; then again, maybe he won't. If Rover smells a bitch in heat and he jumps the wall to get to her, that's instinct. Neutering, in that case, might stop the fence jumping. The problem lies in the fact that Rover has also found out how neat it is to jump the fence and run around the neighborhood. When that happens, fence jumping itself becomes a learned behavior and neutering won't touch it. Many of the instinctive things that male dogs do quickly give rise to learned behavior. Your veterinarian, if he's truthful, will tell you you have a fifty-fifty chance that neutering is going to solve the problems posed by Rover's being male.

If you give your dog buttermilk, he won't have fleas.

Old wives' tale. This is one of my all-time favorites. The "old wife," who lives in Albuquerque, New Mexico, said fleas don't like the taste of buttermilk in the dog's blood. In Albuquerque, New Mexico, there are no fleas. This one reminds me of the joke about the man snapping his fingers in the air. Another man asks, "Why are you snapping your fingers?" The first man says, "It's to keep the elephants away." The second man says, "There are no elephants around here." The first man says "See? It's working."

If you cut the hair away from in front of a Sheep Dog's eyes, he won't be able to see as well.

Wrong. Humans, not God, created these hairy breeds. Imagine brushing all your hair in front of your eyes and living with it that way. Please, Human, groom your hairy dog.

If you cut a dog's whiskers, he loses his balance.

Just plain wrong. Do people honestly believe that groomers shave around each whisker? This one is said of cats as well. A woman called me in tears because her little girl had cut the cat's whiskers. She was certain that the cat would never be able to get around normally and that it would now be blind in the dark. I was able to talk her out of having the cat euthanized. Of course, the whiskers grew back, and everybody lived happily ever after. I can only hope that the little girl was not allowed to have scissors around the cat again.

All dogs want to please.

Very old wives' tale. The old wife was last seen running away from a dog that didn't want to please. Be careful, this one can get you hurt.

Female dogs, and only female dogs, can ruin your lawn.

Just plain wrong. Yes, a female dog's urine will burn your lawn. Pause with me here for a moment of reality. A male dog's urine will burn your lawn as well, until he starts lifting his leg on things that are upright. If it's summertime and Rover is still squatting, his urine will burn your lawn. I had a landscaper tell me one time that I could have a beautiful lawn or I could have dogs but I couldn't have both. As it applies to my grass and the summertime heat, he was right.

Once a dog tastes blood he's going to kill from then on.

Myth. If this were true, you wouldn't dare give Rover a piece of raw meat, because if you did, there wouldn't be a cow safe anywhere.

When a dog howls with a siren, it's because it hurts his ears.

Myth. When a pack of wolves has to spread out the distance between themselves on a hunt, they keep in touch by howling. The siren hits a pitch that some dogs can relate to.

Dogs' mouths are sterile and they can heal their own wounds.

Boy, is this one ever wrong! And the belief can create serious health problems. When wild canines lick a wound, they keep the wound open so it won't close off, which allows infection to begin. But the wild canine doesn't have time to lie down and concentrate for long periods of licking, so the wound doesn't grow to serious size. And if a wild canine is seriously injured, licking his wound is not going to cure him. He will die, as Rover would if not given medical attention. If your dog is injured, please don't think he can heal himself. *He can't.*

A SHORT CHAPTER: HELPFUL HINTS AND THINGS TO KEEP IN MIND

1. If Rover doesn't housetrain as quickly as you think he should, he's not being naughty or spiteful, he's simply confused.
2. The difference between puppy chewing and destructive chewing is the item chewed.
3. "No" means that whatever Rover is doing, you don't ever want him to do it again. For everything else, use a specific command.
4. Pay attention to what Rover is all about and respect the way he wants to play.
5. There has to be a definite peck order. There is no democracy or equality in a pack. There has to be a top rung, second rung, and on down the peck order ladder. This includes you. Remember, you are Rover's pack.
6. You can soothe and comfort a human. You cannot use a soothing voice to comfort a dog.
7. There is no such thing as jealousy.
8. Remember counterpressure/natural resistance.
9. When you're walking Rover and he is on the street side, remember allelomimetic behavior—he'll "copy, follow, mimic" what he sees.
10. About winter: If Rover is an outside dog, consider whether he *should* be an outside dog. Does he have a winter coat to build? If Rover is an outside dog:
    Keep the doghouse close to the house and family activity.
    Start Rover's drinking water tepid to warm; it will chill very quickly.
    If you leave food out for Rover it becomes as cold as the environment. I imagine it would be like eating hard ice cream or small chunks of ice.

11. About summer: If Rover is an outside dog, consider whether he *should* be an outside dog. Does he have a heavy coat that he can't shed enough to stand the heat? If Rover is an outside dog: Put ice cubes in his water and make sure it's not in a bowl that will attract and hold heat.

    If you leave food out for him, he will have to eat the ants, roaches, water bugs, and so on that find it inviting.

    Make sure that he has a shaded area so he can get out of the sun.

12. Your goal is to know what Rover is all about, both as a breed of dog and as an individual.

CONCLUSION

My clients always ask me about my dogs. I thought I'd take this opportunity to tell you a little about Larri and Fido. Both are females. Larri
was named after a character in an animated fantasy movie called *The
Wizards*. When anybody asks me what kind of dog Larri is, I tell them,
"Mother Nature had a bad hair day when she created Larri." Larri is
very ugly. I haven't kept it from her; she knows she's ugly, and as soon
as she was old enough, I told her she was adopted. I had a client tell
me, after seeing Larri, that she'd make a good poster dog for spaying
and neutering. Larri does an exceptional job helping me with dogs. If I
want to get a dog distracted, I tell Larri, "C'mon, Lar, let's go to work."
She runs around the dog and gets him excited while I tell the Human
what to do. If she's distracting a dog when I don't want her to, I say, "Lar,
that's none of your business." She leaves the dog alone. If I'm working
with a Rottweiler or Doberman and I just want to entertain, I'll say, "Lar,
let's go to work"; then, as she's coming toward me, I'll say, "Don't worry,
Lar," and she'll drop where she stands. I do this to entertain the client
and demonstrate a dog's potential.

Now a little about Fido and how she got her name. When I was working as a tech in an animal clinic I realized nobody gave their dogs the
two supposedly common names Fido and Rover. I always said that if
anybody came in with a dog named Fido or Rover I'd give them a hundred dollars. That started in 1975, and I'm still the only one I know with
a dog named Fido. She's a Toy Poodle with problems. Poodles are famous for being easy to housetrain; Fido's nine months old, and I think
she's starting to understand the concept. I wanted to see if I would be
able to teach her to work with me, so I let her out when I was working
with an especially sweet-tempered Golden Retriever. Fido didn't see
Heidi when she first came out, so she bounded out the door, excited to
be with me. When she saw Heidi, she literally screamed and jumped

at least four feet into my arms. I've heard hundreds of dogs scream or cry but never have I heard a dog scream like a human child. Heidi looked a little befuddled and somewhat apologetic. Heidi's Human was as amazed as I was that a small dog could jump that high straight up. I'm going to see if I can teach Fido to help me with puppies. Wish me luck.

If I have achieved what I set out to do in this book, you know a great deal more about dogs and the way they think than you did before. I'm hoping that this newfound knowledge will help you to raise your Rover in a loving home for as long as he or she shall live.

I have a bumper sticker on my car that says, "A dog is for life, not just for Christmas." That's what I've tried to get across in this book. Another life in your home, whether that life be a dog, a cat, or a gerbil, is a responsibility not to be taken lightly.

When you call an animal a stray the word takes responsibility from the Human and puts it onto the animal. One of the definitions of "stray" is "varying from the normal path." Humans, Humans, Humans! Dogs and cats don't intentionally vary from the normal path. There is no such thing as a "stray" dog or cat! They are abandoned and rendered homeless by Humans, not by choice.

A Dog's Prayer

Treat me kindly, my Beloved Master, for no heart in all the world
is more grateful for kindness than the loving heart of me.

Do not break my spirit with a stick, for though I should lick your
hand between blows, your patience and understanding will more
quickly teach me things you would have me know.

Speak to me often, for your voice is the world's sweetest music, as
you must know by the fierce wagging of my tail when your
footsteps fall upon my waiting ears.

When it is cold and wet, please take me inside, for I am no longer
used to the bitter elements and I ask no greater glory than the
privilege of sitting at your feet beside the hearth. Though you had
no home, I would rather follow you through ice and snow than
rest on the softest pillow in the warmest home.

Keep my pan filled with fresh water for although I should not
reproach you were it dry, I cannot tell you when I suffer thirst.
Feed me clean food, that I may stand well, to romp and play and
do your bidding, to walk by your side, and stand ready, willing, and
able to protect you with my life, should your life be in danger.

Then, my Beloved Master, should the Great Master seek to
deprive me of my health and spirit, do not turn me away. Rather,
hold me gently in your arms as merciful sleep is administered, and I
will leave you knowing with the last breath I draw, my fate was
ever safest in your hands.

—Author Unknown

Breeds

BRED TO DO • HOUSETRAINING•

PERSONALITY •TRAINING•

BEST ENVIRONMENT

NOTE: Bold type indicates best environment for each breed.

Afghan

BRED TO DO. Way back when, this Rover was used as a shepherd and a hunter. We're not talking your run-of-the-mill hunter here. Rover hunted wolves, jackals, and the odd leopard. Wild cats do the same thing our domestic cats do when they're confronted by a dog. They turn to the side, puff up, hiss a warning to back off, and then attack. (With domestic cats it's not called an attack; we soften our voice and call it a pounce.) Or they'll stand their ground. Rarely will they say, "Oh, no, it's a sixty-pound dog!" and flee. This 60-pound dog is facing a 300- to 500-pound cat that has no intention of leaving. Well, they must have done a good job or I wouldn't be including them in my list of breeds. In this day and age Afghans are mostly luxury dogs. They seem to love this day and age and the lap of luxury. After knowing what they were bred to do, I can't say I blame them.

HOUSETRAINING. Afghans will fall apart before your very eyes if you put too much emphasis on the discipline. Keep verbal discipline low-key. The hardest part of housetraining a hound is knowing the difference between the nose down looking for a place to "go," and the nose down following a scent. Housetraining will go much faster if you get Rover's urine on a rag, put it where you want him to eliminate, and take him there every time. If his scent is concentrated in one area, he won't have to spend as much time finding just the right spot. Afghans are intelligent dogs, so if there's no confusion, Rover will housetrain easily. Pay close attention to his grooming. Rover's hair tangles and mats easily.

PERSONALITY. You wouldn't think so after knowing what these dogs were bred to do, but these beauties are very sensitive. They're sensitive to you, your home, and the environment. Rover will be upset if you cry, be happy if you're happy, and be restless if there's discord among the Humans. Rover will also be sensitive to changes in barometric pressure. If you notice that he wants out, then wants right back in, then paces until you let him out, you can bet there's a weather change coming.

What Rover was bred to do goes so far back in history that it's in the

DNA. Almost all puppies will pull on your pajama legs or robe as you walk down the hall in the morning, but Rover won't tug, he'll nip and push. Being a shepherd, he honestly can't imagine how you got into the kitchen before he came along. The hunter in him will show up when his nose hits the ground and he does serious wolf hunting. Don't tell him there are no wolves in the area. Searching is more fun than finding, anyway. Think seriously about what Rover was bred to do, and if possible apply it in play. Read Chapter 5, "Playtime with Rover." If you're not going to use Rover for hunting, you must provide as much free running space and exercise as you possibly can. Depriving Rover of necessary exercise is terribly unfair. Far too many people get this dog for his beauty, and don't stop to think what his needs are. Don't be one of those Humans. The last thing you want is a bored Afghan.

Afghans are on the suspicious side, especially with strangers. Let Rover introduce himself at his own pace. If you push him, he's going to have problems with strangers from that point on. Don't think in terms of shyness. If you do, you'll read all the wrong things into Rover's attitude. Just watch him and you'll be able to see a marked difference between suspicion and shyness. Absolutely, positively do not say "It's okay, it's okay." (See Chapter 7.)

TRAINING. You will be amazed at Rover's intelligence and trainability. Use a kind and gentle hand and this dog will learn almost anything you want to teach him. Due to his intelligence I usually recommend challenging him. By that I mean, don't stop at basic obedience. Use your imagination, or pick up a book or two on different kinds of training. If you're a jogger, Rover will make a wonderful running companion. Make sure you condition him as you did yourself. If you're not a jogger, make sure you see to it that Rover has plenty of exercise. It's a must, physically and behaviorally.

BEST ENVIRONMENT: **Jogger**—Walker—Teenagers—Children 6 to 11—Children of any age—Elderly—Latchkey—**Active environment**—Sedate environment—**Multiple dogs okay**—Apartment—**House with yard**—**Room to run**—**Needs daily exercise**—Camping—Hiking

---

Airedale

BRED TO DO. Actually these dogs were bred to hunt and kill otters, water rats (which means they had to swim out into the river to kill rats), wolves, and wild boars, but the Airedale's abilities seem to be limitless. He's worked in the military carrying messages; he's been a police dog and trained for guard and protection.

HOUSETRAINING. It takes time and patience to housetrain an Airedale. You'll find that even as a puppy he will concentrate on something and tune everything else out. Getting him to go outside will be something like this: "Rover, it's time to go out." Rover, watching a bug, says, "Okay, I'm coming." A couple of minutes later: "Rover! Come on, let's go outside!" He was just beginning to come when the bug moved. You can't honestly expect him to come now, can you? "I'm coming." "Rover! Now!" His concentration on the bug is finally broken, because he really really needs to eliminate. He's on his way to you, but he just couldn't hold it any longer. Oops. Hang in there, Human.

As a pup, he'll live to play. Take advantage of that. When play stops, scoop him up immediately and get him outside. He'll have an elimination almost as soon as you get him out.

Airedales are misunderstood. They aren't "slow" and they're not stubborn. You just have to understand that if you're going to get Rover housetrained, you have to be patient and come up with new and different ways to get his attention. Believe me, when you finally get through to him about this housetraining stuff, it'll hit him all at once. "By George, I think he's got it."

PERSONALITY. Have an Airedale along with other dogs at your own risk! When these dogs fight they get serious, with intent to injure, almost immediately. You must understand the dynamics that go into the relationship between two dogs, and your role in that relationship. If there's any confusion at all, fights will begin and somebody will get hurt. If you have other dogs along with your Airedale, read Chapter 10, "Living with Multiple Dogs." Read it until you are sure you understand every word.

Remember, Airedales are not stupid or slow. (I will admit they can be incredibly tenacious.) If you have children of any age, watch Rover's patience and gentleness with them. The younger the child, the gentler Rover is. He'll play with them until they drop, and then help you tuck them into bed at night with a gentle kiss. Make sure you show him that you love him as much as he loves you. If Rover isn't shown love, he'll become visibly depressed. He will walk with his head down, he'll become a picky eater, and he can become very destructive. Airedales have a tendency to become too serious. All that's needed is plenty of love and playtime.

TRAINING. All the different things this dog has been used for required serious cooperation with Humans, which should tell you that Airedales love to do a job. They are proud dogs and comfortable with who they are, so when Rover does decide to learn something he'll throw himself into it completely and do it better than most. Train Rover with a firm but kind hand and a show of respect. You're going to come up against a strong will, and you may see out-and-out defiance. Hang in there, Human; once he accepts the fact that you're serious he'll come along just fine.

I always recommend going beyond basic obedience with these dogs. If they get bored, they get into trouble. I had a client in Santa Fe who owned a ranch. The foreman's house was about 1/4 mile from the main house. Carol, my client, was having problems with Chigger getting into the stable area with the horses and driving the corralled cattle nuts. We tried everything I could think of, to no avail. He was bored and needed something to do, so finally we gave him a job. We taught Chigger to take messages back and forth between the main house and the foreman's house. Not only did this stop Chigger terrorizing the horses and cattle, but he got so good at it that he could take messages to the foreman when he was two or three miles out with the herd. See? All Chigger wanted was a job to do. Yes, yes, yes, this was a modern ranch, Carol and the foreman have cellular phones, but it is a well-kept secret.

Please don't ignore Rover's potential.

If you have two left feet and you're all thumbs, this is the dog for you. Rover will wait patiently while you fumble with his collar and leash and the doorknob. He'll also be understanding when you stumble over sprinklers and fall into bushes.

> BEST ENVIRONMENT: Jogger—**Walker**—Teenagers—Children 6 to 11—
> **Children of any age**—Elderly—Latchkey—**Active environment**—
> Sedate environment—Multiple dogs okay—Apartment—**House with
> yard**—Room to run—Needs daily exercise—Camping—Hiking

Akita

BRED TO DO. These dogs are dog fighters! Way back when, the Japanese bred and used Akitas as fighting dogs. Even though they haven't been used in blood sports for a very long time, the tendency to be aggressive toward other dogs is still there. If you have an Akita or you're thinking about getting one, please take my advice and *have only the one dog*. If there is any confusion in the peck order between an Akita and another dog there will be—not "might be," *will be*—fights. I'm not talking a skirmish or squabble. I'm talking serious fighting, the kind that lands one or both dogs in the emergency room. If you plan to ignore my advice, please read the chapter on Living with Multiple Dogs. Make sure you understand the dynamics of the relationship between two dogs, and your role in that relationship.

Akitas were also used as big-game hunters. From what I've read and been told they were very good at their job.

HOUSETRAINING. I'm not sure why, but I've found that there are some breeds that are not clean. Akitas are one of them. This trait can make housetraining a nightmare. If you put Rover in a small area when you're not with him, make sure it's large enough for him to have eliminations away from where he eats and sleeps. If he realizes that lightning didn't strike him when he lay in his own urine, it won't bother him from that point on. Akitas, like most northern breeds, love to be outside. It's going to be tempting to give Rover too much time outside before he's completely housetrained. Try your best to keep him inside until he's trustworthy.

PERSONALITY. *Akitas are diggers!* I yell this at you because I've seen too many Akitas lose their happy homes due to digging. Mother Nature, in her ever-intruding way, tells Rover to dig in the soil to get cool and in the snow to get warm. But he'll realize as he grows up that digging is not necessary to get warmth, and that coolness is found in shade or near the air-conditioning vent. The more emphasis you place on the digging, the longer it will go on. I know ignoring it is not easy, especially as you watch your lawn and rosebushes bite the dust. Decide that you'll re-landscape when Rover has outgrown the digging.

Your Akita's relationship with you will be totally different than his relationship with other dogs. You may be surprised and you'll definitely be impressed by Rover's loving and mellow nature. He will love you to pieces and hope he gets just a little in return. These are very unassuming dogs. Plan on a lot of wrestling-type play. I know, I know: You've been told not to play any games that might teach aggression. Watch two dogs play sometime and you'll notice that during play all bets are off. The dominant dog will go down and on his back as much as the subordinate dog does. Both dogs chase and are chased. Both dogs will stand on their hind legs and wrestle like bears. If at some point you notice Rover getting bossy, believe me, it isn't because you wrestled or played tug-of-war with him. Read Chapter 5, "Playtime with Rover."

I don't usually recommend Akitas with children younger than ten or twelve. Not because he wouldn't get along with them, but because of his power. A child is going to have to be able to hold his own if he plays with Rover or takes him for a walk.

TRAINING. Akitas look powerful, but they are far more powerful than they look. I always recommend obedience or structured training of some kind. Use a firm but kind hand. Teaching him to sit is going to be easy. Getting him to sit on command is a project. If you don't want to bother with standard obedience training, at least teach him to walk correctly on a leash. At all times, keep in mind that Rover is probably considerably stronger than you. I will never forget working with an Akita named Lobo. His Human, a large man named George, and I were working with Lobo in high stress. Everything was going quite well until Lobo saw two kids with McDonald's hamburgers before George and I did. That dog hit the end of that leash with so much power he broke the clasp on the leash and split the ring on the collar. The blood stopped circulating in my body for what seemed like hours, and I noticed George looked a tad pale. Lobo made a beeline for those two kids and their hamburgers, stopped short, said a pleasant "Hi," and loped back to George and me. I distinctly remember saying, "Well, that's enough high stress for today. I think it went quite well, don't you?" I noticed the blood still had not reached George's face, and he was looking at the broken leash clasp and collar ring he held in his still-clenched fist. He looked at me, nodded, and started toward his car. If Lobo hadn't followed him, I believe George would've driven off without him and probably gotten home before realizing he'd left his dog behind.

Being obedient for obedience' sake is not in the Akita's makeup. Be prepared for back talk. Be prepared to put your hands on your hips, stomp your foot, and say, "Rover! Sit now!" He may follow the command when he knows you're serious; then again, he may not. If you work with him, Rover will pull your kids in a wagon and be happy to help you bring in the groceries (nonfood items, of course). Respect Rover's coat in the hotter months. He's going to be uncomfortable. Don't expect too much of him in the heat of the day.

BEST ENVIRONMENT: Jogger—**Walker (in cooler weather)**—
Teenagers—Children 6 to 11—Children of any age—Elderly—
Latchkey—Active environment—**Sedate environment**—Multiple dogs
okay—Apartment—**House with yard**—Room to run—Needs daily
exercise—**Camping**—Hiking

Alaskan Malamute

BRED TO DO. Malamutes were bred to be sled dogs, and they are still very successful in that capacity.

HOUSETRAINING. Since Rover's a direct descendant of the Nordic Wolf, having eliminations outside will be natural. He's going to love being outside. You're going to hear, "Please oh please oh please let me stay outside and play. Can I, huh huh can I?" Stand your ground and keep outside off-limits except for eliminations until he's housetrained. As puppies, Malamutes are active and curious. You will have to keep an eagle eye on Rover. He can urinate very quickly in mid-play and spends very little time looking for a place to go, so there's no warning that he needs to go out. Introduce him to outside in a positive way a few times, and you'll have him housetrained before you know it.

PERSONALITY. *Malamutes are diggers!* I yell this at you because I've seen far too many northern dogs lose their happy homes because of digging. Mother Nature tells them to dig in the soil to get cool, and in the snow to get warm. The more emphasis you put on the digging, the longer it will go on. If you put Rover's own stool in a hole, he'll dig a new one. Any hole you fill in he will dig up again, because the soil is now loose. If you discipline after the fact, you'll only be yelling at the hole, and confuse Rover. Read Chapter 3, "Dos and Don'ts of Discipline."

You'll notice that he doesn't dig down, he dens out. If possible leave him one favorite hole. You may have to make a conscious decision to have a nice yard next year. As he grows, he will learn that the air-conditioner vents are cool and he can get out of the cold anytime he likes. Most likely, he will stop digging before he's a year old.

Let's think about what it means to Rover to be a sled dog. Canines are pack animals. Add to that the fact that Malamutes were bred to work with a pack and cooperate with Humans, and you've got quite a dog. These dogs are very self-assured and, as adults, mellow. They are aware of their power but don't abuse it. The loyalty of this dog is something to be acknowledged and respected. If a Human can't keep his or her Malamute, especially after the dog's five years old, it is unlikely that Rover will ever completely adapt to a new Human and environment. Without that one Human that he bonded with as a puppy, he could become clinically depressed.

I never hesitate to recommend this Rover with children. You'll notice that as an adult Rover will lie quietly in the shade and in an unassuming manner watch every move the kids make. If there are six kids playing in the yard, Rover will know where each child is. If they want him to play, he will, gladly. I don't recommend this treatment of any dog, but if the kids want to dress him up in Dad's suit, Rover will allow it. If they want to ride him, he will allow that as well.

These dogs would make great Service Dogs—Seeing Eye, Hearing Ear, Wheelchair Companion. The reason you don't see them in that capacity is because of their coat and skin. Nature gave Malamutes an extra inch of fat for insulation, and three coats. In the warmer months these dogs really become visibly uncomfortable. They don't become lazy, as most people think; they're listless because of the heat. They simply cannot handle too much exercise in the warmer months. But even if they can't be Service Dogs per se, I don't hesitate to tell Rover's Humans to get him into a "therapy dog" program if they want to do some kind of volunteer work. They are terrific with the elderly and the young and sick. I've seen it myself several times. Rover will gently put his head on a lap or sweetly kiss a hand or fetch a ball if that's what a child wants.

Don't think you have the perfect family dog. Malamutes are strong-willed, somewhat independent, and can be just plain obstinate.

TRAINING. Yup, I said "strong-willed, somewhat independent, and just plain obstinate." I do recommend obedience work. You have a powerful dog on your hands, and you need to be in control. Be firm but kind. You're going to see back talk with almost every command, but mostly "Sit." He's going to love "Down" if you teach it to him correctly. Training will automatically put you in the lead position, and being in the lead position with a Malamute is important. Malamutes have natural protective tendencies. If they find themselves at the top of the peck order ladder they will take on more responsibility than they know how to handle. The last thing you want is a dog with the power of a Malamute believing he needs to take care of himself. Read Chapter 9, "Natural Protection," and see if you can give Rover a job, at least around the house.

Teaching him to walk correctly on a leash is important. If he sees other dogs, you're going to want total control on the leash. He won't hesitate to fight if a dog challenges him. Try not to let him meet other dogs on a walk; there's no point to it in the first place and it could cause problems for you in the second place. Help the kids teach him how to pull them in a wagon. Remember that these are cold-weather dogs and truly suffer during the warmer months. Don't ask too much of Rover during the heat of the day.

> BEST ENVIRONMENT: Jogger—Walker—Teenagers—Children 6 to 11— **Children of any age**—Elderly—Latchkey—**Active environment (in cool weather)—Sedate environment (the rest of the year)— Multiple dogs okay**—Apartment—**House with yard**—Room to run— Needs daily exercise—**Camping—Hiking**

American Bull Terrier (Pit Bull)

BRED TO DO. These dogs were bred to fight bulls. Fortunately, that "sport" no longer exists. Unfortunately, dog-pit fighting is still done by the absolute scum of the earth. (Probably lost some readers with that one.)

HOUSETRAINING. I don't know why, but some breeds aren't clean. Bull Terriers are one of them. Make sure that when you confine him he has enough room to move away from his urine and stool. If he has to lie in his own waste and finds out his mother wasn't there to scold him, he'll have no problems with it from that point on.

Bull Terriers are strong-willed dogs with defiant minds of their own. Rover will housetrain quickly if you stick to the method, to the letter. Keep everything on a tight schedule so he doesn't have a chance to take over. Believe me, he'll try! The problem is that he'll do it in such an endearing way that you won't know it's happened until you realize you're cleaning up after him all the time. Keep in mind he's a Terrier, so keeping an eye on him is going to take some doing.

PERSONALITY. After the movie *Patton* came out, and then a few years later when "Spuds McKenzie" came along, the Bull Terrier had very short periods of popularity. The main problem I was called for was Rover killing cats or small livestock. A Bull Terrier named Spotz tried to take on the family cow. The cow was not physically hurt, but she wouldn't tolerate being milked for a few days. Whenever I'm asked about a dog getting along with ducks, chickens, hens, and the like, I always say, "Dogs are carnivores." Most humans don't want to hear that. They want me to come up with some magical way for everyone to live in harmony. With Bull Terriers I try to paint a morbid picture, in hopes that Rover's owners can avoid seeing the real thing. I tried to tell Cowboy's Humans, but they were positive that if they worked really hard at it they could make everyone get along. You're ahead of me, and you're right. There were two surviving chickens and three ducks. They found six dead chickens and four dead ducks. I'm not sure exactly why Bull Terriers are cat killers, but I think the cats that get in trouble are the ones that stand and fight. If they run like hell, they survive.

As your only pet Rover can be the best you've ever had. If you want another dog, that will be fine as well. These dogs were bred to defend themselves, not start a fight. They are real characters. They love to play, and will be glad to show you how to play. They are so solid that's it's uncomfortable to have them in your lap, but allow them on the couch at your side and they're in seventh heaven. This dog would walk on coals and go through hell for you if you asked him to. He'll stand proud as your guardian and defend you to his death. I don't hesitate to recommend this Rover with kids. Because of his power, it's best if the kids are old enough to hold their own in play.

I must mention Shirley. Her Humans had only Shirley until she was five years old. Then they brought home a baby. They were concerned about how Shirley would take to the baby, so they called me. When I came by, the baby had been home about three hours. I had them put the baby in an infant seat on the floor, and called Shirley over to introduce them. The only way I can describe Shirley when she saw the baby is to say, "She went all soft." Her gentleness put a lump in my throat. It was love at first sight. The baby is three years old now, and I'm told the two are inseparable.

TRAINING. This dog has the power of a much larger dog, so I do recommend some obedience. You're going to have to be on the firm side with Rover. These dogs can be bullheaded (no pun intended). You need to work hard on "Halt" and "Come." If he goes after a cat, for instance, you're going to want him to stop and come to you immediately. You're going to get back talk from Rover, but it'll be subtle. It'll go something like this: "Rover. Rover. Rover! Are you paying attention?" Response: "Oh—I'm sorry, did you say something?" When you're working with him throw some play in now and then. He'll pay attention longer if he has recess. Be kind as well as firm, throw in a wink, and he'll follow you anywhere.

BEST ENVIRONMENT: Jogger—**Walker**—Teenagers—Children 6 to 11— **Children of any age**—Elderly—Latchkey—**Active environment**— **Sedate environment**—Multiple dogs okay—Apartment—**House with yard**—Room to run—Needs daily exercise—Camping—Hiking

---

American Eskimo

BRED TO DO. To tell you the truth, I'm confused. I'm not quite sure what American Eskimos were bred to do. In fact I, still think of this breed as Spitz. Whatever they were called or bred to do, they are super watchdogs.

HOUSETRAINING. Rover is going to be timid and overwhelmed by the vastness of the backyard. When you begin the housetraining process, carry him to where you want him to go. If you let him walk to the spot, you'll notice it takes a very long time and he acts as though he's walking through a mine field. If you gentle him through it, it won't take long until he barrels out as if he's done it all of his life. Be careful not to put too much emphasis on verbal discipline. These dogs can easily become shy eliminators, dogs that hide to have eliminations. American Eskimos are very clean dogs and they want a clean area. As long as you stick to the method and pamper him in the beginning, Rover will housetrain in no time.

PERSONALITY. When you read or hear that a dog is a good watchdog, you can take it to the bank that he's a barker. This Rover is no exception. Introduce him to the "Quiet" command so that you can stop the barking at once when necessary. Don't tell Rover he's a small dog; he won't believe you anyway. He'll watch and guard your house and territory as if he were paying the bills.

These dogs are very sensitive and somewhat high-strung. Rover will be unhappy if you are, worried if someone in the household is sick, troubled if you fret, and happy if you're happy. If there is arguing in the house, you'll notice Rover is restless and agitated. He's also going to be sensitive to changes in the barometric pressure. If you notice he wants out, then turns around and wants back in, then after a few minutes wants back out again, you can put money on a weather change. I have a client who says that between Snowy and her husband's arthritis she never has to watch the weather report.

Too much chaos will send Rover into a corner or under a bed, in a heartbeat. So this is not a breed I recommend with children. American Eskimos are obviously uncomfortable around kids and will avoid them if at all possible. If you raise this Rover with kids, he'll learn to tolerate them as he grows. But the children's friends can cause problems. At some point it is likely that Rover will begin to growl and snap. You could easily become one of the owners who says, "Don't bother Rover when he's sleeping. Leave Rover alone when he's eating. Leave Rover alone when he has a rawhide." I also hear, "Judi, he growls if I move him on the couch. I don't dare try and get him off the bed." Humans, hear me! If you know the potential for this kind of behavior, you are forewarned. Now read this book and become forearmed. Given the chance, this Rover can be loving, trainable, and fun to have around. He really doesn't want all the responsibility of taking care of everything, including himself.

TRAINING. Handle Rover with tender loving care. These dogs are quick learners, but if you're too firm or harsh in your handling they will fall apart before your very eyes. I do recommend obedience training. Anytime you're training, it automatically puts you in control. Use a gentle hand. The training will go faster and be easier on both of you if you work with Rover in five- to ten-minute spurts, with play in between. Pay close attention to the way Rover wants to play, and go with it.

> BEST ENVIRONMENT: Jogger—**Walker**—**Teenagers**—Children 6 to 11—
> Children of any age—**Elderly**—Latchkey—**Active environment**—**Sedate**
> environment—**Multiple dogs okay**—Apartment—**House with yard**—
> Room to run—Needs daily exercise—Camping—Hiking

American Staffordshire Terrier (Pit Bull)

BRED TO DO. *They were not bred to fight!* Unfortunately, they've been trained to fight. Whenever I'm called out to the Animal Control Center for some reason, I see these wonderful dogs with missing ears, missing eyes, and an unbelievable number of scars. Rarely are they adopted. The situation is so incredibly sad.

Staffordshire Terriers were bred in England as guard dogs. I have three clients who have trained their Staffs to guard and have been so happy with their expertise, they tell me they won't have any other breed for that job.

HOUSETRAINING. If you have children, let them get involved with the housetraining. Rover will want to be wherever the kids are, anyway. The hardest part of housetraining a Staff is getting him to hold still long enough to let you know he needs to go. When a dog is as active as Staffs are, housetraining takes a little longer. You'll have to follow the method to the letter and may need to borrow another pair of eyes. Rover will housetrain faster if he is never confined away from you. If you do confine him away from you, he will become so distressed that when you do pay attention to him, he'll urinate out of sheer excitement at seeing you.

PERSONALITY. One of the neatest things about this Rover is that he can do a job very well but still be a fun pet. Jake, in Santa Fe, guards a jewelry store when it's open, then goes home at night and plays with the kids. Staffs throw every part of their being into whatever they do. That includes, affection, play, training, and love.

Start out when Rover is very young, keeping your homecoming low-key and quiet. I know this is hard to do, because we like it when our dog is happy and excited to see us. If you're not quite sure you want to keep the homecoming low-key, all you have to do is imagine Rover at sixty pounds of solid muscle jumping on you and dancing around every time you come home. That visual image should convince you.

I don't hesitate to recommend Staffs with children, because they're wonderful with them. I do however, caution about the size and power of this dog. If your children are small you're going to have to work at seeing to it that Rover is calmer in play with them than he is with you. If the kids are ten and older, they're going to enjoy Rover a great deal. He'll be able to match them game for game, whatever the game is. If they want him to climb a mountain with them, he'll not only climb the mountain, but carry their stuff on his back if they want him to.

American Staffordshire Terriers are really neat dogs. They are very active without being hyper, great with kids, and all they want in the world is to love and be loved.

TRAINING. Most definitely I recommend you work with Rover on obedience. This dog is far too powerful to let him become unruly. You'll have to use a firm hand in the beginning so that Rover understands this is not playtime. If you're too gentle, he won't respect a thing you say. In the beginning, he isn't going to sit still while you put on his collar and leash. He's going to wiggle and squirm, go down on his back, play with the leash, play with your hands, then get up and jump around. He's not being naughty, so don't treat him as if he is. Keep your hand movements slow and steady, so that you're not petting him and stroking him without realizing it. When the dancing starts, back off, take a deep breath, and wait him out. The hardest part of any training with a Staff is getting him to pay attention long enough to learn. You'll notice that when he understands "Sit," he'll do it, but his body will be one quivering mass of energy ready to explode.

Don't let Rover get the upper hand on the leash, or he'll drag you all over the place. With his power, if he were to see another dog that he wanted to visit, he'd be out of control before you knew what hit you. Once he settles down and starts learning, you'll be amazed at what he'll learn for you, just because you want him to.

> BEST ENVIRONMENT: **Jogger—Walker**—Teenagers—**Children 6 to 11**—Children of any age—Elderly—Latchkey—**Active environment**—Sedate environment—**Multiple dogs okay**—Apartment—**House with yard**—Room to run—**Needs daily exercise (through play is fine)**—**Camping**—Hiking

Australian Shepherd

BRED TO DO. Obviously, bred to herd—cattle, sheep, horses, and anything else that needed herding in Australia. They did their job very well, and still do. Very little training is necessary to get Rover herding. If you ever have the privilege of seeing Rover do his thing there will be no doubt in your mind that he was born to it.

HOUSETRAINING. These little babies are always running; they even run in their sleep. The problem during housetraining is that, being shepherds, they do most of their running behind you. You ask, "Judi, why is that a problem during housetraining?" Human, darling, if Rover is behind you, you can't see him eliminate, so you can't praise him. Ah! I hear you laugh now, but just wait until you're standing outside with Rover, swinging the upper part of your body around to see where he is. He will be right by your feet, *behind* you. Aussies also love to be outside, so getting him back in the house after he's done his job is a bit of a problem. Get right in front of him, and both of you run back into the house. If you stick to the method and there's no confusion, Rover will housetrain quickly. An Aussie's hair is very fine, so keep an eye on the grooming around his anus.

PERSONALITY. As a pup, Rover will nip at your pajamas, slippers, or robe as you go down the hall into the kitchen. Now see? All along you thought you could make it down the hall by yourself. Rover can't imagine how you managed it before he came along. If you have other dogs, cats, and/or kids, Rover will gather them together and herd them to dinner. These dogs are smart, and time has to be spent outsmarting them. I had a client, Toni, with an Aussie named Dundee. Toni had three other dogs and occasionally gave all four table scraps. Somehow, Dundee figured out when there would be leftovers. He would run around, act like he needed to go outside, get the other dogs excited, then herd them all out the door. Dundee, though, didn't go out; he ran under the dining table and waited for the leftovers he knew were there.

As adults, Aussies will climb that peck order ladder and end up dominant. If you're prepared for it, you'll recognize the signs and stop the climb. If Rover becomes dominant, he will take on all the responsibilities that go along with that position. One of those will be taking care of himself. He will become very defensive, and everything and everybody will become a threat. That includes you! I've worked with several Aussies that have gotten to this point, and I'm here to tell you they can be tough to handle. It's correctable, but don't let him bite someone before you correct it. Read Chapter 6, "The Peck Order Factor," and avoid the problem altogether. Because of their tendency to dominate, I hesitate to recommend this breed with small children. If he perceives them to be out of line, he won't hesitate to discipline them. Rover has the potential to be great with older kids, especially if they play with him. Rover will love to play, so play with him to his heart's content. Aussies are alert, smart, and very loving. Don't give up on yours if he starts to get bossy. You need to be aware of the fact that Aussies are very active dogs, and not enough exercise can cause destruction, chronic barking, and digging. Obviously you don't want Rover to get bored.

TRAINING. If Rover seems to have blue eyes, or one blue eye, he is going to be light sensitive. The eyes are not really blue, they are albino. You'll notice that when the sun is bright, he will cock his head and/or stand in your shadow to avoid the sun getting in his eyes. Respect that when you're working with him. It may appear that he's not paying attention to you when, in fact, he's trying to avoid looking up.

Aussies can easily become one-owner dogs. I always recommend that all family members get involved in the training and the play. Too often I see Aussies that respect only one human.

> BEST ENVIRONMENT: Jogger—**Walker—Teenagers—Children 6 to 11**—Children of any age—**Elderly**—Latchkey—**Active environment—Sedate environment—Multiple dogs okay**—Apartment—**House with yard—Room to run**—Needs daily exercise—Camping—Hiking

Basenji

BRED TO DO. I can't wait to tell you what Basenjis were bred to do. I think this is *sooo* cool. Basenjis were bred in Africa to guide hunters through the forests and warn of dangerous animals. The hunter said, "Rover, guide my safari today." And Rover, bless his brave little heart, puffed out his little chest and said, "Okey-dokey," and off they went. Now if I were a dog and I was leading a hunting party to warn of dangerous animals, I think if I saw an eight-hundred-pound lion, I'd have a tendency to let out a bark. Not the Basenji. He would go on point. Africans also used him for hunting and flushing. Another neat thing to know about Basenjis is that they are one of the oldest breeds.

HOUSETRAINING. Basenjis are one of the cleanest breeds around. They are also very proud dogs, even as puppies. Keep the verbal discipline low-key. Putting too much emphasis on the negative is totally unnecessary. Show Rover outside a few times and he'll practically train himself. He may have a problem letting you know when he needs to go out. I can guarantee you he's not going to bark to let you know, or even whine for that matter. Go to some place like Cost Plus or Pier One Imports and get a string of brass bells on a nylon rope (in Albuquerque, they're about eight dollars). Hang the bells from the door handle or knob, and show Rover that when he hits it with his paw or bumps it with his nose, it will ring and you'll open the door.

When a Basenji is housetrained, he's really housetrained. Don't put him in the position of having to hold it for prolonged periods of time.

PERSONALITY. If you have a Basenji, there's a good possibility this is the only breed you'll ever have. Basenjis have a devoted following. If I'm asked about a good breed for the elderly this is one of the first breeds I recommend. Not that they don't get along with children—they do—but one of the traits that make them good with the elderly is their quiet affection. They love to play, but they don't need a lot of exercise. They'll run around the backyard with a child, but also take a calm, slow walk with an elderly gentleman or lady.

Rover's patience never ceases to amaze me. It's not something I like, but I've seen kids dress Rover up and push him around in a doll carriage. If he were a human, I'd say, "Why do you tolerate that?" "How can you let those kids do that to you?" Rover would calmly say, "Don't worry about me, Judi. The little darlings aren't causing any harm, and they do seem to enjoy it. I don't mind as long as they're having a good time." Of course, the conversation would serve to make me feel intolerant and somewhat witchy.

TRAINING. Rover's intelligence should be acknowledged and respected, and above all not wasted. You will be amazed, when you start working with Rover, by how quickly he learns. He'll know all the commands in a short period of time, and then he'll say, "What else do you want to teach me?" I do recommend doing some training. Not for the reasons I usually give—power, size, unruliness, and the like—but because Rover wants to learn, and he takes great pride in doing something well. When I did obedience classes with four or five dogs, and I had a Basenji in my class, I knew neither his Human nor I would have to do much teaching. I'm almost positive the dog learned just from watching the other dogs. I used to ask the owner, "How much training have you done with Rover?" Invariably the owner would say, "None." After I heard that answer a few times, I came to the conclusion that Basenjis are either born knowing basic obedience, or they're smart enough to figure it out by watching. You can always tell when Rover is pleased with himself after he's learned something. His walk will turn into a prance and the look on his face says, "Damn, I'm good."

I'm sure you know that the Basenji is "barkless," but what you may not know is that when Rover does bark, it's best to respect it and see what he's barking at. If he comes and jumps on you to get your attention, there is something going on that you need to pay attention to.

If you have two left feet and you're all thumbs, this is the breed for you. Rover will walk patiently with you as you stumble over sprinklers and fall into bushes. Not only will he be patient with you, he'll do it with such pride he'll make you look as if you know what you're doing. He'll sit by the door with quiet dignity while you fumble with the doorknob and your keys. With most dogs I teach a "Wait" at the door, but with Rover, he just seems to know it.

The first time you see Rover's pride in doing something well, you'll realize what a special little dog you have.

> BEST ENVIRONMENT: Jogger—**Walker**—Teenagers—Children 6 to 11—
> **Children of any age—Elderly—**Latchkey—**Active environment—
> Sedate environment—Multiple dogs okay—**Apartment—**House with
> yard—**Room to run—Needs daily exercise—Camping—Hiking

Basset Hound

BRED TO DO. Bassets were bred to hunt. One of the animals they were supposed to hunt were foxes. I keep trying to picture a Basset hunting a fox. The hunters must've let the Basset start the day before. I mean, you must admit they're a tad slow.

HOUSETRAINING. As with almost all of the Scent Hounds, the hardest part of housetraining is knowing the difference between the nose being down to explore and the nose being down looking for a spot to go. I don't know why, but some breeds simply are not clean. Bassets are one of those. If you confine him when you're not with him, make sure he has enough room to eat and sleep away from his urine and stool. If he lies in his own urine once, he'll discover lightning didn't strike, and it won't bother him from that point on. Bassets aren't easy to housetrain, period. Stick to the method to the letter and muster up as much patience as you can. Think of the years ahead, and the time spent housetraining doesn't seem so long. Plus, your Basset is worth the effort. You'll get him there.

PERSONALITY. *Most Basset Hounds drool.* There, now you know the absolute worst about Bassets. With his nose, he can find almost anything for you; the problem lies in getting him to come back and tell you he found it. Bassets are simply not in a hurry to do anything. If Basset Rover were human, he'd be leaning back in a rocking chair, a wheat straw in his mouth, contributing to the conversation with a "Yup" and a "Nope." This is a breed I don't hesitate to recommend for the elderly and for children who for some reason can't be very active. Bassets are mellow, passive, and wonderfully affectionate. I don't think they have an aggressive bone in their bodies, and I don't think it would occur to one of them to bite. It's just not in them.

I laughed when I saw a man on TV explaining how to determine intelligence in dogs, and his idea of the most intelligent. One of his tests was to put a blanket over a dog and see how long the dog takes to get out from under it. If you throw a blanket over a Basset, he will say, "Cool, dude, the light was starting to bother me." Rover is slow-moving not stupid.

His ears will always be dirty. If there's dirt to be found outside, he will find it and track it in. He will never chase a ball, or anything else for that matter. But he will be forever loyal and always love you with every fiber of his being. Once you get him through the housetraining, you'll find you rarely have to even tell him "No," much less punish him for anything. If you do have to punish him, you'll have to do it only once, because it will break his heart and he won't do whatever it was again.

TRAINING. Be kind and very patient with Rover. He really won't want to be bothered with this obedience stuff. I've never worked with a Basset that didn't use every trick in the book to stop the lesson. You'll notice when you're walking him, at some point, he may just lie down. When you give him a command he'll suddenly have an itch that has to be scratched, or he'll yawn like he parties all night and just doesn't feel well enough to go on with the training. Now that I think about it, he'll love "Down." Seriously, train Rover because you want to, not because you need to.

Absolutely do not take Rover to a large obedience class. The chaos will be more than he can handle, and he'll just lie down and won't budge. That's embarrassing—not to him, to you.

BEST ENVIRONMENT: Jogger—**Walker**—Teenagers—Children 6 to 11—
Children of any age—Elderly—Latchkey—Active environment—**Sedate
environment—Multiple dogs okay**—Apartment—**House with yard**—
Room to run—Needs daily exercise—Camping—Hiking

Beagle

BRED TO DO. Beagles were bred to hunt rabbit, pheasant, and quail. They were also used to hunt the fox for the hunters. They usually did this in packs. I can imagine a rabbit outrunning a lot of breeds, but not a Beagle. Their agility and coordination is amazing. If you ever take Rover somewhere where he can run flat out, believe me, you will be impressed.

HOUSETRAINING. I'll tell you right off, Beagles are one of the hardest breeds to housetrain. I'm convinced that part of the problem is the fact that they don't have a serious bone in their hyper bodies. The moment you pick Rover up to take him outside you'll be holding perpetual motion. He will lick every corner of your face, play with your hair, and struggle to get down all at the same time. As soon as you get him outside and put him down, he'll hit the ground running. If he were a child he would sound something like this: "Did you see that bird? How does it stay in the air like that? Did you see that? I think I saw a lizard. I'm going to get it now. Why are you just standing there like that? Do you want to play?" When you find an accident in the house, and begin the verbal discipline, he will look at you, pause for a split second to wonder what you're upset about, then be off and running again. My mother used to call kids like this "whirlwinds." The name fits. It is going to take you quite some time to get Rover housetrained. Stop and think that you're going to have him for at least twelve years, so the time spent housetraining really doesn't seem that long.

PERSONALITY. Hold on to your hat and bar the door. You are the proud owners of a Beagle. A lot of energy, a lot of personality, and a lot of love wrapped up in about twenty to thirty pounds. This dog will be the joy of your life and your cross to bear.

This breed has changed somewhat over the years. They've always been active, but now they're hyperactive. They've always been affectionate, but the Beagle of today can bowl you over with affection. They've always been curious, but now they not only want to be where you are and watching what you're doing, they want to do it with you.

Beagles should never be latchkey dogs! If everyone in the household is gone four or more hours at a time on an average day you should have two dogs. If Rover is left alone too much too long he will become a fence jumper, chronic barker, and serious digger, plus he may become very destructive. Believe me, having a lone Beagle is a whole lot more trouble and expense than getting another dog. If you get a Beagle it must be with the understanding that he's going to require a lot of exercise and attention. I also recommend Beagles with kids. In fact, the more kids the merrier. If Rover were a child he could do his homework, talk on the phone, and watch TV at the same time. Believe me, a bunch of kids won't faze him. Unless you have kids that can wear him out daily, you must plan on seeing to it that Rover gets plenty of exercise. If you're a jogger, Rover will gladly be your jogging buddy; just make sure you condition him as you did yourself.

The biggest problem I run into with Beagles is their unruliness. One of the first things Beagle owners say to me is, "Judi, we can't let Rover in the house anymore because he immediately gets into things he's not supposed to. He runs around forever and won't calm down. He knows he's not supposed to be on the furniture, but he jumps all over it and then jumps off before we can do anything about it, and then he . . . and then he . . . and then he . . . and he doesn't pay any attention to 'No,' it's like he doesn't hear us." He gets into things he's not supposed to because at some point you chased him to get whatever it was away from him. You may have only chased once or twice but that's all it took for

Rover to love the chase game. Pick up items you really care about and leave a few items out that you know he'll go after. When he grabs and runs, *don't chase;* he'll come back shortly so that you can see what he has. Then he'll run off again, saying, "Looky what I got. I'm going to chew it up. You better get it from me or I'll ruin it." When he sees you're not going to play the chase game, he'll drop whatever it was and go on to something else. You're going to have to do this a few times before he finally gets the message. Think of all of the other unruly things he does and see if there is some way you can get back in control. Remember, to your Beagle everything is a game or a potential game. Please don't banish this dog because he's unruly. I've seen too many Beagles spending their lives in the backyard, getting attention only when they're fed. If you can't seem to manage him, give him to someone who can.

TRAINING. Definitely work with Rover on obedience. You'll need a firm, patient hand. The main thing you have to be careful to do is avoid giving positive reinforcement for what turns out to be negative behavior. He will attempt to turn everything from putting his collar and leash on to getting out the door into a game. When you try to put his collar on and he starts wiggling, if you buy into it at all you're going to have problems from then on. It won't be because he's being naughty, either. It'll be because he got all kinds of wonderful hands-on attention. That's positive reinforcement for what becomes negative behavior. I've always thought that if Beagles were human, they'd be the kids who drop out of high school because they're bored. If all you do is basic obedience, you're not coming anywhere near what Rover is capable of learning.

BEST ENVIRONMENT: **Jogger—Walker—**Teenagers—Children 6 to 11— **Children of any age—**Elderly—Latchkey—**Active environment—** Sedate environment—**Multiple dogs okay—**Apartment—**House with yard—Room to run—Needs daily exercise—Camping—**Hiking

---

Bearded Collie

BRED TO DO. Beardies were bred to herd and drove. They are still used as sheepdogs and drovers in Scotland. Their tenacity and love of their work is what makes them such desirable herders. They'll work right along with the herdsman in the worst weather.

The Beardies I've seen over the years never fit the description in the breed books.

HOUSETRAINING. Beardies love to be outside, even if it's raining, blowing, or snowing. At first Rover will be at your heels the majority of the time. This will help in getting him outside, but once you're out you're going to have a tough time watching him eliminate so that you can praise him. You'll know what I mean when you find yourself standing in one spot trying to pivot your upper body so that you can see Rover. He will be right at your heels, behind you. You may have a bit of a tiff over where you want him to go. Beardies are very independent dogs, and they want to make their own decisions. Watch where he wants to be and if at all possible let him go there. Beardies are clean dogs and usually housetrain smoothly.

PERSONALITY. Read the definition of "independent" so you understand what your Beardie is all about. They're manipulators as well. I've seen a Beardie go down on his back in seeming total submission, then right himself and corner someone with a growl. Pay close attention to the peck order in your family, or Rover will slowly but surely become dominant. You won't be aware of his climb until you try to discipline him for something or take something from him, or move him when he's comfortable. You could easily become one of these Humans who has to say, "Don't bother Rover when he's eating. Leave Rover alone when he's sleeping." This is not a breed I recommend with kids less than twelve to thirteen years old. This dog will not hesitate to discipline a naughty child. He may get along with the children in his family, as long as they respect him, but he will not like the kids' friends. If you watch him, you'll notice that Rover is not comfortable around younger children, whether they're yours or someone else's.

It sounds as if I don't have anything good to say about this breed, and I don't want to leave you with that impression. This is one of the few breeds that I don't mind being a latchkey dog, as long as Rover's not left alone much more than eight or nine hours. Every Beardie owner I've worked with says he will never have any other breed of dog. They're wonderfully affectionate and very smart. Beardies love to play, so pay attention to the way Rover wants to play and go with it. Read Chapter 5, "Playtime with Rover." Please pay close attention to Rover's grooming. He can't see through the hair in front of his eyes any better than you could. Remember, God did not create Bearded Collies, people did, and it's our responsibility to take care of them.

TRAINING. I've found the best way to reach a dog that is this independent is through praise. Pleasing you is not a Beardie's desire. You're going to have to teach him that pleasing you is neat. Praise him for the slightest thing. You can't possibly overpraise.

I definitely recommend training your Beardie. Any training you do sets him up for praise. I don't necessarily recommend straight obedience training. Breeds that are as independent as Beardies have a hard time relating to "Sit," "Stay," "Down." You must, however, work with him walking on a leash. Beardies don't take kindly to other dogs, so you'll want to be able to control him on a walk. Work with Rover on things that apply to your environment. As smart as Beardies are, there's little you can't teach them. One Beardie, Bluebeard, learned how to grab the handle on a garbage bag and drag it to the curb. He also knew how to put his toys away, get his leash, and wipe his feet before coming in.

> BEST ENVIRONMENT: Jogger—**Walker—Teenagers**—Children 6 to 11—Children of any age—**Elderly—Latchkey—Active environment**—Sedate environment—**Multiple dogs okay**—Apartment—**House with yard—Room to run**—Needs daily exercise—Camping—Hiking

Bedlington Terrier

BRED TO DO. Bedlingtons were bred as ratters. They were very good at their job, and they knew it; without hesitation, they would take on the occasional badger. I've been told of Bedlington owners in England who continue to use this dog as a ratter.

HOUSETRAINING. I've known Bedlingtons that housetrained in less than ten days; I also knew one that took several weeks. If Rover doesn't like the spot you've chosen, he's simply not going to go there. You might as well let him pick his spot and try to work around his choice. To avoid a lot of back talk, keep verbal discipline short and to the point. Pay close attention to Rover's grooming. Don't let the hair mat around his anus.

Even though Bedlingtons look like house dogs, they love to be outside. So the hardest part of housetraining could be getting him back in the house after he's eliminated.

PERSONALITY. It's not easy to describe this dog because he's such a combination of aggression and lapdogginess. This is the only analogy I could come up with: If Rover were a man, he'd be hardworking, loving, and responsible with his family. He would, however, stop off sometimes to have a beer with the guys, and more than likely he'd get into a barroom brawl. After the fight was over, he'd straighten his clothes, slap his friend on the back, and say, "I love a good fight." If Rover were a woman, she'd be a loving, responsible wife and mother, and she'd own the bar the fight was in. So your Rover will walk at your side as you've trained him to do, but he'll try and take on any dog that crosses what he believes to be *his* path. This dog has a serious mind of his own and won't hesitate to voice his opinion. Don't let all of that back talk fool you, though, because under it all beats the heart of a lamb. He'll exasperate you all day, then curl up in your lap to watch TV with you in the evening. If you have a Bedlington and another dog, read Chapter 10, "Living with Multiple Dogs." If fighting starts, your Bedlington is going to get very serious quickly.

Please don't have a Bedlington and other small animals—gerbils, hamsters, ferrets, etc. I've known one, but only one, that got along with the cat. When someone asks me how their dog will get along with small livestock I always say, "Dogs are carnivorous." I've found that humans can handle that bit of knowledge, but can't handle the dog making a kill and not eating it. The hunting instinct is strong in some dogs, but their food is in a bowl on the kitchen floor. They don't eat their kill because they're not hungry. Remember, this dog was used as a ratter. Hunting and killing are a part of who he is.

You must at all times be the Head Honcho. Even though breeders have sought to soften the breed's aggressive tendencies, and have succeeded for the most part, I still run into some real tough Bedlingtons. I don't normally recommend these dogs with children, because they have very little patience and won't hesitate to discipline a child they decide is naughty.

TRAINING. Be firm but kind. If Rover decides he doesn't want to learn something, he will dig in his heels—and, believe me he won't learn it at that point. Go on to something else and try again later. The training sessions will be much smoother if you work in short spurts with play in between. If Bedlingtons were human, they'd be called moody.

BEST ENVIRONMENT: Jogger—**Walker—Teenagers—**Children 6 to 11—
Children of any age—Elderly—**Latchkey (don't take advantage)—**
Active environment—Sedate environment—Multiple dogs okay—
Apartment—**House with yard—**Room to run—Needs daily exercise—
Camping—Hiking

Bernese Mountain Dog

BRED TO DO. Way back when, the Romans used this dog as a fighter; then somewhere down the road they used the fighting ability to guard herds. Any predator that came close to Rover's herd never did it again. Rover made his point, one way or another.

HOUSETRAINING. Rover is going to want to be outside, but stick to the method until he's housetrained. You're going to see some back talk from Rover, even when he's a pup. If you want him to have his eliminations in one area, you're probably going to have to insist on it. If he were a child the training would go something like this: You'd take him to his spot, and he would say, "I don't wanna go there, I like over here better." You'll pick him up, take him to where you want him to go, and as soon as you put him down, he runs to his favorite spot. If he's faster than you, he'll get to his spot, squat and go, then run off. Getting Rover housetrained is going to be a tad frustrating. Keep in mind all the wonderful years you have to look forward to. Comparatively speaking, housetraining time is minimal.

PERSONALITY. The Bernese is a very old breed, and what it was bred to do is a part of who Rover is. Rover is going to be an independent thinker, your protector, and, it will seem at times, your adversary.

Bernese *do not* make good latchkey dogs. You would think, given their independence, that being alone wouldn't bother them too much. You would be wrong. These dogs tend to be unruly and get out of control easily. If Rover's left alone too much, the out-of-control factor takes over the second he sees you. If you have children twelve and over they'll need to be able to hold their own with Rover, but he'll play with them until they drop. His stamina is a trait to be respected and admired. The Bernese is one of the breeds I recommend if someone wants a hiking and/or camping buddy. He'll outhike you, know he's done it, and love every minute of waiting for you to finally get up the hill. When you set up camp and establish the invisible site boundaries, Rover will either stand guard and pace a bit, or he'll lie down but remain at the ready, in case he's needed as your protector.

It really doesn't make any difference how many members of the family there are; Rover will attach to one of you, and wouldn't hesitate to walk to the ends of the earth if that was your desire.

Rover has a year-round winter coat. If you live someplace with warm springs, hot summers, and warm fall weather, this is not the dog for you. He will be hot and very uncomfortable for at least eight months out of the year. Remember, he comes from Switzerland.

TRAINING. Bernese are very trainable, and I highly recommend taking them through some type of obedience. Use a firm but kind hand. If you get too overbearing Rover will dig in his heels and openly defy you, or try and turn the session into a game. Rover doesn't have even a smidgen of patience, so the hardest commands for him are going to be "Wait" and "Stay." He won't mind "Down," as long as you don't expect him to stay down for any length of time.

> BEST ENVIRONMENT: Jogger—**Walker—Teenagers**—Children 6 to 11—Children of any age—Elderly—Latchkey—**Active environment—Sedate environment—Multiple dogs okay**—Apartment—**House with yard—Room to run**—Needs daily exercise—**Camping—Hiking**

Bichon Frise

BRED TO DO. Bred to be pampered. Bred to be carried. *Bred to be pleased, not to please.* These dogs are called sleeve dogs, because nobles would carry them in a big bell sleeve.

HOUSETRAINING. Your Bichon will housetrain for you quickly if the weather is warm, the wind isn't blowing, it's not raining, it's not dark, the grass isn't too high, and you carry him out and back in again. Believe me, he will sit and stare at you until you pick him up. I'm going to let you vary the usual housetraining method just a bit. When you take Rover outside, let him play a bit after he's had his eliminations. He's going to have to learn that outside is an okay place to be. Just don't tell him that the peons have to go outside too. Pay close attention to his grooming.

PERSONALITY. You have to keep in mind at all times that Rover thinks that he *is* royalty not that he was bred *for* royalty. To say that Bichons are affectionate is an understatement. Anytime you carry him or let him in your lap he'll be in seventh heaven, and he'll think that all is as it should be. If you sit down long enough to look up a phone number, there's your lap, and there's Rover in your lap. Several breeds need to be groomed and don't like it, but to your Bichon grooming is a form of pampering and he'll love it. He will be happier if you groom him in your lap. If you take him to be groomed, don't mention that a common Poodle will be groomed in the same salon.

I'm being somewhat facetious here because I want you to understand that the Bichon is the epitome of the lapdog. He is also not the least bit shy about letting you know his demands. You will never have to guess what's on his mind. He will look right at you and say, "Do you have any idea to whom you are speaking?" Get used to that look, because you'll see it often. Bichons love to play, but you could go broke buying him toys, trying to find the one he likes. Give him something of yours that you don't mind giving up, like a satin slipper, a small leather purse or shoe, a stuffed animal, or a small pillow. He's going to love the fact that your scent is all over the item, and he'll enjoy bringing it to you so that both of you can play.

I'm never quite sure if I should recommend this dog with children. I've seen some that won't hesitate to discipline a naughty child, others that hide when kids are around, and others that choose a child to sleep with. I think the key is the child himself. If he is old enough to be gentle, and is a natural lover of animals, Rover senses it. He'll love a child that loves him.

TRAINING. This is a breed that I recommend teaching tricks to. Now, don't get your dignified back up and say, "Teaching tricks is demeaning." That's just plain silly. Rover doesn't know the difference between a trick and an obedience command. Rover will love the attention you give him when you're training him, and he'll love being the center of attention when he does what you've taught him. He will do anything you teach him with dignity, but the key in getting him to follow a command is praise. Remember, he couldn't care less if he pleases you, but if you praise a lot he'll learn that pleasing you is kinda fun. Bichons are also intelligent dogs. So don't let their brains go to waste.

BEST ENVIRONMENT: Jogger—Walker—**Teenagers**—Children 6 to 11—Children of any age—**Elderly**—Latchkey—**Active environment (as long as he's involved)—Sedate environment—Multiple dogs okay—Apartment**—House with yard—Room to run—Needs daily exercise—Camping—Hiking

---

Black and Tan Coonhound

BRED TO DO. The name of this hound tells the story of what he was bred to do. But he also worked to bring down stag, bear, and opossum.

HOUSETRAINING. As with most of the other Hounds, telling the difference between nose down looking for a place to go and nose down to explore is the hardest part of housetraining. Make sure you get some of his urine on a rag and put it outside. When you take him to that spot, his nose will go down automatically, and he'll know his scent immediately. Coonhounds can be on the timid side, especially as puppies. If you notice that when you take him out, he seems unsure of everything and wants to run right back in the house before he's had an elimination, you'll have to gently bring him back out and try again. Do not say "It's okay, it's okay."

PERSONALITY. I recommend that Coonhounds be used for what they were bred to do. They love to work, and they are very good at their job. If you have Rover as a pet and have loose cats in your neighborhood, don't be surprised if you hear one screaming, "Would you please do something about your damn dog so I can get out of this stupid tree?" Rover, on the other hand, will be wonderfully proud of himself, and wonder why you don't get your trusty hunting rifle. The cat will stay in the tree until he can get down with at least some dignity intact.

If you don't plan on using Rover, make sure he gets the exercise he needs. If you're a slow jogger or fast walker, this is the dog for you. If you're a runner or biker, you'll be a mile ahead before you realize you've lost Rover to a scent that interested him. You must give him time to use his nose. If he has to keep a fast pace with you, with his head up all of the time, he will be a very unhappy Hound dog.

Coonhounds are vocal! I yell this at you because I want you to know that it can become a real problem. He will howl and/or bark. He will also "talk." If he wants to get something across to you, you'll hear a mumble, a grumble, something between a howl and a whine, then back to a mumble, a grumble. Howling is the way these dogs stay in touch with each other and the hunter on a hunt. It's part of what Rover is all about. If you use him, it probably won't be a problem. If you have him strictly as a pet and give him little or no exercise you're probably going to get complaints from your neighbors.

I've heard these dogs called aggressive. I wondered about that until I was fortunate enough to see one work. They are indeed very aggressive and totally focused when doing their job, but I've seen none of that around the house with family. However, children must be old enough to be kind and gentle with Rover. If they're too young or too rough Rover will avoid them altogether.

TRAINING. As to what he was bred to do, very little training is necessary. He'll need to learn how to stay in line and when to turn everything over to the hunter. As for obedience, he'll learn easily as long as you're calm and controlled. Not *controlling,* controlled. If Rover senses that you aren't sure of yourself, he might take advantage. He won't be subtle about it, either. He'll look you square in the face and say, "If you don't know what you're doing, how am I supposed to know what you're doing?" Confusion and frustration will reign.

BEST ENVIRONMENT: **Jogger**—Walker—Teenagers—**Children 6 to 11**—Children of any age—Elderly—Latchkey—**Active environment**—Sedate environment—**Multiple dogs okay**—Apartment—House with yard—**Room to run**—**Needs daily exercise**—Camping—Hiking

---

Bloodhound

BRED TO DO. Bloodhounds are famous all over the world for what they were bred to do. I read somewhere that you can take a teaspoon of dander and perspiration, spread it on the walls of a room fourteen stories up, and a Bloodhound can find the scent in a three-mile radius, in a city as congested as Philadelphia. That absolutely blew me away. Since then I've had the privilege of watching one work. Obviously this is one of the breeds I recommend using for what they were bred to do. Not because he won't make a good pet—he will—but because an ability like his shouldn't go to waste. These dogs are happiest when they're working. I know it's hard to tell when a Bloodhound is happy, so you'll have to take my word for it.

HOUSETRAINING. Keep the verbal discipline low-key. If you put too much emphasis on the discipline, Rover will fall apart before your very eyes. He wants to please, and as long as you stick to the method he should housetrain smoothly. The hard part in housetraining is the same with almost all Hounds, and that's knowing the difference between his nose down following a scent, and his nose down looking for a place to go. Make sure you get his urine on a clean rag and stake it outside. He'll be able to follow his own scent immediately. This Rover is timid, so be careful when you first start taking him outside. If a plane flies overhead, a neighbor's dog barks, or someone is mowing their lawn, he's liable to cut and run for the house. You'll have to go get him and bring him back out. Gentle him through this stage and he'll learn that the world isn't going to fall in on him. *Do not say* "It's okay, it's okay."

PERSONALITY. These dogs are sweethearts. They're affectionate and truly lovable. As he grows, you'll see Rover's disappointment when he realizes he's too big to sit in your lap. He'll try every once in a while, just in case by some miracle he shrank. Rover can work in severe weather and cross even the roughest terrain, but when he's home he wants the lap of luxury. He wants to nap on the couch or on a sheepskin in front of the fire. He wants to sleep with you in your bed. If he starts out at the foot of your bed, don't be surprised if when you wake up, he's sound asleep on your pillow. Rover is a mild-mannered pet at home and turns into Super Searcher when he's called to duty.

Bloodhounds are very unassuming. They don't have a clue as to their power and I honestly can't imagine one biting somebody. I don't hesitate to recommend this dog with children. But watch your kids, Human. Rover will allow them to do anything they want. I saw a three-year-old boy repeatedly pound on a Bloodhound with a toy hammer. The parent did nothing to stop it. Jinx took it for a few minutes, then finally moved out of reach of the child. I wanted to use the toy hammer on the parent.

These dogs can be problem barkers or howlers if they're bored or frustrated. You may see some temporary personality changes in your Bloodhound twice a year. He will be preoccupied and somewhat hyperactive, and his attention span may be shorter than usual. The two times a year are spring and fall. Stop and think of all of the new scents that have to be filtered through—not just growing things in spring, but open windows in the kitchens of the area. Barbecues being fired up, swimming pools being readied, and the smells heat brings out in cars and on roads. You can imagine for yourself what autumn brings.

TRAINING. As I've said this dog should, without a doubt, be used for what he was bred to do. Speak to someone who works in canine search and rescue in your area, and find out what they recommend about training. I've heard some say obedience training is a must, and others say it's not necessary. I've never known a Bloodhound that actually needed obedience training. Rover will do anything you ask of him. Whatever you decide, be sure to use a gentle hand.

> BEST ENVIRONMENT: **Jogger—Walker—**Teenagers—Children 6 to 11— **Children of any age—**Elderly—**Latchkey (they can be if they're used)—Active environment—Sedate environment—Multiple dogs okay—**Apartment—**House with yard—Room to run—Needs daily exercise—**Camping—Hiking

Blue and Red Heeler

BRED TO DO. Bred to herd, mostly sheep in Australia. And I must say that they were and are very good at their job.

HOUSETRAINING. The Dingo part of Rover is going to make housetraining easy. It just won't seem right to him to have eliminations in the house. The major problem is Heelers' speed. One second he'll be at your side, all set to go out, and the next second you'll say, "Where did he go? He was just here a second ago." In fact you'll be saying that same line for years to come.

PERSONALITY. Some breeds of dogs go as far back as recorded history. The Heeler is only about two hundred years old. In terms of the process of breeding in certain traits, that isn't very long. If your Rover has strong Dingo traits, he's going to seem a bit on the feral or undomesticated side. You'll see him go down into a hunting posture. He'll crouch, a bit like a golfer settling in for a drive, then suddenly spring forward and go into a dead run. If you see a Heeler crouch ready to herd and a Dingo crouch for hunting, it's hard to tell the difference. That hunting crouch is what breeders seek when breeding a dog to herd.

The Heeler's speed and grace are something to see. I run into a lot of Heelers named Spinner or Twister, many of them have an amazing ability to jump straight up and spin in midair.

With Dingo traits, Rover will be suspicious of strangers and will take his time getting to know someone. Let him go at his own pace. The more "domesticated" Heeler, on the other hand, won't know a stranger. If you see more Heeler traits, you'll have a more lighthearted Rover, unless for some reason he believes he needs to be responsible for his own care. He's going to love playing. "Frolic" is the only term I can think of that describes Rover's running around. If you've ever seen a colt frolic you know what I mean. The more Dingo-ish Heelers will play, but not with the same abandon. Heelers can make great Frisbee dogs. They can hit the air from a standstill, and with a running start.

These dogs are totally devoted to their family. If for some reason Rover has to be given away, he's going to have a hell of a time adjusting to a new family. It doesn't make any difference what age he is at the time, he's going to go through displacement again. It will also take him some time to give or accept much affection from his new family. Speaking of family, I do recommend Heelers with children but not the very young. Rover is far too vivacious for them. He needs a child six years old or older, who can keep up with him.

TRAINING. I don't usually recommend that Heelers start structured obedience training until they're seven to eight months old. If you start him too soon he's still too much of a puppy and on the hyper side. Let Rover mature a bit first. Don't hesitate to teach him things that are important around the house and with the family. When you do start his training you'll need a firm but kind hand. Except for taking walks on a leash, I've found that training goes much more smoothly if it lasts not much more than fifteen minutes at a time. If you insist on training for twenty to thirty minutes, you're going to be hitting your head against a brick wall for ten to fifteen minutes of that time.

I enjoy working with Heelers in any capacity because they throw their entire personality into whatever they do. When you're working with your Rover, watch him closely and you'll see him decide whether or not he likes a command. Most of them don't mind "Sit," but they don't much like "Down." If you're seeing more Dingo traits, training Rover to do almost anything is going to be like pulling teeth. With these dogs I recommend training off the leash as much as possible. I've found they respond much faster if they're not restrained.

> BEST ENVIRONMENT: Jogger—**Walker**—Teenagers—**Children 6 to 11**—Children of any age—Elderly—Latchkey—**Active environment**—Sedate environment—**Multiple dogs okay**—Apartment—**House with yard**—**Room to run**—**Needs daily exercise**—Camping—Hiking

Bluetick Coonhound

BRED TO DO. Obviously bred to hunt raccoon. He's also used for hunting fox and cougar. I always think of things from the dog's point of view, and I can't help but wonder what went through this dog's head when the hunter told him to hunt down a cougar. Cougars are not small cats, and they don't like being told where to go or what to do. Rover holds his ground, though, and does his job very well.

HOUSETRAINING. The time of year could be a factor in how long it takes you to housetrain Rover. If it's spring or summer, the instant you take him outside, his nose is going to hit the ground, and he'll hunt down beetles, lizards, spiders, and anything else that happens to be moving along the ground. He'll stop mid-hunt, squat, have an elimination, and be off again. As with almost all the Hounds, the hardest part of housetraining your Bluetick will be telling the difference between his nose down checking out many scents, and his nose down looking for a spot to go.

PERSONALITY. Compared with a Beagle this dog is sedate. Compared with other Hounds he's hyper. He needs to hunt and he needs a lot of exercise. If you're a slow jogger, this is the dog for you. I say *slow* jogger because you have to allow Rover to use his nose. You may be jogging along and suddenly find yourself going off in a direction you had no intention of going. Rover picked up a scent that fascinated him, and you're going along for the ride. If he has to run head up all the time, he'll cease to enjoy the time with you.

If you have cats in your neighborhood, don't be surprised if you hear one screaming, "Would you *please* do something with your damn dog so I can get out of this stupid tree?" Rover will be at the base of the tree, very proud of himself and expecting you to be proud of him. If you try to call him off without telling him what a good boy he is, he's not going to understand. He will say, "Are you kidding? I can't leave now. The cougar will get away. Aren't you going to do anything? I got him in the tree for you." The cat is watching all this and wondering how he's going to get down and away with dignity intact.

Blueticks are fun dogs and they love to play. I've never seen one that didn't have a bit of clown in him. This is not a dog you have to worry may become too serious. Blueticks are good with kids, but they don't bond with them unless the child is the one giving all the exercise or doing the hunting. If you don't plan on using your Bluetick, make sure you don't neglect his need for exercise. If he gets bored or frustrated he'll release it in some way: barking, wall jumping, or destruction.

TRAINING. I do recommend obedience training. You'll notice that until Rover is an adult, he's going to seem flaky, spacy, and just a little off center. The obedience training speeds the maturing and calming. Use a firm but kind hand. I've found that if you punctuate training sessions with play or exercise the training will go more smoothly. If you plan to use Rover for hunting, very little training will be necessary.

BEST ENVIRONMENT: **Jogger—Walker—**Teenagers—**Children 6 to 11—**Children of any age—Elderly—Latchkey—**Active environment—**Sedate environment—**Multiple dogs okay—**Apartment—House with yard—**Room to run—Needs daily exercise—**Camping—Hiking

---

Border Collie

BRED TO DO. They were and still are bred to herd. They aren't too picky about what they herd. Rover will herd sheep, cattle, horses, and even geese. If you have children, he will happily herd them in for dinner.

HOUSETRAINING. Poodles are the easiest breed to housetrain. Border Collies come in a close second. If you stick to the method, you'll have very little trouble. The only problem will be the herding instinct. He'll follow you out, follow you to the spot, and stay behind you the entire time. You'll find yourself standing in one place, turning the upper part of your body back and forth to see where he is so that you can praise him for going.

PERSONALITY. Along with being one of the best herd dogs, Border Collies are one of the best dogs around, period. This breed is so special that Border Collie breeders and owners are trying very hard to keep it out of the AKC. The American Kennel Club has decided to accept Border Collies as an AKC breed. The breeders and owners of this dog know what can happen to so many breeds once they are part of the AKC show and breeding circuit. They don't want that to happen to their dog. I applaud their efforts. This is a wonderful dog just the way he is, and I'd hate to think what could happen if he becomes a part of the AKC. (Oops, just lost some readers.)

This Rover is one of the first breeds that come to mind if I'm asked about a good dog for kids. He's good with kids of all ages, shapes and sizes. If you have an image in your mind of "a boy and his dog," this is the dog you can imagine. Borders are loving, affectionate, and smart. In the years since I opened my practice I don't think I've seen more than a handful of Borders with behavior problems. One of the reasons, I'm sure, is because this has never been the "in" breed to own, and I hope it never is.

If you have very young children, Rover will baby-sit for free. If you have a hyperactive family member, Rover will play until they both drop.

If all you want is a good companion Rover will be that, too. You're probably thinking the Border Collie is the perfect dog. *Wrong*. When this Rover goes through displacement (discussed in Chapter 4, "Puppy Chewing and Destructive Chewing"), he goes through it big-time. He's going to do some destructive chewing. If you understand why he's chewing everything in sight, you'll know how to handle it. I've seen this Rover lose his happy home due to destruction, so please learn what you can, and see him through the tough times.

Border Collies do not make good latchkey dogs! Another dog will help, but these are very people-oriented dogs and won't be happy waiting eight to ten hours for you to come home. Rover can easily become a fence jumper if he's left alone too much. The neighbor children won't mind if he visits. I worked with a Border named Jessie who jumped the wall every day at the exact same time. Every day, Jessie was sitting at the bus stop waiting for the kids to come from school. She would run along with each one as they split off in different directions to go home. The problem was that none of the kids belonged to her. My client didn't have kids, and he was gone ten hours a day. He spent every minute he could with Jessie but it didn't help her through the long days. I assured him that we could stop the jumping, but I warned him that she could become depressed. I was right; she ate very little, she chewed her paws until they were raw, and she became a terrible barker. When he called me again, I had to tell him that the kindest thing he could do for Jessie would be to give her to a family with kids and a stay-at-home parent. As it turned out, one of the kids whom Jessie walked home from the bus was in real need of a special dog, and Jessie fit the bill perfectly.

TRAINING. There is very little you can't train this dog to do. Borders thrive on praise and will do anything for it. Be kind and Rover will turn somersaults for you. If you're too firm, Rover will fall apart. And what you don't train Rover to do, he'll probably figure out for himself. Randy loved ice and every time his Humans got ice they gave him a cube. They bought a new refrigerator with the ice in the door. He only had to watch his Humans get ice a few times before he figured out how to push the ice button and get his own ice. I told them as long as Randy didn't abuse the privilege, there was no need to stop him. With the ice right there for him to get, I couldn't think of a way to stop him anyway, other than getting a new refrigerator or installing a cover.

BEST ENVIRONMENT: **Jogger—Walker**—Teenagers—Children 6 to 11— **Children of any age—Elderly**—Latchkey—**Active environment— Sedate environment—Multiple dogs okay**—Apartment—**House with yard—Room to run**—Needs daily exercise—**Camping**—Hiking

Borzoi

BRED TO DO. In their day these dogs were among the best at hunting wolves. Because of their beauty, they are now exclusively companion dogs, but the hunting instinct is still a part of who they are. It must be recognized and respected.

HOUSETRAINING. A part of Rover wants to be outside, especially in the warmer months, but there is also part of him that loves the lap of luxury and doesn't want to go outside if the weather is chilly. Borzois come originally from Arabia, so even cool weather might keep them in the house. All in all these are very clean dogs, who want to do what's right. Stick to the method and make sure there's no confusion.

PERSONALITY. Even though the hunting instinct is still a part of who they are, and they respect their ancestors, they're glad they can sleep on a soft bed, and avoid any unpleasant work. Borzois love being surrounded by luxury, and they look the noble part. When you see Rover lying down on a plush rug, with his head high and his legs stretched out in front of him, you can easily imagine him holding audience with the common dogs.

Borzois are docile, and you'll see this gentle nature in everything they do. Rover will get along quite well with kids of any age, but he's not going to get too excited about playing with them. He'll be very reserved around strangers, so you want to make sure he greets people in his own way and in his own time. If Rover barks at somebody, take note. Rarely will Rover bark, so when he does, he means it.

These dogs are very loyal to the ones they love. I have never known a Borzoi that will wander off his own territory. He sees absolutely no point in being any farther from you than necessary. Don't confuse his loyalty with protectiveness, though. As reserved and quiet as these dogs are, they don't get too excited about anything, much less an intruder. The loyalty factor becomes obvious if Rover has to adapt to a new person. He will never be as loyal to someone else as he is to you.

You must make sure Rover gets the exercise he needs. He needs a good long jog or fast walk almost daily. If you don't exercise him, he won't become a wall jumper and he probably won't become destructive or start barking. He will, however, start walking with his head low, and show other signs of being depressed. It will be up to you to see to Rover's needs, because he's not going to get insistent about anything.

TRAINING. Borzois can be very bullheaded if you're asking them to do something they don't want to do or see no point in doing. On the other hand, I've never met a Borzoi that required structured obedience. These dogs are polite and well-mannered automatically; it doesn't have to be taught. I do recommend that you work hard on coming when called, and walking correctly on a leash. If you take Rover somewhere he can run free, you're going to want to be able to recall him immediately. If he sees a rabbit or other wildlife, the hunt-and-chase instinct is going to take over. A Borzoi running is a beautiful sight to see, but you want him to come back to you on command. When you take him for a walk on a leash, you want his attention on you, not on everything around him. Use a gentle hand and voice. I absolutely do not recommend taking a Borzoi to a large obedience class. So many dogs and people will be overwhelming to him.

BEST ENVIRONMENT: **Jogger—Walker—**Teenagers—Children 6 to 11—
Children of any age—Elderly—Latchkey—**Active environment—**
Sedate environment—**Multiple dogs okay—**Apartment—House with
yard—**Room to run—Needs daily exercise—**Camping—Hiking

Boston Terrier

BRED TO DO. Bred for the sole purpose of being a companion. The breeding worked. The Boston is known as a gentleman among dogs.

HOUSETRAINING. Really easy to housetrain. One reason is that when he puts his nose down, it's because he's looking for a spot to go. Rarely will you see his nose down for very long for any other reason. On top of that, Rover is a clean dog, he wants to please, and he's a quick learner. If the children are old enough get them involved in the housetraining process. Rover is going to want to be with the kids anyway.

PERSONALITY. *These dogs snore!* I yell this at you because I've seen this wonderful little guy banished to the other side of the house at bedtime. He doesn't have the vaguest idea what he did so wrong that he deserved to be sent away from you. Don't be a Boston Terrier owner if you can't stand snoring.

This is one of the breeds at the top of my list when I'm asked about a small dog that's good with kids. This sweetheart will take care of your youngest until he sees that the child can take care of himself. I've seen this dog sit patiently while a little girl put a doll's hat on him; the ruffled panties, however, presented a problem. He was then picked up and carried around while the little girl tried to burp him. Rover didn't mind, because he knew he was loved. Bostons are also one of the breeds I recommend for the elderly. He doesn't require much exercise and he loves his master with all his heart. Rover will move gently around a walker or cane or wheelchair. He'll enjoy rides in the car once he's conditioned to it, because it means he gets to be with his Human. Rover will get along in an apartment as easily as he does in a house. If you think of snoring as a fault, it's the only one I know of.

Two main traits stand out in Bostons. They are incredibly patient with children, and they believe themselves to be quite large and powerful. They'll protect your house with the best of the breeds that do that for a living.

You're going to notice that Rover gets cold easily. Don't insist that he stay out any longer then necessary during the colder months. If he sleeps with you, he'll learn quickly how warm it is under the covers. There are wonderful fake sheepskin beds for dogs. If Rover doesn't sleep with you, let him curl up in one of those.

This dog will love you and his family with every fiber of his being, and all he asks is a little of the same in return. Rarely will you have to discipline Rover; when you do, he will be absolutely crushed and will never do whatever it was again.

TRAINING. Given how much he loves his Human and wants to please, there's very little you can't train Rover to do. The only thing I caution you about is working with him so much he starts breathing fast. Wanting to please as much as he does, he'll suffer like an asthmatic before he lets you know he needs to stop. If you have two left feet and are all thumbs, this is a good dog for you. Rover will wait politely while you fumble trying to put his collar and leash on, and he'll wait patiently while you bumble with the front door. As you're walking, he won't giggle when you trip over a sprinkler or fall into a bush.

Rover would be pleased as punch to learn tricks. Don't get your dignified back up. Rover doesn't know the difference between a trick and a command. Besides, he loves laughter and enjoys entertaining.

> BEST ENVIRONMENT: Jogger—**Walker (no major distances)**—
> Teenagers—Children 6 to 11—**Children of any age—Elderly—**
> Latchkey—**Active environment—Sedate environment—Multiple**
> **dogs okay—Apartment—House with yard**—Room to run—Needs
> daily exercise—Camping—Hiking

Bouvier Des Flandres

BRED TO DO. He was bred as a cattle driver, but was also used for police work and guard.

HOUSETRAINING. All you have to do is stick to the method and this Rover will housetrain easily. The hardest part is going to be keeping outside off limits until he's completely trustworthy.

He'll have his eliminations; you'll praise him and start back to the house. You'll look around and notice Rover isn't with you. If he were a child, he would sound something like this: "Please can't I stay out for just a little while?" A foot will stamp. "I don't *wanna* go in now. I just wanna stay out a little longer. Ah, come on, you never let me do anything. I never get to do anything fun." You may have to plan on picking him up to get him in.

Watch the grooming. Don't let the hair grow around his anus.

PERSONALITY. You must pay attention to Rover's grooming. Knowing that he has to be groomed is not going to make him like it. Until he finally resigns himself to it he's going to be like a little boy getting his first haircut. Start getting him used to grooming tools and handling as soon as you bring him home. Groomers will thank you for the effort.

Bouviers are fun dogs to have. They are full of personality and funny little ways. I've never known one that didn't have a little clown in him. Rugrat got his name because he would get hold of one end of a Persian rug and pull it over him, roll a couple of times, and go to sleep. Shawn attached herself to a stuffed dog and would carry it with her everywhere. She would sit in front of the washer and dryer when it had to be cleaned and, when it was dry, take it out of the dryer herself. Dude's favorite game was hide-and-seek. This dog would hide while his Human counted to ten. I wouldn't have believed it if I hadn't seen it myself. Johnny, the Human, would close his eyes and count. Dude would run and hide behind something or under something. He would even pick different places to hide. When it was Johnny's turn to hide, Dude would sit down and turn his back for thirty seconds or so, then start looking for Johnny. The excitement they shared when they found each other was something to see. I've known several dogs that play hide-and-seek with the Human hiding, but never, until Dude, have I seen it reversed. Make sure you pay attention to the way Rover wants to play and, if possible, accommodate him. If your Bouvier ever stops playing, see if there are problems going on. Something has happened to make him believe he needs to be alert all of the time.

You would think that with this funny side of him he would be good with kids. I'm sorry, but this is not one of the breeds I recommend with children under twelve years of age. Rover's not very patient, and he doesn't automatically respect anybody. His respect has to be earned. I know the books will tell you that Bouviers are good with kids, but I have found over the years that that isn't true. What I've seen is Bouviers that tolerate children but won't interact. Rover seems to get along with teenagers much better.

Rover won't hesitate to take care of your house when you're not there, and he does it naturally. Given the responsibility, he will take very good care of you as well. The nice part about Rover's protection is that he'll turn it back over to you as soon as you're home. He'll protect you only if he sees you can't protect yourself. Read Chapter 9, "Natural Protectiveness," because this is a basic part of what Rover is all about.

TRAINING. Definitely do obedience work with your Bouvier. This is a very powerful dog, that could easily drag you all over the place. Keep in mind that Rover's respect has to be earned. You will earn it as soon as you start working with him. Use a kind hand. The training sessions will go along much smoother if you interrupt with play. Work for fifteen to twenty minutes, then play for a few. As good-natured as these dogs usually are, they'll learn almost anything you want to teach them.

> BEST ENVIRONMENT: Jogger—**Walker—Teenagers**—Children 6 to 11—Children of any age—Elderly—Latchkey—**Active environment—Sedate environment—Multiple dogs okay**—Apartment—**House with yard**—Room to run—Needs daily exercise—**Camping**—Hiking

Boxer

BRED TO DO. When bullbaiting and dogfighting were still allowed the Boxer was there with the best of them. Thank heaven these sports are no longer legal. He's appropriately named, because he gets those front paws up in the air and starts a fight like a Human does. In Germany, the Boxer was the first breed trained and used as a police dog. Boxers learned quickly and were very good at their job. I'm not sure, but I think the reason they are no longer used in that capacity is because of health. They are susceptible to tumors in the mouth and rheumatism, and their teeth need frequent cleaning. Boxers are not long-lived, nine years being the life expectancy.

HOUSETRAINING. Boxers don't use their noses too much in exploratory behavior, so when you see Puppy Rover's nose down, it's a sure bet he needs to go outside. Your biggest problem is going to be keeping an eye on him. This dog is perpetual motion. If you have infant gates up to keep him in a certain area, don't be surprised to find the gate untouched and Rover in another area of the house. He will turn everything into a game, and he does it in such an endearing way it's hard not to go along with him. Hang in there with him. You'll get him housetrained.

PERSONALITY. I love the way they describe this breed in the books. The word they use is "lively." That, dear Human, is an understatement almost to the point of being ridiculous. Hold on to your hat and get a grip on the safety bar, because you're in for quite a ride. These dogs are about as close to being clinically hyperactive as one can get without actually being clinically hyperactive. Don't get a Boxer if you're not prepared for the amount of exercise this breed demands.

Somehow, though, Boxer owners don't mind. Boxers have a heart as big as all outdoors; they're incredibly loving and loyal and very smart. I don't hesitate to recommend Boxers with kids, but I do recommend the kids be old enough to hold their own. If Rover gets excited when you come home, he's not going to care that your three-year-old is standing between you and him.

Boxers can be fence jumpers. Remember, standing on their hind legs is natural to them, so jumping of all kinds can be a problem. When Rover's a tiny puppy, you'll want to start teaching him not to jump on you, family members, and company. As to the fence jumping, there are several things that could get Rover going over the fence, but the number one reason is being left alone too much. Rover will not handle solitude well, and he has to have exercise. You come home late from work one day and it goes something like this: "It's about time you came home! I have been waiting for you *forever!* You promised we would go for a walk as soon as you got home. The least you could've done was call. I started pacing while I was waiting for you, and I chewed up a couple of pillows on the couch, took the clothes off the line, and dug some holes in back. Well, don't blame me! You were late!" Please, Human, don't neglect Rover's need for attention and exercise. But remember, his breathing can be a problem. He needs exercise, but not jogging. He'll walk as far as you want, but don't insist that he run.

Don't let someone tell you not to wrestle with your dog because you'll teach aggression. Wrestling is going to be one of Rover's favorite games. If you have the opportunity to watch two dogs play, you'll notice that it's impossible to tell which is the dominant dog. When they play, all bets are off. The dominant dog will go down and over as much as the subordinate dog does. The subordinate dog will stand on the back of the dominant dog in play, when he wouldn't dare do that under other circumstances. Also play tug-of-war if you want to. Read Chapter 5, "Playtime with Rover." Read Chapter 9, "Natural Protectiveness," as well. Rover will take very good care of you if he feels you need help.

TRAINING. Definitely train your Boxer. This dog's power and coordination must be acknowledged and respected. I don't care how strong you think you are; with Rover's upper body strength, he can pull you along on a leash if he has a mind to. You'll need to be firm but kind. I say firm, because this dog is going to jump and try to play while you put his collar and leash on, then he'll jump up, grab the leash, do a few turns, and probably end up on his back, chewing on the leash. If you buy into any of his antics, you're going to have problems working with him from that point on. This dog doesn't have a patient bone in his body. You're going to have to be the patient one.

I don't know why, but I've found the male Boxer settles down and learns faster than the female. If you have a female, get a good strong grip on your patience, and you'll get her trained.

After all that, I have to end by saying these dogs are very trainable. I know it sounds as if I'm contradicting myself, but you'll know what I mean when you start working with your very own Boxer.

BEST ENVIRONMENT: Jogger—**Walker**—Teenagers—**Children 6 to 11**—Children of any age—Elderly—Latchkey—**Active environment**—Sedate environment—Multiple dogs okay—Apartment—**House with yard**—**Room to run**—**Needs daily exercise**—**Camping**—Hiking

---

Briard

BRED TO DO. In the beginning Briards were bred to herd and guard, but they have been used in many capacities. They did everything short of carrying a gun in World War I, and probably would've done that if they'd been trained.

HOUSETRAINING. These dogs, for the most part, are sweethearts, but they have an independent streak that could create a problem. There's a possibility that Rover may not like the spot you've chosen for him to eliminate. It won't make any difference how many times you take him to the spot, he'll move away and go to his. If possible let him decide where he wants to go and the housetraining will go much faster. He's going to love every minute of being outside, so you may have to actually pick him up to get him back in the house.

Don't get a Briard unless you have the time to take care of his grooming. While the housetraining process is going on, check the hair around his anus daily.

PERSONALITY. The first thing you're going to notice is that herding is in every fiber of this dog's being. As a pup he'll herd you down the hall into the kitchen for your first cup of coffee. He can't imagine how you managed before he came along. When he's hungry, he may start pushing you with his nose to wherever you keep his food. When he's outside, he may run around trying to get all the birds in one tree. He was also bred to guard his herd; if the birds would cooperate, he'd be more than happy to take care of them. If you have children, his nanny tendencies can become a problem. When the kids try to leave the house for any reason, he won't want to let them go. He may push himself between the child and the door. Gentry not only barred the door, he would get the kids' school backpacks and run into the backyard with them. Gentry's Humans had to put the backpacks in the car so that the kids could get them after they made their escape through the front door. Needless to say, I don't hesitate to recommend Briards with children of any age.

You'll notice that Rover is going to be cautious with strangers. That's okay! Don't push him. Rover is doing everything in his power to take care of you, and a stranger could be a threat to his family. As soon as he determines that the stranger is not a threat and is accepted by you, he'll relax.

There are very few breeds whose members can be the caretaker without also being the dominant member of the pack. This Rover will take care of you because doing so is a part of who he is, not because he's dominant and has to take on all the responsibility that goes with that position.

Except for the grooming, getting along with this Rover is simple. All you have to do is love him, and you'll get it back tenfold.

TRAINING. Given all the various duties this dog has performed, it's obvious that there's very little you can't train Rover to do. Be kind, and he'll do somersaults for you. If you're too firm or harsh, this dog will fall apart before your eyes. This Rover's hearing is very keen. A wolf can hear a small rodent under ten feet of snow. I don't know if the Briard's hearing is that good, but if not, it runs a close second. No need to shout commands, is what I'm trying to say here. Just for the fun of it, see if you can sneak up on him.

> BEST ENVIRONMENT: Jogger—**Walker**—Teenagers—Children 6 to 11—
> **Children of any age**—**Elderly**—Latchkey—**Active environment**—
> **Sedate environment**—**Multiple dogs okay**—Apartment—**House with
> yard**—Room to run—Needs daily exercise—**Camping**—Hiking

Brittany Spaniel

BRED TO DO. Hunt almost any bird that can be hunted. This dog will point the way to woodcock, partridge, quail, and the odd rabbit. He'll also go into water, if that's where the bird is.

HOUSETRAINING. These are very sensitive little ones, so keep your verbal discipline low-key. If you're harsh, Rover will urinate in submission and you will defeat your purpose. Brittanys are on the skittish side, so when you take Rover out and the neighbor's dogs bark, or the wind rustles some leaves, he's liable to run right back in the house. If you gentle him through these times he'll do fine. Stick to the method, and keep things lighthearted.

PERSONALITY. You have to be careful and knowledgeable to correctly raise a good Brittany. If you hit him, he'll become hand shy. If you raise your voice, he'll drop into a submissive posture and freeze. *Absolutely, positively, don't say "It's okay, it's okay."* (See Chapter 7.) If you plan on using Rover for hunting, read what Brittany trainers have to say about getting him used to gunfire. If it's done correctly, very little training is necessary.

I don't recommend Brittanys with kids. These dogs are just too unpredictable if they're not allowed to use their very keen talents; they just don't know how to handle themselves or the confined world around them. If you have a Brittany only as a pet, make sure he gets plenty of exercise. He'd make a great jogging buddy, but make sure you keep him on a leash. This is for two reasons. One, if you're jogging along and Rover sees a couple of robins, he's liable to stop dead in his tracks and point them out to anybody who might be interested. (I don't know about where you live, but in New Mexico the robins would point right back, with the wrong finger.) Two, if something frightens him, he will cut and run. Faced with fight or flight, Rover will choose flight every time. Given the right circumstances these dogs are sweet-natured and trainable, and they love to please.

Too many Brittanys out there were adopted because of their beauty and size. There are several breeds that can be adopted for those reasons and pose no problem; obviously Brittanys aren't one of them.

TRAINING. As I've said, if you're going to use Rover to hunt, talk to a Brittany trainer or read the Brittany books. As to obedience, he's a piece of cake to train. He'll look to you as his leader the first time he lays eyes on you, and if you want him to sit, he'll sit. You must use a gentle hand, though, if you want him to learn anything. If you have a Brittany and you're not using him to hunt, but you care enough to want his happiness, get him into field trials. Any local breeder of sporting dogs can point you in the right direction.

Getting along with this Rover is simple. All you have to do is love him, and you'll get it back tenfold.

Cairn Terrier

BRED TO DO. Bred as a den burrower, to hunt foxes, otters, rabbits, and badgers. In Scotland, they are still used this way. I want you to stop and imagine this little dog actually going into the den of a badger (badgers can be nasty animals) or a fox, and working until the prey runs out. This could take hours, but the Cairn's tenacity won.

HOUSETRAINING. Put your running shoes on, borrow a second or third pair of eyes, and get ready to housetrain your Cairn. If Rover were a child, training would go something like this: "Rover. Where are you? It's time to go outside." He answers your call from some distant place. "I'm in here." You go to "here," but he's not "here" anymore. "Roooover! Roooover!" All of a sudden he's right behind you. Outside the two of you go. There you are, all set to praise him, but he squats and is off like a shot. Sorry, Human. You're going to have to be faster than that. Cairns are clean dogs and easy to housetrain, if you can keep up.

PERSONALITY. Are you ready for life with a Cairn? Are you sure? I hope you're not reading this because you just brought home "the cutest puppy I've ever seen" and now you want to know what he's all about. I hope you're reading this *before* you bring home the cutest puppy you've ever seen. Let me say right off the bat I hope you have kids. If you don't, you're going to need some. No, Cairns are not hyperactive. They're just very active. There is a difference, I promise. Rover will throw every fiber of his being into everything he does. That means he will play, work, train, and love with passion. If you're looking for a dog that will curl up in your lap while you read a book in front of the fire, you'll need to rethink the Cairn, or wait until he's old.

These truly are wonderful little dogs. I was surprised to learn that Bell was a Therapy Dog, who visits nursing homes and pediatric wards, because I couldn't imagine a Cairn holding still long enough to let the elderly or children pet her. Then I had the good fortune to watch Bell do her thing. She ran from person to person and gave each a kiss on the face or hand. She then got her ball from her Human and played a dog's version of round robin. Don't ask me to describe the game. It was her own invention.

Obviously, I recommend Cairns with kids. Not just kids, but kids of any age. Rover will be gentle with a baby, and play as hard and rough as your six-year-old wants to play. Rover will do better than most as a latchkey dog, because he has an independent streak that has to be respected. Please don't take advantage of the latchkey message. I'm not talking about the ten-hour latchkey. I'm talking about six hours, max. If you are a latchkey owner, another dog for your Cairn might help. I've seen these dogs play just as hard at ten years of age as they did at two.

I want you to read, Chapter 5, "Playtime with Rover," so that you can have a repertoire of games. Plain old fetch isn't gonna cut it. He's going to love rooting, hide-and-seek, and any game involving chase.

TRAINING. I recommend training of some kind with Cairns, because they love the process and the praise. They seem to be born knowing how to walk on a leash, and they love the exercise. Have the kids teach Rover some tricks. Human, don't get your dignified back up. Rover doesn't know the difference between "Sit" and a trick. Clients tell me that Rover is stubborn. He's not stubborn, he's just tenacious. Continue to consider the time it takes for him to get a fox to leave its den.

BEST ENVIRONMENT: Jogger—**Walker**—Teenagers—Children 6 to 11— **Children of any age—Elderly—Latchkey—Active environment—** Sedate environment—**Multiple dogs okay**—Apartment—**House with yard—Room to run—Needs daily exercise (through play is fine)—** Camping—Hiking

---

Chesapeake Bay Retriever

BRED TO DO. This dog is 100 percent American born and bred. As his name implies, he was bred to retrieve. And I'm here to tell you: In that capacity they don't get much better. This dog can handle just about any terrain and any weather. He specializes in water retrieving, and with one good shake on dry land he's as dry as a bone. Pause with me here for a moment of respect. This dog was called upon to retrieve between two hundred and three hundred ducks in day. That blows me away every time I think about it. It's also one of the reasons that I recommend Chessies being used for what they were bred to do. You must admit that it would be a shame to let all that superior ability go to waste.

HOUSETRAINING. This Rover has an independent streak that must be understood and respected. If you pick him up to take him outside, he'll wiggle and squirm and say, "Put me down! I can walk outside by myself!" He's right. He can walk outside by himself, and you'll be surprised how quickly he'll learn what he's outside for. Chessies love to be outside in any weather, so letting you know when he needs to go out will come quickly.

PERSONALITY. These dogs are very sure of themselves. If they were human, they'd be called conceited. Every time I see a Chessie around other dogs I have the feeling he's patronizing them and would prefer not to socialize with the riffraff. He'll give a polite nod to other Retrievers, but that's only because he's polite by nature. He'll love you, and show you affection, and he'll even play with you, but he'll be somewhat stand-offish with the rest of the world. You're going to have to spend some time socializing Rover with other people. As soon as he realizes they can be affectionate and playful he'll try getting along.

I absolutely do not recommend this dog with children. He can't re-late to them; he's uncomfortable around them and won't hesitate to dis-cipline a naughty child. Taylor was brought into a home with three children, five years old, twelve years old, and sixteen years old. Even as a puppy he tried to stay away from the five-year-old. If the child came too close, Taylor would give a low disciplinary growl and move away.

He and the twelve-year-old had a neat game going. The boy was in Little League and did batting practice in the backyard. He'd bat the ball off the ball stand, and Taylor would field it and bring it back. Taylor got quite good at fielding. He could catch most of the balls in midair. The sixteen-year-old was a girl whose boyfriend Taylor did not like one single bit. I still don't know how, but Taylor seemed to know when the boyfriend was coming over. He'd position himself at the front door and make it difficult for anybody to open up. Once the boyfriend finally got into the house, Taylor wouldn't let him out of his sight. He stood and stared, lay down and stared, or sat and stared. It made absolutely no difference to Taylor that everybody in the household liked the boyfriend. I talked the boyfriend into taking Taylor for walks to see if that would help the relationship. They got along fine until they got back to the house; then it was stare-down time again. The girl has had several boyfriends since, and Taylor hasn't liked a single one of them. After I pointed it out, the parents finally realized that Taylor wasn't thrilled with any of their children's friends.

Be careful with your Chessie. If Chessies were human, I think they would be in the Mafia. They'll become dominant in a heartbeat, given the slightest opportunity. I've seen this dog take over an entire household. We had to do some serious work to get the Humans back in the lead position. Read Chapter 6, "The Peck Order Factor," and Chapter 8, "The Head Honcho Human."

TRAINING. Because of the power and the independent streak, I always recommend training of some kind. Whenever you train, it automatically puts you in control, and you're going to need as much of that as you can get with your Chessie. You'll need a firm but kind hand. Actually Chessies are very trainable, if the training makes sense to them.

BEST ENVIRONMENT: **Jogger—Walker—Teenagers**—Children 6 to 11—Children of any age—Elderly—**Latchkey—Active environment**—Sedate environment—**Multiple dogs okay**—Apartment—**House with yard—Room to run—Needs daily exercise—Camping**—Hiking

---

Chihuahua

BRED TO DO. The Chihuahua was bred to be a companion. He's well suited to his task. But personally, I don't think Chihuahuas know they were bred only as companions. I think they think they were bred as guard dogs.

HOUSETRAINING. This tiny one will housetrain quickly—if the grass isn't too high, the wind isn't blowing, there's no moisture on the ground, and you're at his side every second. Never do I recommend "paper training," but they now have these things called Pee Pads. In bad weather or if for some other reason going outside isn't a good idea for this tiny dog, show him a Pee Pad. Chihuahuas are very clean, and once you get Rover housetrained it won't occur to him to go in the house. Stick to the method, and he will catch on quickly.

PERSONALITY. Some dogs know their power and some don't. Chihuahuas don't. If a Great Dane runs and jumps on you and you fall down, he's going to apologize, help you up, and ask if you tripped over something. If a Rottweiler runs and jumps on you, he knows you're going to fall down. If a Chihuahua runs and jumps on you, he gets really annoyed if you don't fall down. I always say that this Rover has more guts than brains. My favorite story about a Chihuahua comes from when I was working in a veterinary clinic. Human and St. Bernard came in first and sat down. Human and Chihuahua came in a few minutes later and sat down. The Chihuahua wanted to get down and run around, and to my horror, his Human let him. The Chihuahua made a beeline for the Saint, jumped up, and got hold of his neck. Except for the fierce growling from the Chihuahua, the room was silent. The people stopped breathing. The Saint slowly picked up his back paw and swatted the Chihuahua like a flea. The Chihuahua rolled a few times, gave himself a shake, and jumped back into his Human's lap. As soon as the Saint and his Human went into the exam room the Chihuahua started growling and barking and saying, "It's a good thing he left when he did, or I'da had him." This tiny little dog has the heart and courage of a Rhodesian Ridgeback.

Chihuahuas have a quality that few people know about: They are clannish and prejudiced. If you put several breeds of dogs in a room, the Chihuahuas will seek each other out and shun all the others.

These babies do not make good latchkey dogs. If you have to be away from the house more than six hours a day, get another Chihuahua. I promise, if you have two, they'll still love you and allow you in their clan.

When talking about breeds of dogs, people tell me all the time that they don't like Chihuahuas because they're snappy yappy little dogs. Hear me, people! They don't start out that way. Please read about body language in Chapter 6, "The Peck Order Factor." With the tiny toy dogs, we hold them at eye level or above our heads the way we do with an infant. Every time we do that, we're telling this dog we want him to be dominant. Do that enough times, and the dog is going to say, "Okay, you want me to be dominant, I'll be dominant." He then takes on all the responsibility that goes with that position in the peck order. Now you have a dog that barks at every sound, growls at friends, and growls at you if you disturb his nap. Chihuahuas can be very loving and affectionate dogs; don't make them responsible for your care.

I do not recommend Chihuahuas with children, especially children less than twelve years old. To Chihuahuas, nothing about children is predictable. They move too fast, they swing their arms about, and they scream and cry. I've seen Chihuahuas that, having been brought into a home with young children, spend most of the time under something or behind something. If a confrontation with a child is inevitable, Rover will growl and most likely snap, or out-and-out bite. If confronted with a choice between fight or flight, a Chihuahua will fight every time.

These babies tremble and shiver a lot. Veterinarians tell me that because Chihuahuas are so tiny and thin-skinned they lose body heat easily, and the shivering helps to warm them. Remember, Human, God did not create this dog, people did. Buy Rover a sweater or coat to wear during the cooler months. If he doesn't sleep with you, he may need a hot-water bottle in his bed.

TRAINING. I do recommend training of some kind. Chihuahuas take great pride in doing something well, so give Rover something to do well. If you raise him right, he'll love to love and be loved, which means he will want to please. I hear all the time, "Judi, he walked on a leash perfectly without any training." Hear me, Human. He walks at your side because he has a tiny stride and he's not fast enough to get ahead of you unless you give him a running start. A Chihuahua walking on a leash always reminds me of how a two- or three-year-old child looks trying to keep up with the parent holding his hand. Rover will love to take walks with you, because he loves and needs the exercise, but please slow your pace a bit so that he doesn't have to run just to keep up.

> BEST ENVIRONMENT: Jogger—Walker—**Teenagers**—Children 6 to 11—Children of any age—**Elderly**—Latchkey—**Active environment—Sedate environment—Multiple dogs okay—Apartment**—House with yard—Room to run—Needs daily exercise—Camping—Hiking

Chow Chow

BRED TO DO. Since Chows are one of the oldest breeds—they date from before 150 B.C.—the consensus is that there is very little this dog wasn't used for, including being a celebration dinner for a wedding or birthday. They were also killed for their coats. Kinda makes you not blame them for being standoffish and suspicious of strangers and new situations.

HOUSETRAINING. How quickly Rover housetrains could depend solely on the time of year. If it's summertime, he's not going to want to leave the air-conditioned house, even if he's a puppy. If it's winter, he's not going to want to come back in. People and books are going to tell you that the Chow Chow's coat keeps him cool in the summer. Wrong. If that were true, Rover would be just as energetic in the summer as he is in the winter. Believe me, Humans, this Rover is going to be uncomfortable when it's hot, no matter who says what. I tell my Chow clients to praise, praise, praise. If you put too much emphasis on verbal discipline, this dog will look you straight in the face and say, "If you ever talk to me like that again I will pee in your boots." It's hard to imagine this furball, with a sweet face, could ever talk to you like that, but you better believe he can and will. Make a big fuss when he has eliminations where he's supposed to, and keep the discipline low-key.

PERSONALITY. All of the stories you've heard about Chows being aggressive, mean, biters, and dangerous around children are true. I hope you're reading this before getting a Chow Chow and not after you've made the commitment. Don't think that if you give him enough love and affection, he'll get along just fine. So many people can't resist this cute ball of fluff, which looks like a little bear. They bring him home and then can't understand why he growls and snaps if he doesn't want to be messed with. Many, many times when I'm called about a Chow Chow, the situation's gotten so bad that if I can't help, the dog will be euthanized or sent to the Animal Control Center. Nine times out of ten I can help, but it's because I understand this breed and know how to tap into his psyche. Now I'm telling you what I know so that you can understand and respect what this breed is all about.

Chows are one of the very few breeds that I recommend as a latchkey dog. (As long as you're not gone more than eight to ten hours.) He'll love it when you're home, but won't mind too much when you're gone. When you're gone, Rover will quietly guard your house and his territory; he takes his work very seriously. Chow Chows are dignified, proud dogs, and rarely will you see one making a spectacle of himself by barking and running along a fence. If you do see your Chow do this, you can bet there's a damn good reason for it.

To his masters, Rover will be affectionate and incredibly loyal. But you must at all times be his Master. If you show yourself to be weak and too passive, Rover will take over in a heartbeat. (Watch his attitude toward you change if you are ill and in bed.) Make sure you're always first through doors, up and down stairs, and over obvious thresholds. Read Chapter 6, "The Peck Order Factor," and Chapter 8, "The Head Honcho Human." The last thing you want is a Chow Chow on defense, with everything and everybody being a threat. When it comes to a choice of fight or flight, this dog will stand his ground and fight every time.

When you have company over, Rover will size them up quickly and then probably go lie down in his favorite spot. He will not join you in the welcomes and handshakes. Don't insist that he socialize. If he wants to approach someone, let him do it in his own time and his own way. Given time, he may actually let someone pet him.

Pay very close attention to the way Rover wants to play, and don't insist that he play your way. If you do, he won't play at all. As you can imagine, Chow Chows can become very serious. If that happens, you've lost him as a companion. Whenever possible, treat him to your light heart, and let him join in the fun.

The minute you get Rover home, start playing with his paws, checking his eyes and ears, opening his mouth, and playing with lifting his tail. Trips to the veterinarian can become a nightmare for everyone concerned if you don't get Rover used to being handled. Chow Chows don't like—let me restate that: Chow Chow's *will not tolerate* being held close, held tightly, or held down. Practice holding him in a relaxed manner before you take him to your veterinarian. His eyes will have to be checked, and he's not going to like this stranger's hands on his face. His ears will have to be checked, and he's not going to like this stranger putting a scope in his ear. And on and on and on. Too often a veterinarian can't properly examine a Chow Chow because the dog won't tolerate being handled. Practice. Practice. Practice.

Rover will get along with the strong-minded elderly; he's perfect for women living alone and wonderful for a couple with no children, who live a rather sedate life. If you place this dog in a family with children, you do it at the children's risk. I hope you've understood what I've had to say about this breed, so that maybe there will be one less Chow Chow euthanized, or waiting to be adopted at the Animal Control Center. If Chows are understood and respected, they can make great companions. The red Chows are usually less aggressive, and the fawns less again.

TRAINING. Rover really doesn't care if he pleases you, so you must teach him that pleasing you is neat. I have all of my Chow Chow clients praise like crazy for the slightest good deed. I started this about five or six years ago and the results have been wonderful. I do recommend some obedience with Chow Chows because it automatically puts you in the lead position and offers an opportunity for praise and affection. Use a gentle hand! I know—from everything I've said, you're thinking you should use a firm hand. But with Rover's independent and aloof nature, a firm hand will stop him cold. He'll dig in his heels and fight you at every turn.

BEST ENVIRONMENT: Jogger—Walker—Teenagers—Children 6 to 11—
Children of any age—**Elderly—Latchkey**—Active environment—**Sedate environment—Multiple dogs okay**—Apartment—**House with yard—**
Room to run—Needs daily exercise—Camping—Hiking

Cocker Spaniel

BRED TO DO. Cockers were bred to hunt small game. They're great at finding the game that may be lost to other hunting breeds. They're tough in almost any terrain, and will put in much more than a nine-to-five day. You'll notice that when Rover puts his nose down he makes short passes back and forth directly in front of him. This always reminds me of a metal detector.

HOUSETRAINING. Keeping this wee one confined during the housetraining process is going to be of utmost importance. If he has the run of the house, there is not a corner he won't investigate, and probably have eliminations in—not to mention the job you'll have finding him to take him outside. You may find him curled up in your slipper, looking ever so cute, but before you melt, take a look in your other slipper. If you stick to the method, Rover will housetrain in a normal period of time. He is going to have accidents off and on all his life. I've never known a Cocker that would cross his legs and hold it for any length of time. If you're not there to let him out when he needs to go, he's not going to wait for you.

PERSONALITY. *Cocker Spaniels test for dominance! They want to be dominant!* I yell this at you because I don't ever want you to say you weren't warned. I have yet to read in a book or hear a breeder admit that Cockers can become serious problem dogs. By the time I'm called, the dog has already bitten someone, or would've if that someone had gotten close enough. I'm rarely called at the first sign of a problem, say when Rover starts growling, or snaps for the first time. The way he begins his takeover is crafty. You'll be brushing him and he'll suddenly yip, turn, and snap. You'll start to pick him up and he'll yip, growl, and/or snap. You'll be scratching him lovingly behind his ear and he'll yip, growl, and/or snap. Human nature usually dictates your first response. You immediately assume you've hurt him in some way, so you stop whatever you were doing and apologize: "Oh, honey, I'm sorry, did I hurt you?" Round One for Rover. No, you didn't hurt him. During Rounds Two and Three, he won't bother to yip; he'll get right to the growl and/or snap. I must admit that a part of me admires this dog's ability to manipulate. You have to agree that it takes superior intelligence to pull it off.

Rover is going to test for dominance, off and on, until he's around five years old. All you have to do is be forewarned. When he tries it the first time, be aware of what's happening, and don't buy into it. When he yips and snaps, give him a resounding "No." He'll know you called him on his behavior, and he won't try again for a few months to a year. Two behaviors will make Rover think he can get away with it. One is holding him eye level or above when he's a puppy. The other is "It's okay, it's okay." Read about body language in Chapter 6, "The Peck Order Factor." Rover can become the best dog you've ever had, or the worst. It's up to you.

I think Webster should have defined the word "mischief" as "Cocker Spaniel." This Rover can get into more trouble than a two-year-old child on the move. Sally was having her air-conditioning system turned on and all the vents cleaned. Boss, one of the best-looking black Cockers I've ever seen, was at her feet following her every move, as he usually did. When the work was completed and the workmen had left, she realized Boss was nowhere to be seen. She called him and heard a bark that sounded as if he was in the same room with her, but she couldn't find him. She started walking around calling him, and every time he barked it sounded as if he was in the same room that she was in. You guessed it: He was in the air-conditioner vents. I'm still trying to figure that out—the vents were at the top of the walls and were only big enough to put your arms in. Sally called the workmen and told them her dog was stuck in the vents. She got on a ladder and called Boss from one vent while the workmen tried to locate him. They finally found where his whine was coming from and pushed him through with a Roto-Rooter kind of thing. Boss came through the crisis just fine. Sally said he went to his bed after dinner and took a short nap, then got up ready to play ball. The relationship you have with your Cocker won't be your run-of-the-mill dog-Human relationship. Rover will make you laugh harder than you ever have at his antics, and get madder than you ever thought you could be at a dog. He'll love you with every fiber of his being and you won't be able to help loving him back just as much.

TRAINING. Yes! Train your Cocker! Whether in obedience, hunting, field trials, or tricks, this Rover needs to be trained. Training puts you in control, which you must be with a Cocker. These are very intelligent dogs and I think it's a shame to let their fine minds go to waste. I've known Cockers that could open the refrigerator and kitchen cabinets. I know one that loves the family's pet goat so much that he figured out how to open the gate and let the goat into the backyard. I know one that we think is psychic. If he sees someone in the family looking for something, he'll join in the search; they figure he finds whatever it is 75 percent of the time. Too many Cockers to count will bring their Human their food bowl and go get their own leash. Work with Rover, if for no other reason than to prove to him you're smarter than he is.

BEST ENVIRONMENT: Jogger—**Walker—Teenagers**—Children 6 to 11—Children of any age—**Elderly**—Latchkey—**Active environment**—Sedate environment—**Multiple dogs okay**—Apartment—**House with yard**—Room to run—Needs daily exercise—**Camping**—Hiking

---

Collie

BRED TO DO. Bred to herd, and still used in that capacity. These dogs are multitalented and have worked as rescue, guard, and Seeing Eye dogs. Not to mention their appearances on the silver screen and television.

HOUSETRAINING. Collies are very clean and very intelligent, so as long as there's no confusion Rover will housetrain easily. When the housetraining begins you may have to do some coaxing to get him outside. Collies are a little on the timid side as puppies, and may run for the safety of the house if something disturbing happens outside—if, say, dogs start barking or the UPS truck goes by or a flock of birds take off all at once or the neighbor walks out into his backyard. Once he realizes that the sky is not going to fall, and that you'll take care of him if it does, he'll relax. After that your biggest problem is going to be getting him back in the house. He will see birds in the trees and he'll go into herding mode immediately, running around trying to get all the birds into one tree. You'll also see his herding mode as he comes up behind you and nips at your slippers or pajamas, believing he's herding you down the hall into the kitchen. He can't imagine how you managed before he came along.

PERSONALITY. *These dogs are barkers!* I yell this at you because I've seen Collies lose their happy homes due to barking and the neighborhood complaints that are a result. Teach "Quiet" so that you can stop the barking on command. With Collies, barking is more a survival mechanism than a watchdog trait. They will bark at anything they perceive to be a threat. Spend as much time as you can building confidence, so that fewer things are threats.

For the most part, the barking is the only major problem you'll have with Rover. Well, wait a minute, I take that back; I forgot to mention grooming. You must stay on top of Rover's grooming, or it'll become a nightmare. When I was working in the animal clinic, I saw far too many Collies come in with "hot spots," skin infections caused by hair matting. Rover will try to take care of his own coat, but it's more than he can handle. Decide that you're going to groom Rover yourself, or take him to a groomer regularly. This is especially important in the summertime. Remember, God did not create this dog, people did, and people have to be responsible for his care.

Absolutely have a Collie and children of any age at the same time. Rover will take very good care of your kids. When Lassie was rescuing Timmy, there was a trainer just out of sight of the camera. But many of the rescues could easily have happened in real life, without a trainer. If the circumstances are such that you or your children need protection or rescuing, Rover will be there for you, doing his best however he can. I'm sure this love of children is the reason Collies are commonly used as Seeing Eye dogs for blind kids.

These dogs are very sensitive. Rover will love it when you laugh, be upset if you cry, and pace if there's arguing. He will also be sensitive to changes in the barometric pressure. If you notice he's restless and agitated—he wants out, turns around and wants right back in, then back out—you can bet there's going to be a change in the weather.

Rover is going to love every member of your family with all his heart, but he's going to be suspicious of strangers. You'll notice that when you have company, Rover will take his time getting to know them. He'll come forward and sniff a little, then back off and watch. Let him introduce himself at his own pace; don't push him. Rover will like some people and dislike others. Even though he won't be obvious about it, you will know when he doesn't like someone. He will also be suspicious of the kids' friends until he realizes they can be trusted.

Collies have a tendency toward weight gain. Make sure you insist on plenty of exercise.

TRAINING. Rover is going to do everything he can think of to get out of school, and you're going to be tempted to use a firm hand. Don't go with the temptation. If you use a firm hand with Rover, he won't learn a thing. Use a gentle hand, and you may need to do some coaxing. These dogs are a walking contradiction. They don't like school, but they learn quickly and want to please. They act as if they really need a nap, right in the middle of learning how to sit, but will get up and play at the slightest hint that a game can be played.

BEST ENVIRONMENT: Jogger—**Walker**—Teenagers—Children 6 to 11— **Children of any age—Elderly**—Latchkey—**Active environment— Sedate environment—Multiple dogs okay**—Apartment—**House with yard—Room to run**—Needs daily exercise—Camping—Hiking

---

Dachshund (Shorthaired, Longhaired, Wirehaired)

BRED TO DO. They were bred to go into the animal's den and flush it out. The shorthaired and wirehaired are still used for this purpose in Germany, Switzerland and Great Britain. In America they're almost exclusively companion dogs. They do the job as companion very well.

HOUSETRAINING. Doxies either housetrain in a heartbeat or take forever. Some never do get totally housetrained. You're really going to have to be diligent in keeping an eye on Rover. And bear in mind how close this little one is to the ground. When you take him out make sure the grass isn't too high. If yours is a shorthair, he's not going to like the cold, so that may be a strike against you. Unless he's between eight and ten weeks of age he's not going through fear imprint, so barking dogs, noisy cars, or rustling leaves shouldn't be a problem. I usually have some idea why there are housetraining problems with a breed but Doxies always stump me. Compare the time it's going to take you to housetrain your Doxie with the years of enjoyment ahead. And I promise you, you will enjoy the years ahead.

PERSONALITY. The only obvious personality difference between the types is that Longhairs seem to be mellower. Dachshunds can be problem barkers! This is because they all think they're Mastiffs. They think they were bred to guard you and your house, and they'll give it their best. I love to watch Rover when he sees or hears something he thinks he needs to check out. His tail goes straight up and bends forward at the tip. It looks like a periscope. If his body can't go on point, his tail sure can.

See if you can let Rover kinda do what he was bred to do, but in your home. Even as a puppy he's going to love crawling into a paper sack or pillowcase. If you have low bushes or vines in your yard, Rover is going to pretend there's a fox in there.

Usually Doxie owners become Doxie people. You could not pay them to have a different breed. But I don't usually recommend Doxies with young children. These dogs don't hesitate to defend themselves if they believe they're threatened. If a child pulls Rover's ear, Rover is going to snap or even bite, in defense. Disciplining him at the time is going to work at the time. But the next time the child pulls his ear he's going to defend himself again. I've heard more times than I care to remember that Doxies are mean to kids. Rover isn't being mean. He's a small dog, and he defends himself with the means available to him. Some breeds run and hide if a child hurts them; others avoid the child altogether. Doxies stand and fight. If you have young children, it's going to be up to you to see to it that they are gentle. Doxies love kids old enough to play dog games.

I must tell you about Shatzie, my sister Bobbie's Doxie. Shatzie would take turns each night sleeping with one or the other of Bobbie's daughters so that nobody's feelings were hurt. That in itself is unusual. And Shatzie was not a morning dog. First thing in the morning, when everybody was getting up to start the day, Bobbie would have to make sure she was at the outside door, holding it open, or Shatzie would get up, walk with her head down, and walk right into the door. The resemblance to myself in the mornings was too close for comfort. If there was ever a dog who should have been named Judi, that dog was Shatzie.

Spine problems and weight problems are common in Dachshunds. Decrease the risk of back problems by not allowing Rover to gain too much weight. I'm going to step over medical lines here and tell you what I always recommend to my Doxie owners: As soon as Rover is old enough to eat adult food, put him on one of the "light" diets and keep him on it. Now, I'm really going to get in trouble with veterinarians everywhere when I tell you that if you have a male Doxie, you shouldn't have him neutered. The loss of testosterone in the male slows down the metabolic rate, so the dog can't burn off calories as fast as before. (However, if your veterinarian recommends neutering for health reasons, by all means take his advice.) If Rover is marking territory, roaming, or the like, and your veterinarian thinks neutering might help, try correcting the problem by psychological means first. If you have no success, listen to your veterinarian.

TRAINING. It's entirely up to you. If you do work with Rover on some commands, he'll learn quickly and do everything with pride. Pay attention to the length of your stride on a walk. Doxie owners tell me, "Judi, he walks on a leash like he was born to it." Well, of course he does, people! As short as his legs are, he'd have to run like hell to get ahead of you, and it's unlikely he's going to have the strength to pull you. This dog is somewhat limited as to what he can do and should do. Don't ask him to do a lot of jumping. He'll jump for you, but he shouldn't. Don't insist that he keep up with your stride on a walk. He will, but it's not fair.

> BEST ENVIRONMENT: Jogger—Walker—Teenagers—**Children 6 to 11**— Children of any age—**Elderly**—Latchkey—**Active environment—Sedate environment—Multiple dogs okay—Apartment—House with yard—**Room to run—Needs daily exercise—Camping—Hiking

Dalmatian

BRED TO DO. To tell you the truth, I don't think anybody knows for sure what Dalmatians were bred to do. There is a possibility that long long ago they were Hounds, and we know they ran along with coaches and carriages. I have a problem with the idea of breeding a dog for the sole purpose of running along the carriage. That would be like breeding a dog just to run alongside a bicyclist or jogger. Something tells me there's more to this dog's history than we know at this time.

HOUSETRAINING. Dalmatians are incredibly clean. As soon as Rover realizes he's soiling where he eats, sleeps, and plays, being housetrained will follow shortly. Warning! Rover will be completely, totally housetrained—then, right out of the blue, he'll break training for three or four days. This relapse will be short lived, so just point out the error of his ways.

PERSONALITY. *Dalmatians take advantage of a weakness!* I yell this at you because I don't want you to fall into the *101 Dalmatians* trap and buy one of these dogs for your children. Contrary to popular belief, Dalmatians are not good with kids. (Breeders just threw my book across the room.) Every other book and every breeder is going to tell you this dog is good with kids. Keep in mind I'm a behaviorist, and I specialize in behavioral problems. I see so many Dalmatians with all kinds of problems, and growling, snapping at, and biting kids is one of them. You say, "Judi, my Dalmatian gets along just fine with my kids." Then I ask, "How does Rover behave when one of the kids is sick?" The response is usually stuttered: "Well, he does seem to get a little bossy. He growled and snapped at my son that one time. But he only did that once or maybe twice and then he was fine." My dearest Human, how many times are you going to let Rover go after you kids before you admit there's a problem? Imagine what would happen if both you and your child were sick at the same time. I'm not talking major illness here. I'm talking a bad common cold or the flu.

Another problem I'm called in on is Rover attacking or trying to attack other dogs. After I've asked a couple of questions, the Humans realize the dogs Rover goes after are always smaller than he. Now are you starting to understand what I mean by "Dalmatians take advantage of a weakness"? I can hear Dalmatian owners screaming at me: "Judi! My Dalmatian is not like that!" Not every Dalmatian is going to be bad with kids or attack smaller dogs. Not every Rottweiler is aggressive. Not every Chow is mean. The point is that the majority of the Dalmatians I see, even the ones I see just for obedience, take advantage of a weakness or vulnerability.

I call Dalmatians the elephants of the dog world. This dog has an incredible memory. Many times, I have worked with a Dalmatian for whatever reason, and then seen that dog again two or three years later. Folks, that dog remembers me. He doesn't just remember *me*, he remembers things we worked on, things I taught him, and things I may have done that he didn't like. Sparky's owner, Kathy, was in a wheelchair. Sparky was two years old at the time of Kathy's accident and the only problem she'd had with him before was that he lunged at other dogs when she took him for a walk. Now Sparky growled at her and jumped on her every time she moved from one room to another. Kathy had to stay with him while he ate, because if she moved he would bite her feet. She called me after she fell off her bed and Sparky stood over her, ready to bite every time she tried to pull herself up. She had an alarm system set up with her neighbor, so she was rescued within minutes. Among the things I had Kathy do to get back in the lead position with Sparky was give him jobs to do. We taught him to help with the groceries, and bring her the remote control; I showed her how to teach him to say his prayers (that one was for the fun of it). When she called me, at least three years later, it was to help Sparky adjust to the new man in her life. When I walked in the door, Sparky gave me a sniff and a look and promptly brought me the remote control. The last I heard, Kathy, her new husband, and Sparky are doing fine.

Dalmatians do not make good latchkey dogs. They have to have human or canine contact all the time. This dog becomes visibly sad and depressed if he's left alone too much. If you're a walker or slow jogger, this is your exercise buddy. He'll love every minute with you and enjoy the exercise. If you really want to tickle him pink, let him walk at your side while you ride a horse.

Dalmatians are very sensitive. Rover will be very aware of your moods, and you'll notice he becomes restless and agitated at weather changes, especially if there's a wind. Dalmatians do not like the wind. I don't know why.

I don't want you to think Dalmatians are all bad; they're not, not by any stretch of the imagination. They're wonderfully loyal and will do anything for their Human. I've never seen another breed come up with games the way this one can. Puppy Heidi would get one end of a tug-away toy and go completely limp while her Human dragged her around. She looked like a seal, and loved every minute of it.

Deafness is very common in Dalmatians. If your Dalmatian is deaf, don't let anybody tell you he can't be trained. Find a behaviorist or trainer in your area who is willing to take the time to help you train him.

TRAINING. Use a kind but firm hand, expect him to learn something, and then act like he doesn't have the vaguest idea what you taught him to do. In Chapter 11, "Obedience," carefully read the section on "Rover, let's go." If you plan on taking Rover for walks there can't be any question as to who is in control. Get him out into high stress and work with him until every single time he sees another dog, he looks at you.

Doberman Pinscher

BRED TO DO. Bred as a watchdog and bodyguard, but must be trained to do the job. This a such a young breed that we're still watching for consistency in personality traits. Unfortunately, breeders feel the desperate need to breed for color, when at this stage in the breed's development, they should be aiming consistently for temperament, personality, and ability. This dog's speed is awesome. A well-trained Doberman can beat a man to his gun at thirty feet. I had to see that one for myself, and it's true.

HOUSETRAINING. Expect some back talk. If Rover is involved in something, he's not going to want to stop just to go outside. Once you get him outside, he's going to put his medium-sized paws on his medium-sized hips, look you square in the face, and say, "I didn't need to go outside, I didn't want to go outside, and I'm sure as hell not going to go where you want me to." Back in the house, he'll immediately squat behind Dad's favorite chair. Let him know that you're unhappy with him. Square your shoulders, put your hands on your hips, look him square in the face, and say, "I am Human, you are Rover, I am superior and I will get you housetrained."

PERSONALITY. I can't give you across-the-board personality traits, because right now few Dobes are alike. A few years ago, black-and-tan females were wired and somewhat squirrely. I see less of that now. Instead I'm seeing red females that not only wouldn't guard or watch but would show a burglar where the silver is. On the other hand, both the red male and the black-and-tan male will watch and guard as if they were born to it, very little training necessary. If you don't already have a Dobe, but you're looking, try to stay away from fawns and blues. Maybe if we don't adopt the mutant colors, breeders will breed with the aim of getting good Dobes. If you get a good Dobe you'll have one of the best dogs around. As an adult (becoming an adult takes about two years) he will be the best watchdog you've ever had. And he'll do a wonderful job as your bodyguard. A good Dobe will do both jobs so well and so subtly you won't know he's doing it. If you're taking Rover for a walk and you meet someone he's not sure of, he will very calmly put his body slightly between you and the someone. Unless you're watching for this you may not even notice it.

Make sure you play with Rover, especially as he grows. These dogs have a tendency to get too serious and somewhat grouchy. Keep the lighthearted side of him active. This dog's loyalty to you and his sensitivity will melt even the hardest of hearts.

The story that a Doberman will turn on his master is just that, a story. These dogs have a strong will, and given the responsibility will take the dominant position in the peck order. When a dog of any breed becomes dominant there is always the chance that he'll "turn on his master."

When the Doberman was first bred, the English Greyhound was bred with it. When I can't figure out how to work with a Doberman, I start watching him as if he were a Hound. It amazes me how the traits I'm seeing begin to fall into place. Polly, for instance, has fought playfully everything her Human and I have tried to do with her. After several weeks she still won't come when called, and argues, playfully, against almost every command. Her Human, Bob, takes her out almost daily to run loose in a mesa area, so I'm taking advantage of that. I showed him how to "range her out" with a clothesline so that she won't go more than one hundred feet and will come when called. This process can take up to a month to achieve, but if she comes when called it's worth the time.

I can't in good conscience recommend Dobermans with kids, because I can't rely on them being trustworthy.

TRAINING. You're going to need a firm but kind hand. You have to earn Rover's respect, it doesn't come automatically just because you're

Human. You're going to have a major struggle with "Sit." This is true of a lot of breeds, but especially with Dobes, and the males especially. I think part of it has to do with the tail dock, (and, in males, with the size of their testicles). Don't let anybody tell you that docking the tail does not hurt. Notice that when a Dobe sits, the tail brushes the ground a little. Neither male nor female Dobe want to sit all the way down.

The other problem you're going to have to watch for is Rover turning everything into a challenge, so that almost everything you do or say becomes a confrontation. The more you insist on something, the greater the challenge. The louder your voice gets, the more Rover is stimulated. From the very first time you work with Rover, whether it's at three months or six months, make sure your attitude is no-nonsense. Be like Queen Victoria, who said, "We are not amused." If you get that attitude in your mind, you'll display it to Rover.

Stay calm from the moment you put his collar and leash on. I'm going to ask you to keep praise low-key. If you praise too enthusiastically, Rover will get so excited he'll forget what you're praising him for, and you'll have to wait until he calms down again before you can go on with the training.

Take my word for it, training your Doberman is going to try your patience. Keep in mind, though, that you can't let a dog with Rover's power and speed go untrained.

BEST ENVIRONMENT: **Jogger—Walker—Teenagers (strong willed)**—Children 6 to 11—Children of any age—Elderly—Latchkey—**Active environment—Sedate environment—Multiple dogs okay**—Apartment—**House with yard—Room to run**—Needs daily exercise—Camping—Hiking

---

English Bulldog

BRED TO DO. Way back when, these beauties were bred to combat bulls. Can you imagine the courage it took to take on a bull? I can imagine this dog being sent into the arena with a bull. "Ahhh, excuse me, sir, have you seen the size of that animal I'm supposed to attack? Do you figure those hard, pointed things coming out of the sides of that animal's head could inflict pain? Okay, let's go over the plan one more time. If I understand correctly, I'm supposed to go into the arena and combat that bull. Right? Okey-dokey, I'm going in the arena now. Here I go. Love to the wife and kids." The bull, during this sizing-up time, is laughing outright at this small, very ugly dog, planning where he's going to dinner after this silly game is over. I have a feeling the bull stopped laughing when he realized how serious and brave the dog was. In bull-baiting days, Bulldogs were mean, ferocious, and out for blood. Once this cruel sport was outlawed, the breeders starting concentrating on a kinder, gentler disposition, and they did their job well.

HOUSETRAINING. When his nose goes down and starts sniffing, scoop Rover up and get him outside immediately. About the only time you're going to see his nose down is when he's looking for a place to go. Bulldogs are clean, and most of them want to do the right thing, so stick to the method and you'll have him housetrained in no time.

PERSONALITY. Bulldogs snore! If you're already sleeping in the guest room because your spouse snores, this is not the dog for you. If you're thinking you still want a Bulldog, so you'll have him sleep in the bathroom or laundry room, think again. Rover isn't going to snore only between the hours of ten P.M. and six A.M., he's going to snore every time he sleeps. That means while you're watching TV, when you have company, and while you're eating.

When a Bulldog wants attention, he wants it *now*. If he wants to play, he's going to make that known. If he wants affection, he's going to make it very clear, and you will pet him *now*. How's he going to do that, you ask? He'll throw a shoulder against your leg, or he'll nuzzle you with his entire snout, or he'll start "talking" to you in a very insistent manner. Whatever method your Bulldog uses, you are going to give him the attention he's demanding.

The breeding to turn a bull-killing dog into a companion dog has only been going on for about one hundred years. When it comes to totally altering a breed's personality, that is not a long period of time. I've seen Bulldogs that wouldn't hesitate to take on a bull or a Human, if they don't get their way. If you choose your Rover from a litter, pay close attention to the disposition of the bitch, and if possible the stud. For the most part these dogs are terrific with kids, but because of the possible personality glitch, I usually don't recommend them with kids less than ten or twelve years old. That's not a rule I've written in stone, because I've seen Bulldogs that are fantastic baby-sitters to kids from infants on up. But though he'll take care of your kids, his loyalty will lie with one love in his life. The Human honored with Rover's love and devotion will be lucky indeed.

My dad tells the story of a English Bulldog he found and brought home in a Cracker Jack box. Skeeter was totally devoted to my dad. Somehow he knew when school let out, and was at the corner to meet him every day. The first time Daddy came home from the army on furlough, he didn't tell Grandma and Grandpa, because he wanted to surprise them. As he was walking up his street, he saw Skeeter waiting for him on the corner, as he'd always done. Grandma said that it was the first time Skeeter had wanted out in front since Daddy went into the army. I've also heard about how Skeeter baby-sat my sister and me.

TRAINING. Because he's such a tough looking character, humans seem to think they need to be overfirm, even harsh, with Rover. Not at all necessary. Rover will learn anything you want him to, if you are kind. I will caution you to work with him in ten-minute spurts, rather than for twenty to thirty minutes at a stretch. As soon as you start working with him, Rover is going to get excited because he has your undivided attention; his breathing will become more rapid and he may do a dog's version of hyperventilating. Anything you teach Rover to do, he will do with good nature and dignity.

BEST ENVIRONMENT: Jogger—Walker—Teenagers—Children 6 to 11—Children of any age—**Elderly—Latchkey**—Active environment—**Sedate environment—Multiple dogs okay—Apartment—House with yard**—Room to run—Needs daily exercise—Camping—Hiking

---

English Cocker Spaniel

BRED TO DO. They were bred to locate and retrieve small game. The English Cocker's mouth is so soft that feathers are not disturbed. In parts of Great Britain, this dog is still being used, and doing a wonderful job.

HOUSETRAINING. The hardest part of housetraining an English Cocker is keeping tabs on where he is. Don't give Rover the run of the house until he is completely housetrained. If he has this privilege too soon, he'll get so involved in discovering every corner of the house, he'll eliminate wherever he is, even if that's the corner of your closet, on your favorite boots. If you watch closely, you'll be able to tell the difference between Rover's nose down following a scent, and his nose down looking for a place to eliminate.

PERSONALITY. This is the dog Disney had in mind when he created Lady, of *Lady and the Tramp* fame. English Cockers are very affectionate and love to please. I don't hesitate to recommend them with children, especially children old enough to enjoy playing with a dog. Rover will follow that child everywhere and be totally devoted. Like the American Cocker, the English version is full of mischief. If Rover's young Human hides behind a bush playing spy, Rover will be right next to him excited about jumping out at somebody. If his young Human wants to check out the forbidden attic or basement, believe me, Rover will be right there encouraging this naughty deed. When asked who broke the lamp, your child may point to Rover and say, "He did." Now, I know most children won't admit to something they've done if there is someone else to blame it on, but when there's an English Cocker present, your child might be telling the truth.

English Cockers have observation down to a fine art. When you're in the kitchen cooking, you may notice Rover watching every move you make. You're thinking that he's begging. You couldn't be more wrong. He now knows which cabinet has the potato chips and which one has the kitchen trash; after watching you for a few more meals, he'll know how to open the refrigerator. He'll watch you going through the backyard gate a few times, and the next thing you know he's sitting on your front porch. I don't know one English Cocker that hasn't at some point figured out how to get out of the backyard. Whether by jumping over, digging out, or opening the gate. When they do get out, they rarely go far; in fact most of them stay on their own property.

If you are a walker or slow jogger, take Rover. He'll enjoy being with you, he wants and needs the exercise, and he'll love following all those neat scents out in the world. You'll notice he'll put his nose down and make short back-and-forth passes right in front of him, a little like a metal detector. Let him use his nose to his heart's content. If he has to be in the correct spot at your side, with his head up, he'll cease to enjoy the exercise. Scenting is a major part of who he is, and must be acknowledged and respected.

English Cockers do not make good latchkey dogs. If he's left alone too much, he'll start roaming, digging, or barking, or he'll turn his frustration in on himself.

TRAINING. Whether you work on structured obedience with Rover is entirely up to you. I do, however, recommend that you work very hard on getting him to come when called. If you have him out, and he picks up a scent, he could easily get so engrossed following that scent that he could be out of your sight in no time at all. Rover's level of concentration when he picks up a fascinating smell is amazing. While working with Freckles and his Humans in their front yard, I saw Freckles pick up a scent, and watched as he walked right into the tire of my truck.

Unless you plan on showing your English Cocker, don't insist that he heel correctly. As soon as he realizes that he needs to keep in touch with where you are, so that the collar doesn't tighten down, he won't pull you on the leash.

BEST ENVIRONMENT: Jogger—**Walker**—Teenagers—Children 6 to 11—
Children of any age—Elderly—Latchkey—**Active environment—
Sedate environment—Multiple dogs okay**—Apartment—**House with
yard**—Room to run—Needs daily exercise—Camping—Hiking

English Setter

BRED TO DO. To indicate to the hunter where the game is. He'll first use his excellent nose to find the game, and then he'll "set" to show the hunter where the game is. Still used as a Setter in both Great Britain and the United States.

HOUSETRAINING. Keep verbal discipline low-key. If you become too harsh, Rover will fall apart and won't have the vaguest idea why he's in such trouble. I've seen these dogs become shy eliminators, hiding behind or under something, because they think urinating is wrong. Rover will love being outside, and he's very clean. If you stick to the method and understand how sensitive he is, he'll housetrain easily.

PERSONALITY. These are sensitive dogs! Rover will be sad when you are, and he'll put his head on your leg to comfort you when you cry. He'll be happy when you are; he'll become agitated and restless if there's arguing. There was a teenager living in Dixie's house, and so there was almost constant arguing. No one noticed that Dixie was losing weight, chewing her paws, and spending most of her time pacing. When her Humans did take notice, they realized Dixie's paws had open sores and her weight was dangerously low. The veterinarian recognized the signs of serious depression and had Dixie's Humans call me. Luckily an argument broke out while I was there, and I knew immediately why Dixie was depressed. Everyone in the household cared enough about her to make some changes, and at last report she's doing fine.

English Setters are sensitive to changes in the barometric pressure as well. If Rover wants out, then turns around and wants back in, but after a minute wants back out, pay attention to the weather; you can bet there's going to be a change.

If your Rover is strictly a companion, please see to it that he gets plenty of exercise. And if part of that exercise means letting him run free, he'll be in seventh heaven. If you can let him run free, pause for a moment and watch the beauty of his movement. It's a thrilling sight.

English Setters are good with kids if they're raised with them. You may notice, though, that when neighbor kids come over Rover will be a little standoffish until he's sure about the new faces. If you let him meet them at his own pace, he'll be playing ball outside with everybody in no time.

TRAINING. You must use a gentle and patient hand to train this dog. Many people think that since English Setters can work under bad weather conditions and rough terrain, they can be trained with a firm hand. Please don't do that to Rover. He'll freeze where he stands if you speak to him harshly.

If you don't plan on using him to hunt, look into getting him into field trials. I have never known an English Setter that didn't need confidence building unless he was used for what he was bred to do. If you aren't using Rover, you'll need to get him out into high stress. Once he realizes you're there to take care of him, he'll relax.

BEST ENVIRONMENT: **Jogger**—Walker—Teenagers—Children 6 to 11—**Children of any age—Elderly—**Latchkey**—Active environment—**Sedate environment—**Multiple dogs okay**—Apartment—**Houses with yard—Room to run—Needs daily exercise**—Camping—Hiking

---

Fox Terrier

BRED TO DO. Obviously, to hunt fox. Fox Terriers would go into the fox's den and if necessary fight toe to toe. You can find both the Smooth-haired Fox Terrier, and the Wirehaired Fox Terrier in just about every country in the world. These were the original circus dogs.

HOUSETRAINING. Almost all you have to do with this wee one is show him where you want him to have his eliminations; then stick to the method. Rover is not a creature of comfort on demand, so outside is going to be no problem for him. Of course, use common sense and consider the weather.

PERSONALITY. *Fox Terriers can be barkers!* I yell this at you because I want you to understand that Rover's barking may become a serious problem. Start introducing him to the "Quiet" command as soon as he discovers his bark.

These are fun dogs to have. They're smart and a little on the sly side. Roxy figured out one time that she could go from a kitchen bar stool to the kitchen counter, and you can imagine how pleased she was with her discovery. The second time she did it she was caught and disciplined. This kitchen had two swinging doors, one from the dining room and one from the hall. When her Human, Julie, went out one door, Roxy went in the other, and up on the counter. Julie could not for the life of her, figure out how Roxy was getting on the counter. Once I pointed out to her what Roxy was doing, the solution was simple. Julie tilted the stools against the counter; problem solved.

Groucho didn't like being left alone, so he would wait quietly behind a chair near the door and scoot out like a shot as soon as Bill or Margie opened the door to the garage. He always got caught, so he came up with Plan B. He would wait behind the door, and at the first opportunity dash out into the garage, where he waited under the car. As soon as one of his Humans opened the car door he was in, and under the seat so fast that he actually got away with it a few times. Told you these dogs were smart.

I don't hesitate to recommend this dog with kids. Because of his size, I advise that the children be six or over. He'll love them and their friends if they'll play with him, because he lives to play and plays to live. Even though he's not a Retriever, he'll play fetch. Even though he'll like company, he won't be thrilled if the company gets more attention than he does. If you're having a conversation that's gone on longer than Rover thinks it should, you'll suddenly have him on your lap, his back paws on your legs and his front paws on your chest, with his face right in front of yours. Don't get too upset with him; just give him a little affectionate attention and he'll be fine. He has to make sure you still love him most.

TRAINING. There's next to nothing that you can teach a small dog that you can't teach a Fox Terrier. As I mentioned, these were the original circus dogs—and, I suspect, the original hams. They love to learn and they learn quickly. I don't necessarily recommend obedience, but I always recommend tricks. Now, now, don't get your dignified back up; Rover doesn't know the difference between a trick and a command. If you take Rover for walks, you'll have to watch him around other dogs. Rover doesn't like most other dogs, and he doesn't hold his feelings in. He may attract the attention of a dog that won't take kindly to being told his mother wears army boots.

BEST ENVIRONMENT: Jogger—**Walker**—Teenagers—**Children 6 to 11**—Children of any age—**Elderly**—Latchkey—**Active environment**—Sedate environment—**Multiple dogs okay**—Apartment—**House with yard**—Room to run—Needs daily exercise—Camping—Hiking

---

German Shepherd

BRED TO DO. Long ago, they were bred and used as shepherds, and they were very good at their job. Later, it became obvious that they were capable of doing many tasks. They've been honored for work done in wartime and in several areas of police work. They've been put to work as guide dogs for the blind, Wheelchair Companions, and Hearing Ear dogs. And, of course, they're stars of television and the silver screen.

HOUSETRAINING. Rover will take almost anything you want seriously enough to at least give it a try. If he thinks, having eliminations outside is worth his effort he'll housetrain in record time, although you may have to negotiate over the spot. If for some reason he doesn't find your backyard to his liking, you're going to have to work harder at getting him housetrained. Either way, you're going to have to make him understand that you think he's the most magnificent dog known to man. He already knows this to be true, but he'll appreciate your saying so.

German Shepherds have the canine world's most sensitive stomach. Ask your veterinarian to recommend the best possible food available to feed him, and stick to that diet only.

PERSONALITY. There are good German Shepherds and bad ones. If you have a good one, he will most likely be the best dog you've ever had. The bad ones aren't too bright, and that fact tends to make them unpredictable. The bad Shepherds developed because judges started giving blue ribbons on the basis of size. (This seems to be a common American habit.) The breeders then started aiming for size and bred what I believe to be retardation—as well as hip displasia, allergies, and eye problems—into what used to be a magnificent dog.

Within the last ten years, police forces have gone to Germany to get their dogs, and conscientious breeders have done the same to recapture the true German Shepherd. I'm starting to see some wonderful German Shepherds. My first clue that more and more good ones were out there again came when owners started complaining that their German Shepherd, "doesn't even bark when the doorbell rings." German Shepherds are very sure of themselves; they know their power and ability. In other words, they don't need to bark when the doorbell rings. An intruder isn't going to ring the doorbell, and Rover has seen you go to the door and handle the person on the other side. One hopes he knows you well enough to know if something is wrong. Your German Shepherd won't hesitate to take care of you if need be: If German Shepherds were human, they would all be Rambo or Bruce Lee.

Now, let's talk a little about how smart this dog is. Were talking serious smart here. Poodles have the uncanny ability to understand the English language, and I believe, German Shepherds have the ability to connect with the human mind. You may notice that you're eating dinner, with Rover at your side, or you'll be watching TV, with Rover at your side, you'll be thinking hard about something, and Rover will suddenly pick up his head, perk his ears, and look seriously at you. You could be thinking about the argument you had at work, or that it's time to feed Rover. Now that I've brought it to your attention, watch your Rover and you'll soon see what I'm talking about. You'll have to watch closed doors in your house. Dogs in general don't like closed doors, but this is especially true of German Shepherds. Given the time and opportunity Rover will be able to open doors, ever so quietly take the lid off the garbage can, and hide your keys if he doesn't want you to leave. Boris knew how to flush the toilet. He only drank water from it, but he'd seen his Humans flush just before they left the bathroom, so he did it too. It took Boris's Humans quite some time to get used to suddenly hearing the toilet flush when they were the only people in the house. Another German Shepherd, Colonel, could turn a battery operated toy on and off.

Pay very close attention to Rover's diet. German Shepherds have notoriously sensitive stomachs. A potato chip can set off anything from gas to mucousy stools to serious diarrhea. German Shepherds are also the biggest babies of the canine world. When they get a vaccination they cry as if they're being killed, and God forbid you should step on Rover's toe. You'll be apologizing for days, because he'll limp for days. I don't think he's faking the pain, it's that his pain tolerance is zilch.

TRAINING. You haven't seen back talk until you've seen it from a German Shepherd. He'll sit for you as a puppy, but will refuse to sit as an adolescent and adult. He's not going to take kindly to heel either. I've gotten to the point with some German Shepherds that I've had the Human teach "Stand stay" instead of "Sit."

When you start walking him on a leash, you're going to have a hell of a time getting him to walk where he's supposed to. He's going to be happiest when your left leg is in line with the back of his shoulder or the beginning of his ribs. Try your best to keep your leg in line with the back of his neck. Once he's totally trustworthy on the leash, you can let him go a little farther ahead. Don't insist that he be so far back that he can't see around you.

I have similar problems with Wolf Hybrids and the Dingo personality in Heelers and Australian Cattle Dogs. There are definite feral traits in German Shepherds, and they must be acknowledged and respected. It's not that these dogs can't be trained; they can, and better than most, but they're going to have strong opinions of some of the obedience commands.

There is absolutely nothing that a dog can learn that you can't teach a good German Shepherd to do. Think about his many and varied uses and apply that information to your environment. Use a firm but kind hand. Your will is going to have to be at least as strong as his, or he'll walk all over you. Remember: I said a firm hand, not a harsh hand.

BEST ENVIRONMENT: Jogger—**Walker**—**Teenagers**—Children 6 to 11—
Children of any age—**Elderly**—Latchkey—**Active environment**—**Sedate
environment**—**Multiple dogs okay**—Apartment—**House with yard**—
Room to run—Needs daily exercise—**Camping**—Hiking

German Shorthaired Pointer

BRED TO DO. Point and say, "Yo! You guys with the guns, the birds are over here." Not to mention follow game and guard. When it comes to hunting, there's very little this dog can't do. And he can do it over any terrain—mountains, woods, marsh—and in any climate. This dog is one of the most popular hunting dogs.

HOUSETRAINING. Make sure the place you choose to confine Rover is roomy. Also, don't confine him any longer than absolutely necessary. This dog has to have room to move! Cabin fever comes quickly. If you stick to the method, Rover will housetrain easily. The hardest part is going to be getting him back in the house after he's had his eliminations. He's going to love every minute of being outside, as long as you're with him. He'll begin to show some independence when he's a little older, but as a puppy he's going to want you with him every minute possible.

PERSONALITY. Maybe someone out there can explain to me why these dogs have to have something in their mouth all the time. Make sure you provide plenty of toys and chewable things. German Shorthaired Pointers are mouth-oriented and can become very destructive while seeking something to chew on. Outside he's going to chew your firewood, your hot tub cover, the garden hose, and any plants he watched you put in the ground. Indoors can become fair game, if you don't keep an eye on him. Everything Rover does he does with passion, and that includes destruction.

I can't really tell you that a German Shorthair is going to get along with kids. I've seen some that are wonderful with children and others that shouldn't be anywhere near children. If possible, pay close attention to the bitch and see if you would trust her with your kids. As Rover gets older he's going to get grouchy, and he won't have much patience with young children.

If you don't plan on hunting with Rover or putting him in field trials, make sure that he has plenty of exercise and, if possible, room to run. He'll get along better with everyone if he's exercised. If you're a jogger or fast walker, take Rover along; you'll both enjoy the sport and each other's company.

TRAINING. You'll find Rover to be very trainable if you use a kind hand. This is one of the breeds that "click in" when they know they're learning something. You'll have to work for a few minutes getting his attention, but once you've got it he's yours. Of the sporting breeds I've worked with, the German Shorthair is among the easiest to train. If he were a schoolchild, he would be the one who's totally self-motivated. You would never have to ask him if he'd done his homework.

> BEST ENVIRONMENT: **Jogger**—Walker—Teenagers—Children 6 to 11— Children of any age—Elderly—Latchkey—**Active environment**—Sedate environment—**Multiple dogs okay**—Apartment—**House with yard**— **Room to run**—**Needs daily exercise**—Camping—Hiking

Giant Schnauzer

BRED TO DO. Seems kind of funny to breed a dog to guard beer bars and butcher shops. He must have done a very good job, because the police hired him, and so did the military.

HOUSETRAINING. It's going to be a little frustrating in the beginning, because Rover will always be busy doing something. Busy busy busy. Even when he's asleep, he'll be busy in his dreams. I always think of the Giants as being like those people who believe there's a place for everything, and everything in its place.

Don't confine Rover any longer than you absolutely have to. If he's confined for too long he's going to get resentful, and you'll see a dog's version of a temper tantrum. If you stick to the method and make sure you keep a close eye on him, he'll housetrain quickly.

PERSONALITY. If the adult Rover were human, he'd be an accountant. He would also organize your kitchen and alphabetize your CD collection. In spite of all this busywork, he's still going to love to play. Don't let Rover get too serious; play with him as much as possible. These dogs are chock-full of personality and character. Rover's going to be the best dog you've ever had one minute, and your cross to bear the next; funny and frustrating all at once. Schnauzers of all sizes are a little loopy as puppies, but at around twelve to sixteen months they settle down and seem to get it all together.

Giants are terrific with kids of any age. Their patience and gentleness with the very young are wonderful to watch. As you teach your child to tie his shoelaces, Rover will be right there watching your every move. When the child tries it himself, Rover will watch every loop and cheer him on. As for older children, as long as they don't insist on perfect fetch Rover will play until they both drop. You and your children will always be able to count on Rover. He will baby-sit your kids; he'll take good care of you and your property. When you have company, Rover will greet the guests politely, then stand or lie down somewhere and watch. You'll notice he barely moves, but he doesn't miss a thing. In fact, Rover takes his butler/bodyguard duties very seriously, which means he can become a real problem at the front door. If you don't have him under control there, he'll maul company with love before they get all the way into the house. Remember, dogs are narcissistic. Everything happens to them, because of them, about them, and for them. You can't explain to Rover that you invited people over to see you. He just thinks it's so neat that you invite people over for him. It's after all the excitement dies down, that he goes into butler/bodyguard mode.

TRAINING. If you have two left feet and you're all thumbs, this is the dog for you. He'll wait patiently as you pick yourself up after stumbling over the sprinkler and falling into a bush. With his pride in doing something well, he'll make you look as if you know what you're doing. Once he gets over his adolescent loopiness he'll be a piece of cake to train. He'll look at you with adoring brown eyes and do anything you ask of him. Giant Schnauzers have natural protective tendencies, and they are truly strongwilled, so I do recommend training of some kind.

> BEST ENVIRONMENT: Jogger—**Walker**—Teenagers—Children 6 to 11—**Children of any age**—Elderly—Latchkey—**Active environment**—Sedate environment—**Multiple dogs okay**—Apartment—**House with yard**—Room to run—Needs daily exercise—**Camping**—**Hiking (as long as he's trustworthy off leash)**

Golden Retriever

BRED TO DO. Go get something, preferably a bird, and bring it back. The Golden's become a terrific companion dog, and I rarely see one used as a retriever. Because of their wonderful temperament they are used in almost every job a dog can have. They are valued highly as Seeing eye and Hearing Ear dogs, Wheelchair Companions, police dogs sniffing out drugs and other contraband, and search-and-rescue dogs.

HOUSETRAINING. Housetraining is not one of the problems Goldens have. They usually respond quickly to the method because all Rover wants to do in the world is please you. If you have children, involve them in the housetraining process. Rover is going to want to be wherever the kids are anyway.

PERSONALITY. *I get more calls about serious destruction from Golden and Lab owners than any other breed!* I yell this at you because I've seen far too many Goldens lose their happy homes because they've destroyed their happy homes. Read Chapter 4, "Puppy Chewing and Destructive Chewing," and concentrate on displacement. Displacement behavior is hard for Goldens to get through. For some reason they become more insecure than most breeds do during that phase. And when I say "serious destruction," I'm not talking holes in the yard, firewood everywhere, or clothes off the line. I'm talking about major tunneling; firewood—

along with rosebushes and small trees—everywhere; hot tub covers being destroyed, and the hot tub itself being damaged; furniture being demolished; fences being torn down; and on and on and on.

Even though it makes you feel better, *please don't discipline Rover after the fact.* If you do, the destruction will continue anyway. For Rover to understand that chewing your hundred-dollar shoes is wrong, he has to make a conscious choice to displease you intentionally. But these dogs urgently want to please; doing something that might make you angry just doesn't make sense. In most dogs, displacement starts at around five and a half to six months and lasts until around eight months. With Goldens it can start a little earlier and end a little past eight months. But once you get Rover through displacement and you can fall in love with him again, all you have to handle is his unruliness and some hyper behavior.

These are a little easier to handle. Start when your Rover is a tiny pup: Stop him from jumping on you. When any large dog jumps on you, you have to catch your balance, but when a full-grown Golden jumps on you he doesn't want you to have any question in your mind that he loves you and he's glad to see you. Every fiber of his being is glad to see you. In fact, every fiber of his being is glad to see anyone. The problem is, all those fibers of being get yelled at for jumping. If you can hang in there with your Golden until he's sixteen to eighteen months old, I promise you the headaches will be worth it. As an adult, he will lie by the hearth and be the dog you see on the calendars. When the going gets tough, keep in mind all the jobs this dog can do. To do them he has to have the desire to please, he has to be intelligent, and he has to be trainable. Hang in there with your Golden. I promise you he has the potential to be the best dog, friend, and companion you've ever had.

According to the latest statistics, Golden and Labrador Retrievers are the most popular dogs in the United States right now. Considering sheer numbers, we're going to start hearing about bite cases involving them, we're going to see more roaming Goldens and Labs, and unfortunately the Animal Control Centers are going to be full of them. My sincere hope is that thanks to the information I've given you here, your Golden will be in the same happy home for his entire life.

Rover will love your kids as much as you do. Whenever I'm working with a Golden and the family is present, I have to insist that the children be out of the area. If Rover knows that *his* kids are around, he has to know where they are and if they're okay. Rover would much rather be with the children than learn how to sit. (Come to think of it, Rover would rather be doing almost anything than learning how to sit.)

The male Golden will almost always end up dominating with other dogs. This surprises most Golden owners, because aggression toward other dogs—or toward anything, for that matter—seems so out of character.

TRAINING. I always recommend waiting until a Golden is seven to eight months old before any kind of structured obedience training begins. Goldens mature late, and if you start obedience too soon, you'll become impatient and frustrated, Rover will become impatient and frustrated, and neither of you will gain anything. Because of his tendency to be unruly, you'll have to keep your praise low-key. If you put too much emphasis on praise, he'll get so excited he'll forget what he's being praised for. Make sure you do praise, though.

This Rover is such a mix of personalities with respect to school. He's like a child who pretends to be sick so he doesn't have to go and whines when he has to do homework, because he'd rather play or watch TV— but somehow manages to get all A's and B's. As you're working with him on a leash, he'll stop and scratch his neck as if he has a terrible itch. I don't care if it's thirty degrees, he'll hang his head and stop beneath a tree and tell you how hot he is. He'll come around in front of you when you're walking, he'll jump up and down, play with the leash, and do anything else he can think of to stop the training session. If for any reason you stop working, Rover will lie down and act as if he's really pooped and needs a rest. The pooped act can appear five minutes after you put the leash on him. Is Rover a manipulator? Oh, yes, one of the best. You're going to lose patience and want to be harsh with Rover. Please don't. You could beat this dog to within an inch of his life and he would still want to please you and continue to be totally devoted. Get a good hold on your patience, remembering it's a virtue, and hang in there. Raising your Golden to maturity may be one of the hardest things you've ever done, but it is a wonderful accomplishment and well worth the effort.

```
BEST ENVIRONMENT: Jogger—Walker—Teenagers—Children 6 to 11—
Children of any age—Elderly—Latchkey—Active environment—
Sedate environment (as an adult)—Multiple dogs okay—
Apartment—House with yard—Room to run—Needs daily exercise—
Camping—Hiking
```

Gordon Setter

BRED TO DO. Used to set at game, and retrieve downed game. Of the Setters, the Gordon is one of the best. They're not as fast as some of the others but they make up for that in perfect retrieving. These dogs are good at hunting in general. They are happiest when working, and are much better pets if they're so used.

HOUSETRAINING. The Gordons have the scent ability that you see in Hounds, and as with Hounds the hardest part of housetraining is being able to tell the difference between the nose down looking for a spot to go, and the nose down following a scent. Gordons do everything methodically, so as long as you're not wishy-washy during the housetraining process, Rover will housetrain quickly.

PERSONALITY. When I'm called in on a problem with a Gordon, the complaint usually has something to do with Rover not having any patience with the human race. I hear, "Judi, he snaps at me for no reason at all." "Judi, he growls at me if I want to pet him." "Judi, we can't get near him when he's eating." "Judi, he paces constantly." I've noticed that Rover gets obviously uncomfortable if there's too much going on at once. I've also noticed that there's a marked difference in attitude between Gordons that are used in hunting (or in field trials) and Gordons that are strictly pets.

If Gordons were humans, they'd be called conceited and snobbish. Whether you're working your Gordon or he's strictly a pet, you must give him as much affection as you have time for. He's kind of like a child with behavior problems. The answer to those problems is an overabundance of physical affection, constant love and attention, and encouragement of anything that builds self-esteem. If you're having problems with your Gordon getting along with this world we live in, treat him like that troubled child and you will be amazed at the changes. It may seem as if Rover just wants to be left alone. Please don't listen to him.

Because Rover tends to be impatient, I don't recommend him with children. If you're working your Gordon, he will get along okay with older children, but these dogs are obviously uncomfortable around younger children.

TRAINING. If you're training Rover for hunting, you'll have to do very little. But if you're new at such training, contact someone who can help you. As to training Rover for basic obedience, I highly recommend it. Use a firm but kind hand, and *praise, praise, praise.* Don't take Rover for granted. Praise him *every time* he does anything you've commanded him to do. Teaching him as much as you can will build confidence, and so will getting him out into high stress.

BEST ENVIRONMENT: **Jogger—Walker—Teenagers**—Children 6 to 11—Children of any age—Elderly—Latchkey—**Active environment**—Sedate environment—**Multiple dogs okay**—Apartment—**House with yard—Room to run—Needs daily exercise**—Camping—Hiking

---

Great Dane

BRED TO DO. Boy, this breed goes back along way. They've been around since at least 400 A.D. and may go back as far as 35 B.C. I'm sure this is why there are very distinct personality traits in each color of the breed. The Dane was bred for battle, hunting, watch, and bodyguard. Recently he's been used mostly as guard and friend.

IN GENERAL. *Feeding a Great Dane is a large dollar investment!* I yell this at you because I've seen far too many Danes with nutrition problems because they are given the cheapest possible food. The old adage "You get what you pay for" applies to dog food.

Danes have absolutely no idea of their size and power. If a Rottweiler jumps on you, that dog has absolutely no doubt that you will fall down. If a Chihuahua jumps on you, he gets annoyed when you don't fall down. A Great Dane jumps on you, and when you fall he helps you up and says, "Are you all right? Did you trip on something?" It doesn't occur to him that he knocked you down.

Dogs engage in something called allelomimetic behavior, which means they mimic and follow. Danes are more prone to this than almost any other breed. I've never known a Dane that doesn't back up to sit on a chair the way a Human does. I've known a number of Danes that when going through displacement will chew on light switches, oven knobs, telephones, and doorknobs. They see their Human handle these things and want to do it too.

Danes have an odd trait that befuddles me every time I work with one: He rarely looks at you while you're training him. He'll appear to be totally preoccupied with something he's watching. When you do get his attention, he'll say, "I'm sorry. Were you saying something?" I think if Danes were kids, their teacher would note on their report cards that "Rover is a daydreamer." Don't let him fool you, though, he hears every word you utter.

All Danes are leaners. If you stand still for any length of time, Rover will lean on you until you move. He may relax against you so completely that you have to warn him you're going to move, so he doesn't fall over.

FAWN

HOUSETRAINING. All you have to do with your Fawn is show him how unhappy you are when he has an accident in the house and praise him like crazy when he goes outside; he'll make the connection quickly. This sweetheart wants to please and he's very clean. Those two traits alone make housetraining a Fawn relatively easy.

PERSONALITY. Of the Danes, the Fawns are the sweetest. They are also a bit more active than the other colors, and need more exercise.

Giving Rover exercise is easy, though, all you have to do is play with him. I don't hesitate to recommend the Fawn Dane with kids of any age. When he's a puppy you'll have to watch him around the young ones, because he's like a bull in a china shop, a fast-growing but lovable giant. Once he grows through the clumsy stage, he'll be ever so gentle with your baby, a little more playful with your eight-year-old, and as boisterous as your fourteen-year-old wants to get.

Throughout my twenty-one years in my chosen career I've been called for only one serious problem with a Fawn Dane. Leo had taken over the entire household of five people. He wouldn't let anybody walk around the house without growling and snapping. He had become totally dominant. When I was told the symptoms over the phone I had a hard time connecting serious aggressive behavior with a Fawn Dane. When I walked into the house, though, I knew immediately what had happened. Throughout the house was futon furniture. If you're familiar with futon furniture, you know that it's usually very low and you don't actually sit on it, you lounge on it. The only furniture that sat everybody higher than Leo was the dining room set. The dog was almost always higher than all of the kids, and higher than or at eye-contact level with the adults. He actually became dominant by default. Getting the peck order back in place was easy, because Leo didn't want to have the dominant role he was given. Keeping it in place was the problem. These people actually had to make a choice between Leo and the decor. When they saw what a great dog Leo could be, they chose to replace the living room and den furniture.

Don't make some of the mistakes I see people make with their Danes. Rover's big, but he's not an outdoor dog. Rover's big, but he doesn't need a lot of exercise and is not a good jogging buddy. Your Fawn will jog with you because he loves you, not because he needs the exercise. He will also stay outside and shiver without complaint, because he loves you. But Great Danes make wonderful apartment dogs. Once you realize that, other things will fall into place.

TRAINING. If your Fawn is a male, he's not going to like the "Sit" command. If he really gives you a hard time about it, respect his wishes and teach him a "Stand-stay" instead. It's a guess, but I think males resist the "sit" because of the size of their testicles. Be kind and gentle, and all other commands will come easily.

BEST ENVIRONMENT: Jogger—**Walker**—Teenagers—Children 6 to 11—
Children of any age—Elderly—Latchkey—Active environment—**Sedate
environment—Multiple dogs okay—Apartment**—House with yard—
Room to run—Needs daily exercise—Camping—Hiking

BLACK

HOUSETRAINING. Black Danes have a very strong will and will use the spot you've chosen for them only if they like it. If your pup chooses another spot, you might as well go along with him. It won't make any difference how many times you take him to your spot; he will cut and run for his. Stick to the method, put your hands on your hips, and tell Rover that you're the boss. Your going to have to remind him of your dominant role off and on for quite some time, so you might as well start now.

PERSONALITY. Practice, practice, practice. Stand in front of your mirror, with your hands on your hips, your feet firmly planted, and repeat: "Rover, I am the boss. I am your alpha Human. I do not live in your house. You live in mine." Now after you've practiced this a few times you're ready to be your Black Dane's master. Keep in mind that most Black Danes care where they stand within the peck order, and they will take over that top rung given the slightest encouragement. Read Chapter 6, "The Peck Order Factor," and Chapter 8, "The Head Honcho Human." Once you gain that top rung and hang on to it, you're going to love your Black Great Dane.

Of all of the Danes, this one has the most natural protective tendencies. He'll be your loyal bodyguard in a quiet, dignified manner and he'll love every minute of doing it. Once he realizes that you're not going to let him run the show, his devotion and love will be unconditional.

If you have children, please study the temperament of the bitch, and if possible, the stud before selecting a puppy.

TRAINING. Yes, you must train your Black Dane! Training automatically puts you in the lead position. You're going to have to earn Rover's respect; it won't come naturally. You'll need a firm but kind hand; if you need to, practice in front of your mirror again. You're going to get some serious back talk from your Black Dane, so be prepared.

BEST ENVIRONMENT: Jogger—Walker—**Teenagers**—Children 6 to 11—
Children of any age—Elderly—Latchkey—Active environment—**Sedate
environment**—**Multiple dogs okay**—**Apartment**—House with yard—
Room to run—Needs daily exercise—Camping—Hiking

BRINDLE

HOUSETRAINING. It takes a little longer to housetrain Brindles. If Rover were a female human, she would be a tomboy. If Rover were a male human, he'd be Pigpen from "Charlie Brown." Brindles love to roll in the dirt, and they're in seventh heaven when making mud pies. One of the things I recommend that a Brindle owner teach his dog is how to wipe his paws before coming in the house. I don't care if there's no dirt in your backyard, Rover will find some. In the warmer months, Rover will love the part of housetraining that gets him outside and hate the part that keeps him in until he's housetrained.

PERSONALITY. The Brindles, for the most part, are good-natured and fun-loving. They can also be unpredictable, and a little squirrely. I've run across enough of them with these traits to make note of it. If you have children study the temperament of the bitch and, if possible, the stud before selecting a puppy. This Rover won't intentionally climb the peck order ladder, but if there is confusion he will become dominant, and won't like it.

TRAINING. I'm probably going to lose some Dane breeders with this one, but if Brindles were children, people would smile and say things like "He's just a little slow" or "He learns—it just takes him a little longer, is all." Use a gentle hand and come armed with patience. He will learn anything you want him to, because he loves you and is totally devoted; just keep in mind that it may take him a little longer.

> BEST ENVIRONMENT: Jogger—Walker—**Teenagers—Children 6 to 11**—Children of any age—Elderly—Latchkey—Active environment—**Sedate environment—Multiple dogs okay—Apartment**—House with yard—Room to run—Needs daily exercise—Camping—Hiking

HARLEQUIN

HOUSETRAINING. Harlequins can be high-strung and somewhat jumpy as pups, so when you first start taking Rover out, he may be a little nervous. Gentle him through it and he'll be fine. As long as there isn't too much chaos during the housetraining process, Rover will housetrain at a normal rate. Keep the verbal discipline low-key.

PERSONALITY. Harlequins are impressionable and vulnerable as youngsters. If you use a harsh hand with him as a puppy he'll begin to avoid you. As he gains some age and maturity he'll become stable and sure of himself. Harlequins have an independent streak that has to be acknowledged and respected. They are also very proud dogs. If you ever have the chance to see Danes of other colors you'll notice that the Harlequin holds his head just a little higher.

I don't recommend Harlequins with young children. They're a bit too independent and impatient to be comfortable around young children.

The guarding instinct is strong in Harlequins, so Rover can get along well as a latchkey dog. When you leave for work in the morning, Rover will immediately go on duty. He'll do his job for as many hours as you do yours. These giants can become too serious, so make sure a lot of time is spent playing.

TRAINING. You must train your Harlequin! You may have to use a somewhat firm hand every now and then, but Rover will learn quickly and do everything you teach him, with a sense of pride in doing something well.

BEST ENVIRONMENT: Jogger—Walker—**Teenagers**—Children 6 to 11—
Children of any age—Elderly—**Latchkey**—Active environment—**Sedate
environment—Multiple dogs okay—Apartment**—House with yard—
Room to run—Needs daily exercise—Camping—Hiking

BLUE

HOUSETRAINING. As long as there's no confusion Rover will house-train quickly. He may want to pick his spot outside, but if you do some coaxing, he'll see it your way.

PERSONALITY. Blues are polite and obedient. Rover will occasionally come to you with definite ideas of his own, and he may even argue his point, but if you can show him that your way is better he'll go along with you. Pay attention to him, though, because occasionally his way works. He may insist on having his way about where he sleeps and what he eats.

TRAINING. The Blues love to learn, so if you use a kind hand with this loving Giant, training will go smoothly. If you are all thumbs and left feet, this is the Dane for you. Rover will wait patiently while you learn how to put his collar on and how the leash should go. He'll pause during a walk if you stumble over sprinklers and fall into bushes.

BEST ENVIRONMENT: Jogger—Walker—Teenagers—**Children 6 to 11**—
Children of any age—Elderly—Latchkey—Active environment—**Sedate
environment**—Multiple dogs okay—**Apartment**—House with yard—
Room to run—Needs daily exercise—Camping—Hiking

Great Pyrenees

BRED TO DO. Just about anything that had to do with life in the mountains. He could rescue people in snow, guard sheep, guide people through snow and rough mountains, and still find time to take care of his family and be a good companion. *Feeding a Great Pyrenees is a major dollar investment!* I yell this at you because I don't want you to buy the cheapest food possible. The old adage "You get what you pay for" applies to dog foods; the cheaper ones are not nutritionally complete.

HOUSETRAINING. Your Pyrenees will give you plenty of warning that he needs to eliminate. It seems that the spot is important to them. These lovable giants love the outdoors and they can easily relate to having eliminations there. Keep the verbal discipline low-key, or Rover will fall apart before your very eyes. All you have to do is point him in the right direction, and as long as there's no confusion, Rover will housetrain with ease.

PERSONALITY. The hardest time in this dog's life is when he realizes he's too big to sit on your lap. He'll try off and on for years, just in case by some miracle he shrank. If you allow him on the furniture, he'll love you to death if you sit on the couch so that he can at least lie across your lap. Even though he was bred to do all kinds of rough-and-tumble things he's not a happy camper if he's kept outside. These gentle giants are very people-oriented. If Rover realizes that his size makes it hard for you to move around the house, he'll find a way to stay out of your way, as long as you let him be a house dog. I hear you out there thinking, "Yeah, sure," but I've seen it several times. Without exception, every time I have been called about a Great Pyrenees, the problems have been created because the dog was kept outside. Don't adopt one of these dogs if you don't plan on letting him be an inside-the-house member of the family. Sometimes, in the winter, he'll prefer to be outside, but once he's cooled off he'll want right back in.

Grooming these dogs can become a nightmare if you don't stay on top of it. Keep in mind that Rover is a cold-weather dog with a cold-weather coat. When he begins to shed his winter coat, help him out and groom him yourself or have him groomed. If his hair becomes matted in the warmer months, air cannot get to his skin and he will develop skin infections called hot spots.

If you have children you can certainly have a Great Pyrenees. Rover will become a nanny to the youngest and best buddy to the oldest. He will know where the kids are at every moment, and when he learns their names he will seek them out if you ask him to. He won't play outside quite as much in the warmer months, but he'll play until he drops in the air-conditioned house. If the youngest children want to use him like a rug, it'll be just fine with him. One of my favorite images of this dog came from seeing Fluffers sound asleep on her side with a three-year-old child curled up against her chest and tucked under her leg. The child's mother said that if she didn't pick her daughter up and take her to bed, Fluffers would stay put until the girl woke up, no matter how long it took.

Rover will never make a jogging or walking buddy but if you are a hiker and/or camper, this is the dog for you. So that you don't become incensed when it happens, I'll tell you now that Rover can and will out-hike you. Not to worry, though—if he gets too far ahead he'll stop and wait patiently until you catch up.

TRAINING. Ask him to climb a mountain, guard your sheep, or rescue you from anywhere, but don't ask him to follow obedience commands with enthusiasm. He's not being lazy and he's not being stubborn, he just doesn't see much point in this obedience stuff. There will be times when he needs to be under control on a leash, so make sure you teach him to walk correctly on a leash, and you might want to teach him to sit, so that he'll do it nicely at the animal clinic. If you teach him "Down" during the summer months, he'll learn it in a snap. How much training you do with your Great Pyrenees is entirely up to you. Use a gentle hand.

BEST ENVIRONMENT: Jogger—**Walker**—Teenagers—Children 6 to 11—**Children of any age**—**Elderly**—Latchkey—Active environment—**Sedate environment**—**Multiple dogs okay**—Apartment—**House with yard**—Room to run—Needs daily exercise—**Camping**—**Hiking**

Greyhound

BRED TO DO. Long ago, Greyhounds were used to hunt and bring down deer, wild boar, and of course, rabbit. With his speed, he could bring down both deer and wild boar without stopping. I think that is amazing, but I'm trying to visualize a deer and a wild boar hanging out together. A loose rabbit doesn't stand a chance. We're talking serious speed in this magnificent dog.

HOUSETRAINING. Get the bells I recommend in the chapter on housetraining and put them on the door handle. I've never known a Greyhound that barked, whined, or pawed the door to indicate that he needed to go out. The bells seem to do the trick. Rover will housetrain at a normal rate as long as there's no confusion. Gentle him through the method, never forgetting that he does love you, he just doesn't know how to show it.

PERSONALITY. I'm seeing more and more Greyhounds in my practice, because retired racers are now being adopted out instead of euthanized. Some problems arise from the Greyhound personality; others result from the three or more years they spent racing. Every single one, without exception, begins running around the backyard or through the house at least once a day. They do this as if they could tell time. It's a perfect example of the compulsive habitual canine personality. These dogs were trained to race, and exercised at set times every day. The fact that the track is no longer there doesn't mean a thing to Rover. When his internal clock goes off, he's gonna run.

The other problem I see is a form of kennelosis. Kennelosis is seen in dogs that have spent most of their lives in a dog run. The result is agoraphobia, a fear of open spaces. It's not severe in the Greyhounds I see, but it needs to be addressed. You'll notice Rover is a little tentative when going through doorways for the first time, especially from indoors to outdoors and vice versa. Human! You are going to be *so* tempted to say, "It's okay, it's okay." In fact, stopping yourself is probably going to be one of the hardest things you've ever done. If your Greyhound is showing signs of kennelosis, it means he's going through some serious anxiety attacks. Tell yourself over and over again: "If I tell him it's okay, I'll be praising him for his feelings of anxiety." I hear you now saying, "Judi, isn't there some way I can comfort him? Please, I have to do something!" I'm sorry, Human, I wish I could tell you that just this once it would be all right. Stiffen your upper lip, square your shoulders, and give Rover a command. He can't follow a command from you and feel anxiety at the same time. Get him through the door or whatever is causing his anxiety, and then you can praise him and pet him to your heart's content.

Greyhounds are naturally reserved. Don't confuse this trait with shyness or anxiety. You're not going to see an obvious show of affection from Rover, whether you've raised him from a pup or adopted him after he retired. Don't think he doesn't love you; he does, he just shows it differently from most other dogs. I'm sure at some point you've known somebody who isn't comfortable with shows of affection. Well, your Greyhound is the same way. I implore you, Human, don't get a Greyhound thinking you're going to have a fun family pet. I've seen too many humans disappointed in their Greyhound when they realize what his personality is all about. But if you want quiet dignity and a regal manner, by all means adopt a Greyhound.

Greyhounds are incredibly clean dogs and they are very vain. It's a good thing they don't need to be groomed. They'd insist on going to the groomer at least once a week. I'll never forget seeing Number Twelve (don't blame me; I didn't name him) after a long, hard rain. The yard was muddy in places and there was dirt runoff on the patio. In his best aristocratic manner, and showing considerable disdain, Number Twelve carefully walked around the mess until he reached the wet—but clean—grass.

TRAINING. *Greyhounds must have a daily run!* If you're a jogger or runner and you want a buddy, this is the dog for you. You must, however, be dedicated to your running. You can't be a weekend jogger or a warm-weather jogger, because Rover is going to need that daily exercise whether you do or not. If you get sick you may have to call on a friend or hire a jogger for your dog.

Greyhounds are born polite and somewhat obedient. If you work with Rover on structured obedience, use a gentle hand.

BEST ENVIRONMENT: **Jogger—Walker—Teenagers**—Children 6 to 12—Children of any age—**Elderly**—Latchkey—**Active environment**—Sedate environment—**Multiple dogs okay**—Apartment—House with yard—**Room to run—Needs daily exercise**—Camping—Hiking

---

Irish Setter

BRED TO DO. Just about any hunting. Irish Setters can handle almost any terrain and weather. Their speed and excellent nose make them sought after.

HOUSETRAINING. Irish Setter puppies are often high-strung and easily startled. Try hard not to let anything traumatize Rover during the housetraining process, especially in connection with the spot you've chosen for him to go. Blarney had a rough start in housetraining. He was eight weeks old when James got him, so he was going through "fear imprint" and the first time James took him to "the spot," the neighbor dog jumped on the wall and barked. Blarney did urinate and defecate at that moment, but out of fear. It took James almost four months to get Blarney completely housetrained.

If you have Rover out, and a child screams or the garbage truck goes thundering by, you're going to have to stand your ground and act as if nothing happened. As soon as he realizes you're there to take care of him, he'll begin to relax, and being housetrained will follow soon.

PERSONALITY. *These dogs require a lot of exercise!* Unfortunately, Irish Setters are often adopted for their beauty and put in a city backyard without nearly enough to do. Years ago I wondered why I saw so many Irish Setters at the Animal Control Center and the Animal Humane Association. Why would anybody adopt such a magnificent dog and then abandon it? I soon learned that Setters are notorious fence jumpers and roamers. Their need for daily exercise was simply not being satisfied in a backyard, and they became too high-strung to make good pets. I can't begin to tell you how saddened I was when I learned of the plight of these truly magnificent dogs. Fortunately, they gained a reputation for being fence jumpers, hyper, and difficult to handle as city pets. I saw fewer and fewer being abandoned and having behavior problems. Just understand that if you don't have the time to meet the exercise requirements of the Irish Setter, you shouldn't adopt one. But if you're a jogger, this is the jogging buddy you need. (However, make sure you condition him as you did yourself.)

The Irish Setter is among the best sporting breeds. I'm sure you've guessed that this is a dog I recommend using for what he was bred to do. If you don't hunt, but you want an Irish Setter, call breeders in the area and find out how to get Rover into field trials.

Considering their scenting ability, you'd think that when Setters took off, they'd trace their way back. No doubt the ability is there. I think they choose not to return home. I've never known an Irish Setter that didn't love to roam. If you take him out into open space you'll notice he'll run dead out for a while; then, when he settles down, he actually meanders.

There's an independent streak in this dog that has to be respected. You're going to get your feelings hurt every now and then because there will be times when Rover won't care where you are or if he's with you. When everybody is gathered in the den watching TV, Rover will be somewhere else in the house, completely content to be by himself.

You'd think that an animal this independent would make a good latchkey dog. Wrong. Either have two dogs, or live somewhere that gives him room to run, or use him for hunting, but don't leave this dog alone in a backyard or house while you go off to work for hours at a time. If Rover is left alone too much, and he can't get out of the yard, believe me, you will get complaints from neighbors about his barking. There's a lot about this dog to love, and he can be very loving, but don't adopt him unless you know you can provide that right home.

TRAINING. This dog's concentration is keen when he's hunting, but it'll wander during obedience training. If you train him for hunting or field trials, you'll be amazed at how quickly he'll learn, but you're going to have a hard time keeping his attention long enough to care about a "Sit." Whether you work with Rover on obedience is entirely up to you, but I do insist on working hard at coming when called. You might want to put some serious effort into the "Halt" command as well, but if the only command you can get out of your Irish Setter is "Come," you've got it made. Whatever you train him to do, use a gentle hand. You're going to get frustrated and want to harden your hand, but the minute you do, Rover will walk away.

Irish Wolfhound

BRED TO DO. Big-game hunting and protection of stock. They will bring down stag and wild boar for the hunter, and hunt wolves and coyotes for the rancher and farmer. They are still used in this capacity.

HOUSETRAINING. If only one family member does the housetraining it will go much faster. This dog is going to bond strongly to one master no matter what you do, but if you want Rover to be a part of the entire family, it's not that difficult: One of you do the housetraining, another do the feeding; everyone get involved in play, exercise, and training. I don't care how young he is, he's never going to be tiny, so taking him to an accident in the house is going to take some coaxing if he doesn't want to go with you. And carrying him to the spot you've chosen is going to be impossible in a very short period of time. So, the second you bring him home, start teaching him that following you anywhere is the neatest thing in the world to do. These dogs are smart and cooperative, so as long as there's no confusion the housetraining process should go smoothly.

PERSONALITY. I hope you have some idea as to how big thirty-eight inches at the shoulder is. Irish Wolfhounds are the tallest dogs in the world. I'll never forget the first time I saw a Harlequin Great Dane and an Irish Wolfhound standing side by side. I'm here to tell you it gave me a totally new concept of size. The first time I met an Irish Wolfhound he stood on his hind legs, put his paws on my shoulders, and hit seven feet tall. Teaching Tiny not to jump on people was a physical challenge I'd never been faced with with before. His tallest owner was five eleven and I'm five feet, period. We did it by using a fifteen-foot canvas line (usually used with horses) and a pinch collar. As it turned out, we only had to pull him off twice before he realized we didn't want him to jump on people. He was praised for *not* jumping two or three times, and that was it. As I've said, these dogs are very cooperative.

It's hard to imagine, but Irish Wolfhounds make great companion dogs. Rover will lie at your feet as you watch TV, he'll take any kind of walk or jog you want, and he'll love you totally, with every bit of his great big heart. If you are a walker, jogger, runner, or biker, and you want a buddy, this is the dog for you. Make sure you condition him as you did yourself. He'll enjoy the exercise with you, but you should take him someplace he can run totally unrestrained. Running free is an absolute must. If he's not allowed this outlet, he'll seek it out for himself. You'll be jogging along, and the next thing you know, he'll be off at breakneck speed. He may just take off out of the yard, and run until he's exhausted. By that time he could very well be lost. When you see your Irish Wolfhound run dead out, it will take your breath away. The stride and speed are beautiful.

These dogs really are sweethearts. They're very affectionate, and they're gentle in spite of their size. In fact, I think they know they're the world's largest dog, and they're gentle by choice. I don't hesitate to recommend Irish Wolfhounds for children of any age. You'll have to watch Rover with the kids until he grows through the clumsy-puppy stage, but after that you can trust him with your very youngest. Fatima the cat and Daisy the Irish Wolfhound were the best of friends, and when Fatima had a litter she didn't hesitate to let Daisy help. Daisy would lie down in front of the nesting box and Fatima would place the kittens between Daisy's island-sized paws. Daisy and Fatima would then share the kitten-cleaning duties. I was called in because Daisy became depressed when the kittens were adopted out. She recovered shortly, but her Humans decided to have Fatima spayed so that Daisy wouldn't have to go through that loss again.

TRAINING. You should get Rover used to a collar and leash within a week or so of adopting him. Obviously you don't want to wait until he's old enough to take you for a walk. I'm sure I don't have to remind you of how powerful your Irish Wolfhound is. If you're walking him, and he wants to check something out, *the two of you* will check something out.

He won't have to put too much effort into taking you along. As gentle as Rover's soul is, he's not going to overpower you intentionally. These dogs are mellow and train easily, but because of their size, I've seen Humans think they need to use a harsh, controlling hand. That's totally unnecessary. Rover will learn almost anything you want him to, because he loves you and wants to please. Because Rover will bond to just one Human, I recommend that all family members work with him.

BEST ENVIRONMENT: **Jogger—Walker—**Teenagers—Children 6 to 11— **Children of any age**—Elderly—Latchkey—**Active environment—** Sedate environment—**Multiple dogs okay**—Apartment—House with yard—**Room to run—Needs daily exercise—Camping—Hiking**

Jack Russell Terrier

BRED TO DO. Like most Terriers, he was bred to hunt small game in its lair. The Jack was appreciated because he could burrow into very small holes.

HOUSETRAINING. Like most Terriers, the Jack Russell is very active and forgets he needs to go outside. Even as puppies these dogs are eager explorers, so you'll have a hard time telling if he's just checking stuff out or looking for a place to go. Absolutely, positively don't give Rover the run of the house too soon. If you do, it will take you forever to get him housetrained. As curious as this wee mite is, there won't be a corner he won't check out. He'll have eliminations in so many different places in the house you won't be able to keep track. Plan on keeping more than one eye on him. Keep his eating schedule as precise as you possibly can. You'll be able to keep track of his patterns this way, and it'll help greatly with the housetraining.

PERSONALITY. I'm beginning to see more and more of these dogs. From what I've seen, I'm not too concerned about this breed becoming popular. These little ones are lighthearted and fun to have around. Even breeders who breed strictly for the money won't be able to breed disposition problems into this sweetie. For some reason the adult males do a lot of territory marking, even in the house. And Jacks get very possessive about *their things*. Their toys are really *their* toys. His food and water dish are his and his alone. If you have other dogs, Rover isn't going to share. I'm pretty sure that when he starts marking, it's because his things have been threatened in some way. George started marking at the corner of the dishwasher when his Human decided to wash his bowls. Lora washes his bowls in the sink now, it's much faster. The females are possessive as well; if their things are threatened they cache them and constantly check to see if they're okay.

When you have Rover out make sure he's either on a leash or you have total vocal control. These little ones are courageous and curious to a fault. When it comes to checking something out, they have more guts than brains. Your Jack won't hesitate to introduce himself to a snake, a skunk, a porcupine, or anything else that piques his interest. If you have a child with this same curious nature the two will be inseparable. Just imagine Rover seeing something run under a rock and having a child of his very own who will lift the rock to see what's beneath it. Speaking of kids, Jack Russells are good with them, as long as there's respect for what belongs to whom.

TRAINING. Jack Russells are very trainable. They want to please and they love to learn. The only problem you'll have with Rover is getting him to hold still long enough to start the lesson. You'll notice he does acrobatics naturally, so if you want to, you can teach him things along those lines. Make sure that you spend a considerable amount of time on coming when called. You'll want to be able to recall him the instant you see him walking over to a skunk.

BEST ENVIRONMENT: Jogger—**Walker**—Teenagers—**Children 6 to 11**—Children of any age—Elderly—Latchkey—**Active environment**—Sedate environment—**Multiple dogs okay (as long as he doesn't have to share)—Apartment—House with yard**—Room to run—Needs daily exercise—**Camping (if you can keep an eye on him)**—Hiking

---

Keeshond

BRED TO DO. Anything a dog is capable of doing, the Keeshond did on Dutch boats. Think about the diversity of jobs! He had to catch rats, be a watchdog, stay alert to danger, and swim whenever the job required it. If Rover were human, he could work for Temp Force; they could send him on almost any job.

HOUSETRAINING. These dogs are pure unadulterated puppy when they're puppies. Sounds redundant, I know, but you'll see what I mean when you bring one home. He's going to have a hard time relating to this housetraining stuff because he won't take anything seriously and won't understand why you're being such an old grump about where he pees. You'll have to stick to the method to the letter, and you'll have to commit yourself totally to getting him housetrained. Once he grasps the concept, he'll housetrain quickly.

PERSONALITY. For some reason Keesh owners are surprised to learn that Rover loves water. This dog is known for his swimming ability. He will play in your sprinklers and may play in his own water bowl. (Get him a large, heavy porcelain bowl.) You're going to be surprised the first time you see Rover wet and realize that he's not really that wet. The water rolls right off.

Keeshonds are incredibly alert. Very little will go on in your home or neighborhood that Rover won't be aware of. If he were human, he'd be the neighborhood gossip. When you see your Keesh alert to something, don't fall into the trap of whispering, "What is it? What do you hear?" That will encourage barking, and Keeshonds can become bad barkers anyway. You will also lose his watchdog abilities, because he'll start alerting to things just to get your attention.

Female Keeshonds are very feminine. Roverette will eat delicately and politely. If you offer her a scrap of food she'll sniff it first to see if it's something she wants.

Rover will throw himself into play completely; he'll throw himself into watching and guarding as well. When a Keeshond does anything he does it with passion and because he loves doing it.

I hesitate to recommend Keeshonds with young kids—these dogs are so lively and rambunctious they can be overwhelming. Keeshonds can be worriers, too. If you have a very young child, Rover will pace when the child cries, and just plain worry when the child is upset. When he's with kids old enough to hold their own, Rover relaxes. I'm going to repeat: Keeshonds are worriers. If you become ill, Rover will stay with you and jump every time you stir, in case there's something he can do for you. When Carol became seriously ill with the flu, Katie lost weight from worry. She took it upon herself to guard Carol and watch the house; when she knew Carol was asleep she went from room to room, window to window, and door to door without stopping until Carol woke up. She then took up her duty station at the foot of the bed. Carol told me that when she became well, Katie slept for almost twenty-four hours.

TRAINING. Keesh are naturals at watch, and I believe that any dog with natural protective tendencies should get training of some kind, because it puts you in control. When you think of all of the different jobs this dog did, it's a shame to let that kind of ability and intelligence go to waste.

One trait that you may notice in your Keesh is laziness. It seems to come out of nowhere and I can't find any explanation for it. It's not caused by having a heavy coat in hot weather—it happens in winter as well. Don't fight it. It's obviously a part of Rover, and it has to be respected. If he has an attack of the lazies, just wait it out. It'll pass, and then you can go back to the training.

BEST ENVIRONMENT: Jogger—**Walker**—Teenagers—**Children 6 to 11**—Children of any age—Elderly—Latchkey—**Active environment**—**Sedate environment**—**Multiple dogs okay**—Apartment—**House with yard**—Room to run—Needs daily exercise—**Camping**—Hiking

---

Labrador Retriever

BRED TO DO. To retrieve in water and marsh. A lab will plunge right into water without skipping a beat. The word "caution" is not part of his vocabulary.

HOUSETRAINING. The biggest problems I've found Humans have in housetraining their Lab are these: They have a hard time getting him back in the house, and he's so klutzy it's impossible to be serious with him. Lab puppies are all skin and heart. If you stick to the method, and there's no confusion, Rover will housetrain easily. (Note: I didn't say "quickly.") Once he's housetrained you may have to remind him every now and then until he's four to five months old. His strong desire to please will help.

PERSONALITY. Please read Chapter 3, "Dos and Don'ts of Discipline," and Chapter 4, "Puppy Chewing and Destructive Chewing." It's important that you understand these chapters, so that you can begin helping your Lab through the months ahead. Here's the most important advice I can give you about your Labrador: *Hang in there until he's an adult.* He is definitely worth the wait. There are going to be times when you think, "I can't stand this anymore! I'm going to have to find Rover another home! That's it! He's destroyed for the last time!" I've got my fingers crossed hoping that you're reading this *before* you bring a Lab home. More than likely, though, your Lab is about six months old and driving you nuts, and you're desperately hoping to read something that will help. This will definitely help you understand what's going on, but you may cringe when I tell you how long you're going to have Destructo! I'm sorry to say that you're going to have to live through several months of unruliness and destruction. I get more calls about serious destruction by Labs and Goldens than any other breeds. For some reason, these dogs have a really hard time with displacement behavior, harder than other breeds do. The anxiety is worse, the feelings of insecurity are stronger, and the feelings of isolation and abandonment are more intense.

As to Labs' unruliness, I find that in most cases it's predictable. It's at its worst when you come home after being gone for any length of time. He loves you more than anything else in the world, and he's been alone for a while not knowing if you're ever coming back. His unruly excitement at seeing you comes from all of that love, and relief that you came home. Rover's unruliness may also become a problem when you play with him. He gets so excited in play that he's no longer in control, and then can't stop. If he's been outside for a while, and you walk outside after being indoors, you're going to get jumped on and mauled. The unruliness is all caused by love and excitement. Start teaching him "Off" from the minute you adopt him and bring him home. From the very beginning, keep homecoming as low-key as possible.

Your Lab will be the best dog you've ever had, and your cross to bear for months to come. When he's sixteen to eighteen months old he's going to be the perfect calendar dog. He'll lie at your feet in front of the fireplace. He'll be a wonderful companion to you and your children. I'll say it again: Hang in there, he's worth the wait.

Enough advice and bad news. Labradors are wonderful dogs. They're so affectionate that you will never feel unloved. They are one of the first breeds I recommend if someone wants a large dog that does well with children. If I'm working with a Lab on obedience, I always have to ask that the children not be there. If the children are present Rover is constantly checking to see where they are and what they're doing, so he's totally distracted. This dog will take care of and protect your children of any age. With some breeds I caution that this can get out of hand: The dog begins to protect the children even against family members. With Labs that's rarely a problem. Rover trusts completely that you can take care of your children and yourself.

I've learned recently that Labs and Goldens are now the most popular dogs in the United States. So, because of sheer numbers, there will be more Labs and Goldens (and crosses with Labs and Goldens) in animal shelters. There will be more reported bite cases involving them. We'll see more abandoned Labs and Goldens, and I'll be seeing more behavior problems than I do now. I can't even begin to stop poor breeding practices, but I can implore you to study the bitch and stud before selecting a puppy, and remind you again that you're going to have to stop several times in the next few months to take a deep breath and count to ten. Your Lab is most definitely worth your time and patience.

TRAINING. Please wait until Rover is seven to eight months old before you start structured training. Labs mature late, and if you start him too young you'll get absolutely nowhere; and when he's old enough to handle the training, your attitude toward training in general, and training Rover in particular, will be very negative. For a dog to work as a Seeing Eye, Hearing Ear, and Wheelchair Companion, and in contraband search (and the list goes on) he has to be trainable and have a desire to please. Obviously Labs are trainable, and they love nothing more in the world than to please you. You're going to need a firm but kind hand. When training begins, Rover is going to start testing your patience from the moment you try to put his training collar on. Once you get through the collar and leash struggle, he's going to stop often to scratch an imaginary itch, he'll walk right in front of you in an attempt to stop the walk, and at some point he'll just lie down as if he just can't do any more work today, he's just too exhausted. If you show him a ball, his exhaustion will mysteriously disappear. If your Lab were a child, he'd be the one who would fake a stomachache to get out of going to school; he'd daydream in class and rarely show any signs of studying for a test; but his report card would have all A's and B's. When you're working with him you must keep your praise constant but low-key because of his leanings toward being unruly. If you're too hearty with your praise, Rover will become so excited he'll forget what he's being praised for—and remember, he's already trying to turn everything into a game. Labs love to be working members of the family, so teach him things that will allow him to be that. He can bring in the newspaper, your slippers, and his own leash, help with the groceries, and do anything else you can think of. Everything about this dog is worth your time and effort.

BEST ENVIRONMENT: Jogger—**Walker**—Teenagers—Children 6 to 11—
Children of any age—Elderly—Latchkey—**Active environment**—
Sedate environment (as an adult)—**Multiple dogs okay**—
Apartment—**House with yard**—Room to run—Needs daily exercise—
Camping—Hiking

Lhasa Apso

BRED TO DO. The Mastiff was outside the castle. If an intruder got past the Mastiff, the Lhasa Apso was inside to alert of strangers and possible danger by barking.

HOUSETRAINING. One of the biggest advantages of housetraining a Lhasa is that these dogs were bred to alert, so letting you know when he needs to go outside will come easily and quickly, and the house-training process can take half as long as usual. As Rover gets a little older, not only will he let you know when he needs to go out, but if you don't pay any attention to him he'll come and get you. If he were a child, he'd tug on your arm until you paid attention.

The other advantage is that though Lhasas have excellent hearing, their sense of smell is nothing special. When Rover puts his nose down and starts sniffing, you can bet he's not doing it for fun, he needs to go outside quickly.

Lhasas are born bossy and willful. There is going to have to be a meeting of the minds about the spot you've chosen for his eliminations. He's going to have definite opinions, and may not give you any say in the matter. Pay attention to his chosen spot, and see if you can work around it. Prepare yourself, because if you are the proud owner of a Lhasa Apso there will be many arguments ahead.

PERSONALITY. Did you just bring home the cutest puppy you've ever seen? I hope you've already read this. I've never known a Lhasa that wasn't bossy. I think the Lhasas got confused and now think they're Mastiffs. You're really going to have to pay attention to body language with these wee ones. Read Chapter 6, "The Peck Order Factor." Rover is going to climb that ladder anyway, and if you constantly put him in a physically dominant position—holding him above your head, letting him lie on top of you, letting him sleep on your pillow—you'll be telling him over and over that you want him to be dominant. If you start his climb on that peck-order ladder, he'll climb to the top in a New York minute.

Children in the family should be in their teens—or, if younger, very kind and gentle with animals. This dog is not going to tolerate being picked up and carried by a young child. Lhasas don't hesitate to discipline a child they think is naughty. Their perception of what's naughty may be very different from yours. Some breeds that don't get along well with children will attempt to avoid them. The Lhasa, on the other hand, insists that the child stay out of *his* way. There are also breeds that get along well with children if they're raised with them; not so the Lhasa. I've have several Lhasa owners with children in my clientele; harmony can exist but it takes considerable effort and time.

Rover will be very affectionate and playful with you, but I find that if an outsider is present, even one Rover knows, he'll put his little snub nose in the air and act as if he wouldn't lower himself to play. Play with your Lhasa as much as possible. Climbing that peck-order ladder is tough work, and if he reaches the top rung, he's going to become very serious. As long as he continues to play and show affection, you increase the possibility he'll never reach the top. Of the small breeds, the Lhasa could be the best watchdog. Remember, his job is to bark and warn you of strangers or possible danger. Because of this breeding Lhasas can make good latchkey dogs. (Don't take advantage of this and leave your dog more than nine hours. If you have to be gone longer, get Rover another dog.) When you're gone Rover goes on duty to watch the house. That's part of his job. When you're home he lets you know of possible problems; that's the other part of his job.

TRAINING. I rarely use the term "stubborn" of a dog. Usually dogs are tenacious, not stubborn. This Rover is the exception. You really haven't seen back talk until you've seen it from a Lhasa. I don't care how many times Rover sat for you. The time is going to come when you'll tell him to sit and he'll say, "Nope. Not gonna do it. Not gonna sit. I know you've said it five times, I'm not gonna sit." Go ahead, Human, put him in a sit, and watch him stand up as if he sat on a spring. You'll have to hold him in the "Sit" position, praise quickly, and stop the lesson. I don't insist on obedience training with Lhasas, but I do highly recommend correct behavior at the front door. Barking and running to the door when the bell rings are part of Rover's job, and he has absolutely no idea that you heard the doorbell. In a very short period of time Rover will be totally in control at the front door, and he will decide whom you can talk to or let in. Rover is not going to respect you automatically. You will have to earn his respect, and you can only do that if you are the Head Honcho.

BEST ENVIRONMENT: Jogger—Walker—**Teenagers**—Children 6 to 11—
Children of any age—**Elderly—Latchkey**—Active environment—**Sedate
environment—Multiple dogs okay—Apartment**—House with yard—
Room to run—Needs daily exercise—Camping—Hiking

Maltese

BRED TO DO. Maltese were bred to be carried, bred to be pampered, bred to be pleased. They are one of the breeds called sleeve dogs. Nobles carried them around in their big bell sleeves and kept them in their laps.

HOUSETRAINING. Maltese are *very* clean dogs and will avoid eliminating within shouting distance of where they spend their time. (Not just where they eat and sleep). The housetraining process can get complicated if Rover has decided he doesn't like your backyard. You'll speed the process if you carry him out and back in; this is one of the few puppies I advise letting play outside before they're completely housetrained. You're going to have to convince Rover that outside can be a fun place to be. It is very possible that you may have to provide Pee Pads, and allow Rover to go in the house every now and then. He's not going to like going outside if it's raining, snowing, or really windy.

PERSONALITY. Of the sleeve dogs I think the Maltese are the sweetest. He will let you know that he is of royal blood, but he'll do it so sweetly that you won't mind his conceit. These dogs are very affectionate, and if you show Rover love, he'll return it to you tenfold. He will be totally devoted to his Human. If for some reason you can't keep your Maltese, please spend as much time as necessary finding a new home. He's going to have a terribly tough time adjusting, and he will actually grieve your loss. Maltese are long-lived, so you could have this affectionate, sweet, devoted little dog until he's sixteen to eighteen years old.

I don't usually recommend children with a Maltese. If he's raised with them, he'll avoid the very young and tolerate the others. I've seen several Maltese that spend most of their time under the bed or coffee table or chair when the children are present. They're simply not comfortable around kids. If it comes to fight or flight, Rover will choose flight every time.

If you want a dog that you can pamper and carry around, this is the dog for you. I know of several people who take their Maltese to work with them. Maryann has a small bed for Misty in a desk drawer. Tammy sleeps in the "in" basket on Mark's desk, and the Prince has a bed right by the cash register in a bookstore, where he graciously allows customers to pet him. Remember, though, Rover was bred to be pleased, not to please. He won't hesitate to give you the cold shoulder if he feels you're not paying him enough attention.

TRAINING. These dogs are born polite. Train Rover only if you wish to. If you do work with him on commands, make sure you give an overabundance of praise. You have to teach him that pleasing you is neat. If for some reason you feel it would be beneficial to get Rover into high stress, you don't have to put him on a leash. Carrying him will give the same results.

> BEST ENVIRONMENT: Jogger—Walker—**Teenagers**—Children 6 to 11—Children of any age—**Elderly**—Latchkey—Active environment—**Sedate environment**—**Multiple dogs okay**—**Apartment**—House with yard—Room to run—Needs daily exercise—Camping—Hiking

Mastiff (Old English)

BRED TO DO. There are eight breeds of Mastiff, the Old English being the most common. Once upon a time the Mastiff was used as one of the most vicious of the fighting dogs. Breeders have taken great care to breed the fighting dog out of the Mastiff and, for the most part, they've done an excellent job. When no longer bred to fight, the Mastiff went on to guard livestock and property and to bodyguard.

HOUSETRAINING. This Rover is very territorial, even as a tiny—ah, small—ah, *young* puppy. He'll want to be outside to lay claim to his territory. As long as there's no confusion, Rover will housetrain for you easily. These dogs love to be loved, so lavish praise on Rover when he does what he's supposed to do where he's supposed to do it.

PERSONALITY. Even if you're using your Mastiff as guard, don't isolate him from you and the family. As I said, these dogs love to be loved, and they love to love. Of the massive breeds of dogs (the ones normally weighing close to two hundred pounds) I've found the Mastiff and the Rottweiler to be the most affectionate and most needy of affection. Rover will do his job beautifully, and enjoy doing it, but he wants nothing more in the world than to be with you. Mastiffs do not make good strictly outdoor dogs.

I don't hesitate to recommend Mastiffs with kids, especially ones old enough to play. You'll have to watch him with the children as he's growing, because he's going to be on the clumsy side to say the least. He will be affectionate and loving, but any dog weighing close to two hundred pounds needs to be respected and reckoned with. Teach him "Off" from the moment you bring him home. Don't wait until he's big enough knock you down by brushing up against you. Once he's grown, his gentleness with children is something to see.

When a Mastiff is doing his job as guard, if he encounters an intruder, he will knock the person down, put his cavernous mouth around the person's neck, and hold him there. If you want to make Rover a happy camper, play with him right. Get a soccer ball or basketball, let some of the air out of it, and kick it along the ground. Rover will run to it and hold it there until you kick it out from under him. I've have never seen a Mastiff that didn't enjoy this game.

I don't know why this is so, but the major problem I'm called in on with Mastiffs is their insecurity when leaving their own territory. Most Mastiffs don't like riding in the car, even if they've been conditioned to it. They're not thrilled with going for walks, if the walk takes them too far from home. As I've said, these dogs are very territorial and don't like being away from their territory. Taurus got so upset he went right through a window, just after getting home from the animal clinic. He had to make a return trip the clinic to get stitches in his leg. The following year, he tore through a screen door to get to a man who was talking to his owner. That time he had to be returned to the clinic to stop the bleeding of his gums. He now gets his boosters by way of a house call. When Brutus was walked, he would begin to tremble as soon as he was out of sight of his home. He'd shy away from any kind of confrontation with another dog, a person, blowing leaves, or low flying birds. If he and his Human walked too far, by the time he could see the house again he was a blithering idiot. I'm convinced that Mastiffs have a touch of agoraphobia, and it's a part of who they are. It doesn't make any difference what method of therapy I prescribe, the Mastiff shows only some improvement. Start getting Rover out and about from the minute you get him home. *Make sure that at no time do you say, "It's okay, it's okay."* (See Chapter 7.) I don't very often suggest socializing a dog just for the sake of socializing unless the owner plans on showing the dog. With Mastiffs I make an exception. Don't, however, begin the socializing when Rover's between eight and ten weeks of age. That's the age of fear imprinting. (By the way, if you've trained Rover as a bodyguard, he'll do his job no matter where the two of you are. He will overcome his anxiety if there is a threat to you.) You must at all times be in the Head Honcho position. Rover has to understand that you can take care of him if need be. If he feels he's his own caretaker when he's off his territory, his anxiety can easily turn to panic. Mastiffs are truly great dogs, so the time you need to take to socialize Rover will be worth the effort.

TRAINING. Absolutely do obedience work with your Mastiff. This dog is far too large and powerful to be untrained. Work hard on the "Sit" so that you can use it to get him through stress, and work hard on "Rover, let's go" so that you can get him into some stress and remain in control when he says anxiously, "Can we go home now?" Rover has natural protective tendencies and you must have control over a dog that has two hundred pounds behind his role as your protector. Use a kind hand and

Rover will do almost anything to please you. Remember he loves you with every fiber of his island-sized being.

> BEST ENVIRONMENT: Jogger—**Walker (you'll have to insist)**—Teenagers—Children 6 to 11—**Children of any age**—Elderly—Latchkey—Active environment—**Sedate environment**—Multiple dogs okay—Apartment—**House with yard**—Room to run—Needs daily exercise—Camping—Hiking

Miniature Pinscher (Min Pin)

BRED TO DO. Actually they weren't bred for any particular purpose, other than for their look, but they make great watchdogs. This breed is ancient.

HOUSETRAINING. As long as the weather isn't too cold, Rover will housetrain smoothly. Just about all you have to do is show him where you want him to go and take him through the process a few times; he'll catch on quickly. If you are housetraining during the colder months, make sure that when you take him out he really has to go.

PERSONALITY. *These dogs are barkers!* Whenever you hear that a breed makes good watchdogs, you can bet they're barkers. The Min Pin is no exception. Work with Rover on the "Quiet" command so that you have some control. Also, read Chapter 6, "The Peck Order Factor." Your understanding of that chapter, especially the section on body language, will help you a great deal in raising your Min Pin. These little sweethearts know how to use their teeth and won't hesitate to snap and bite if they become dominant. For this reason I always hesitate to recommend this Rover with children younger than eleven or so. I can hear you Min Pin owners now: "Judi, my Min Pin gets along great with my five-year-old." I'm sure he does, but I'm also sure he's good with your five-year-old by avoiding the child. This

Rover just isn't comfortable around youngsters. They're much too erratic and unpredictable for him. If a young child pinches Rover, he's not going to run off. When it comes to fight or flight, Rover will stand his ground every time.

Now that I've given you the negatives, I'll fill you in on what neat little dogs Min Pins are. Rover will be totally devoted to you. He will love you with every fiber of his being, and expect little in return. These dogs are also very intelligent. Don't ever underestimate Rover's ability to figure something out, all on his own. Duke had a Teddy Graham addiction, and he learned how to open the cupboard that held his coveted Teddy Grahams. Lady, a Shih Tzu, liked Teddy Grahams, too, but not nearly as much as Duke. Duke hated it when he got his Teddy Grahams out and Lady would beg him for some. He figured out the best way to handle this: He'd get a mouthful and drop them in front of Lady. She would eat what he so kindly gave her, and he could eat his in peace. Duke and Lady's owners had several other snacks in that cupboard, but Duke touched only the Teddy Grahams. He also didn't abuse the privilege.

TRAINING. Yes! Absolutely train your Min Pin. These dogs are popular on the show circuit, because they're born hams, and they love being in the spotlight. Use a gentle hand, and Rover will do somersaults for you.

> BEST ENVIRONMENT: Jogger—**Walker—Teenagers**—Children 6 to
> 11—Children of any age—**Elderly**—Latchkey—**Active environment**—
> Sedate environment—**Multiple dogs okay—Apartment**—House with
> yard—Room to run—Needs daily exercise—**Camping**—Hiking

Miniature Poodle

See "Standard Poodle."

Miniature Schnauzer

BRED TO DO. Can be an excellent mouser, and takes the job of protecting your territory very seriously.

HOUSETRAINING. Actually housetraining a Schnauzer goes smoothly as long as you don't get too insistent about the spot you want him to go, and if you keep the verbal discipline quick and to the point. If you put too much emphasis on verbal discipline Rover will dig in his heels, put his little paws on his little hips, and tell you, using dog expletives, just what you can do with your verbal discipline.

PERSONALITY. These little ones are born thinking they are the Number One dog of the Western World. We have absolutely no self-image problems here. The Miniatures have the same desire to protect what is theirs as the Giants and Standards do. The Miniature, though, can become a nuisance barker. Teach Rover the "Quiet" command very early, so that you can stop the barking on command. I've found that most people want their dog to bark when the doorbell rings. (The point of this totally eludes me.) Be careful what you wish for, because you'll get it: This sweetie will take over total control at your front door. You'll have to pick him up to stop him from charging people. Or you may have to put him in the backyard or another room so that you can carry on a conversation. If he were a person, the scenario would sound something like this: Rover says, "Just relax, I'll get the door." You ask, "Who was at the door?" Rover answers, "I didn't like the looks of him so I sent him away." "But who was it, Rover?" "It was that Ed McMahon dude with a check for you."

Rover will take responsibility for the front door, for the house when you're gone, for the house when you're not gone, for the yard, and eventually for himself. These dogs can easily become growlers and snappers, and it usually happens because of the Rover Peter Principle, meaning he's been promoted to his level of incompetence. I see far too many Miniature Schnauzers in my practice with behavior problems directly related to being the dominant force in the household. Read Chapter 6, "The Peck Order Factor," and apply it so that your Rover isn't one of the many. These dogs are a little like the little girl with the curl: When they're good they're very very good, and when they're bad they're horrid.

I don't usually recommend Miniatures with children. Rover won't hesitate to discipline a child he perceives as naughty, whether the child is two or fifteen. I've seen this Rover get along beautifully with children in the family, while the children's friends become a problem. I've also seen Miniatures that get along beautifully with all children, love company, and are totally devoted to their family. Growling and snapping never cross their mind.

You'll notice quickly that Rover has a tremendous amount of energy. He'll play almost any game you can think of at the drop of a hat, and he'll have as much energy at ten as he did when he was a year old. General's Humans had a pool in their backyard and one of his favorite games was to drop a ball into the pool from the diving board, jump in after it, swim to the other side of the pool, run back around to the diving board, and start again. When the family played tennis, it was General's job to retrieve out-of-bounds balls. Schatzi would lie down next to the playpen when the baby was in it. She'd watch the baby carefully; whenever he threw something out of the playpen, Schatzi would get it, jump into the playpen, give the toy back to the baby, and jump back out, ready for the next retrieval. As I said, when Rover's good he's very very good.

TRAINING. Schnauzers are very trainable. They love to learn, and they're proud when they can do something correctly. Given Rover's energy level, except for walks, your best bet is to work with him no more than fifteen minutes at a time (except in taking him for walks). If you try to stretch it out much past that, he'll become impatient and grouchy.

One of Rover's favorite things to do is go for a walk. He loves seeing and walking through the world around him. Once he learns how to walk on a leash, he'll beg and beg and beg to go for walks. Be kind, but nononsense. You're going to get some back talk, so be prepared for it. One of the ways Rover will back talk is by following the command, but somewhere else and on his own time. For example, let's say you've told

Rover to sit. He will first look at you and say, "@#*&#!" Then he will move four or five feet away from you and sit.

> BEST ENVIRONMENT: Jogger—**Walker**—**Teenagers**—Children 6 to 11—Children of any age—**Elderly**—Latchkey—**Active environment**—Sedate environment—**Multiple dogs okay**—**Apartment**—House with yard—Room to run—Needs daily exercise—**Camping**—Hiking

Mixed Breed

I don't want to leave out this very important breed of dog. After all, every breed was at one point a Mixed Breed. If you have a Mixed Breed of unknown origin, you'll notice everybody has an opinion as to what the mix is. It's very possible that your Rover could be a mix of three or four breeds. Just love him for what he is, and don't worry about his ancestors. Once, when I asked a client over the phone what breed her dog was, she said, "I don't know. He's just your basic brown dog." All puffed up with my years of experience, I told her I could probably tell her what mix he was. Well, when I saw him, I had to agree with her. George was just your basic, generic brown dog. He was a little on the neurotic side, but we got that under control, and he's doing fine now. If you do know what the components of your mixed breed are, read what I have to say about those breeds. You'll come close to figuring out how to raise your Rover.

Newfoundland

BRED TO DO. They are wonderful rescue dogs, especially in water. One was given an award because he rescued some twenty people, pulling them ashore in a lifeboat after a shipwreck.

HOUSETRAINING. The hardest part of housetraining a Newfoundland is catching him quick enough between play and sleep to get him outside. If he were human, the dialogue would sound something like this:

"Rover, it's time to go out." "Okay, just let me sleep a little longer." "Rover, it's time to go out!" The head goes under the covers. There's a muffled "I'm coming." "Rooooveeeer!" The pillow goes over the head. Hang in there, Human, you'll get him housetrained if you're patient.

PERSONALITY. When James M. Barrie wrote *Peter Pan*, the dog Nana was patterned after his own Newfoundland. (He changed her hair color.) Newfs are terrific dogs. I've had clients tell me, "Judi, it's almost as if he understands when I talk to him." That's very possible. This Rover seems to be somewhat attuned to Humans. You can trust him totally around your kids (of any age) and their friends. I saw one that stopped a little boy from going into a field of stickers, and know of another that pulled a two-year-old girl out of the swimming pool. (Occasionally I run across a Newf that takes care of the kids a little too much. If Rover takes over the caretaking role when you're there, you'll need to let him know that you're the primary caretaker and you're perfectly capable of taking care of your own kids.) Speaking of swimming pools: If you have one, don't be surprised if Rover jumps in and joins you in your afternoon swim. He loves water, he's got a very heavy coat, and in the summer months he going to seek out any cool place. Between his thick coat and the fact that he's black, he's going to be somewhat sluggish in the warmer months. Pay close attention to Rover's grooming, especially in hot weather. His hair mats easily, and he can suffer from "hot spots," a kind of skin infection. Remember, God did not create this dog, man did, and man needs to take care of him.

Newfoundlands do not like chaos. If everyone comes over for the Fourth of July picnic, you'll notice Rover somewhere in a corner or under something, paws over his ears. As much as he loves your kids, he's not going to join in when one of them has a slumber party.

Newfs can be latchkey dogs, if you don't take advantage. Try very hard to come home directly from work and spend the rest of your day and evening allowing Rover to be with you. Newfs are very polite and unassuming, so having him at your side when you're home is not going to present any problems.

Though Rover will take wonderful care of your kids, don't expect him to do any guarding or watching of the house when you're gone. If an intruder talks to Rover before intruding, Rover will lie back down and let the intruder do his intruding.

TRAINING. Do not take your Newfoundland to a large obedience class. (He may get along okay if the class is small.) A large class is more activity and stress than Rover can handle. If you *have* taken him to one of these classes, at some point he probably lay down, and refused to move. He'll say, "This is it. There's too much going on and I don't wanna do this anymore. I have a headache and I want to go home. You can stay if you like, I'll wait for you at the car." If you see this attitude, you might as well just pack up and go home, because he's not going to take one more step with you unless it's out the door. Either train Rover yourself or find a trainer who works one-on-one. These dogs are intelligent and are born knowing some obedience. Rover's favorite command is going to be "Go lie down." The obedience he doesn't already know, he'll learn quickly. Well, "quickly" might not be the correct word. Rover does nothing quickly. As an adult, he will always look as if he's in slow motion. He'll sit for you on command; it'll just take him longer than it does most other dogs.

BEST ENVIRONMENT: Jogger—Walker—Teenagers—Children 6 to 11—**Children of any age—Elderly—Latchkey—**Active environment—**Sedate environment—Multiple dogs okay—**Apartment—**House with yard—**Room to run—Needs daily exercise—**Camping (especially if it's near water)—**Hiking

---

Norwegian Elkhound

BRED TO DO. Boy, this breed is old! I was told that Elkhounds were around when hunters were using slingshots. They were—and in some places still are—used to hunt elk. The Elkhound would utter a high-pitch bark to attract the elk, and then bob and weave to get the elk to leave the herd. I always think of things from the dog's point of view. Can you imagine what must have gone through his mind the first time he saw an elk, antlers and all? It must have crossed his mind that elk are very big and, with all those pointy things on their heads, could be dangerous. When the hunter said, "Rover, go find an elk, draw it away from the herd, and lead it back to me." Rover said, "Ahem, excuse me, sir, ah . . . did you happen to see the size of one of those elks?" The hunter said, "Yup," and the dog said, "Okey-dokey, just thought I'd ask. I'll be back in just a bit." He then threw out his courageous chest and, with his big Elkhound heart, went off to do his job. Which, by the way, he did very well. Elkhounds were also used in some parts as sled dogs.

HOUSETRAINING. I haven't figured out why, but for some reason Elkies housetrain faster if only one person does the job. My theory is that Rover's relationship is different with each Human, and at the same time that he's being housetrained he has to adjust to each person. As he grows he'll do that with ease.

As puppies, Elkies are busy, busy, busy. You'll have to watch Rover closely or he'll get involved in something and totally forget he's supposed to go outside. Elkies are very clean dogs, so that will speed the process.

PERSONALITY. This dog has the unique trait of treating humans as individuals. Rover seems to know who likes to be licked and who doesn't, who will play with him and who won't, and how each individual wants to play. He'll roughhouse with one child and sit quietly while another plays with dolls. He will be every family member's best friend and close companion. I'm sure you can guess that I don't hesitate to recommend an Elkie with children of any age. If he wasn't raised with children, and he's suddenly presented with one, he'll be a little standoffish at first. Give him the time he needs to introduce himself, and once he gets used to all of the new smells and strange movements of this small human he'll accept the child with no problem.

Elkies have a gentle soul and a very mild manner. Rover may suffer in the warmer months, but he'll never complain to you. It will be up to you to see to it that he's not carrying part of his winter coat into May and June. I always tell my Elkie owners to get their dog groomed in April and then again in June. Remember, God did not create this dog, people did, and it's our responsibility to take care of him.

Elkies are hardy, sturdy little dogs. If you're a hiker and want a buddy, this is the dog for you. He will follow you over any terrain and up any mountain. Check his paw pads to make sure they're not getting bruised, because Rover will never complain to you that his feet hurt.

TRAINING. Remember your Elkie is a hunter, so if you're hiking or camping somewhere and he sees a rabbit, he's going to go dead out running after it. You must work hard on coming when called. You also might want to put serious effort into the "Halt" command. Use a gentle hand. If you become too harsh, Rover will go down into submission posture and you'll lose that part of the lesson. Let me explain. If Rover goes into a submissive posture, he will be all the way over on his back or on his side with one leg up. As soon as you bend over to get him up, he'll get more submissive. To get him up on all fours, you'll have to stand up and move away. And once submissive posturing begins, Rover will go back into it as soon as you give him another command. You'll have to stop the lesson altogether and try again later, with a kinder voice and hand. Elkies are very trainable and love to learn—or for that matter, do anything that keeps them close to you.

> BEST ENVIRONMENT: Jogger—Walker—Teenagers—Children 6 to 11—
> **Children of any age—Elderly**—Latchkey—Active environment—**Sedate**
> **environment—Multiple dogs okay**—Apartment—**House with yard**—
> Room to run—Needs daily exercise—**Camping—Hiking (during the**
> **cooler months)**

Old English Sheepdog

BRED TO DO. Bred to drove and guard. They were also used as herd dogs, retrievers, guard dogs, and, oddly enough, sled dogs. For some reason I have a hard time picturing an Old English Sheepdog pulling a sled.

HOUSETRAINING. Because these dogs' personalities vary so much, it's hard to give any general advice. The foot pads of Old English puppies are very tender, so make sure the spot you've chosen is comfortable to stand on. Rover's not going to go to a spot covered with gravel, hot sand, or hot cement. Pay very close attention to his grooming. Old Englishes' hair is fine and mats easily. If you stick to the method, and avoid any confusion, Rover should housetrain at a normal pace.

PERSONALITY. Please pay close attention to this dog's grooming! He can't see any better with hair in front of his eyes than you can. Remember, God didn't create this dog, people did, and it's our responsibility to take care of him. I'm happy to say that I'm not seeing as many Old English as I used to. I don't know if AKC shows contributed to the downfall of the Old English personality, or if a short run of popularity caused the problems. Old English have always had an independent streak, which is true of many herd dogs that are also used to guard. If that trait is exaggerated through careless breeding, we have a dog that depends solely on himself, and displays unfounded aggressive tendencies. I've always been a little leery of recommending the Old English with children. This dog is just too unpredictable to be totally trustworthy.

That having been said, if you find yourself with a good Old English Sheepdog, you are truly blessed with a wonderful dog (but still not one I'm comfortable with around young children). The independent streak I mentioned can be an advantage. Rover won't feel he needs to be at your side every minute, and he won't mind entertaining himself. As long as you don't take advantage of him, he can be a latchkey dog. At his best, your Old English is affectionate, playful, and mellow. He can devote himself to just one human or the entire family. The one trait that I've seen consistently in the Old English is their understanding that there is a sucker born every minute. Not sure about that? Watch Rover the next time you sit down to eat: He'll have his head or paw on the leg of the Human who gave him a scrap of meat three months ago. If you asked him what he was doing he'd say, "Oh, nothing. I just thought Judi looked a little down. I wanted to let her know I was there for her." He'll bring in a toy while you're watching TV and lie down with it between his paws. All you have to do is get a glance at that face and I'll bet you money you won't be able to resist playing with him. (He'll bet he's irresistible, too.) There is a good possibility that Rover will want to play fetch games. As an adult he will have a nice soft mouth. The soft mouth is the reason these dogs were used to retrieve.

TRAINING. If you have a good Old English, training will go smoothly. Just make sure you don't want him to do anything in a hurry. These dogs are never in a hurry. When you tell Rover to sit, give him what I call an Old English minute before you reinforce the command.

There's very little you can't teach Rover to do, so don't underestimate his ability to understand and learn. You may have to use a firm hand now and then to let him know you're serious. The Old English needs strong leadership from his Human. If you can't provide it, he'll take leadership on himself.

> BEST ENVIRONMENT: Jogger—**Walker**—**Teenagers**—Children 6 to 11—Children of any age—**Elderly**—**Latchkey**—Active environment— **Sedate environment**—**Multiple dogs okay**—Apartment—**House with yard**—Room to run—Needs daily exercise—**Camping**—Hiking

Pekingese

BRED TO DO. Actually they had no purpose other than to be carried and pampered by royalty. This is going to have to be our little secret. If Rover got wind of it, he'd be very insulted. He thinks he's Ace Rover, Watchdog Extraordinare.

HOUSETRAINING. You're going to know immediately when Rover needs to be taken outside. That's just about the only time you'll see him with his nose down. You're really going to have to stay on your toes, though. Peke puppies are very active; they can stop, pee, and go back to playing without skipping a beat. Watch that Rover doesn't find a favorite spot in the house. This could easily happen, because Pekes don't like to be bothered when they're busy. While your priority is going to be getting Rover housetrained. Rover's priority is going to be to continue to do whatever he was doing when you so rudely interrupted him. If he does find a favorite spot, put a bookcase on top of it and start again.

PERSONALITY. Pekes have more guts than brains. Their courage is amazing. Rover wouldn't hesitate to protect you from a lion. When I was in England I lived in a small village where nobody locked doors. There was a greeting card and gift shop whose owner lived in the back of the store. (This is very common in England.) She didn't have an alarm system; she had three Pekes and a ladder. When she closed the shop she put the ladder close to the front door and let her Pekes loose. There was *one* burglary attempt. The doomed burglar sneaked into the shop after dark and was met by a Peke around his neck, another on his arm, and a third chewing his calf. The story goes that he was the one to call the police. I asked the shop owner how she trained her Pekes. She looked at me in the very haughty manner that the English seem to be born with, and said, "My dogs don't have to be trained."

Pekes are sensitive dogs and very alert to their environment. Rover will be happy if you are; he'll try to comfort you if you're unhappy, and become restless and agitated if you're angry or if there is arguing in the house. Your Peke will absolutely love you to pieces. He's going to love every minute of the time he can be in your lap or be carried. He won't flinch at grooming, and in fact can become depressed if he's allowed to become matted.

You must read Chapter 6, "The Peck Order Factor." I've never known a male Peke that wasn't at the top of the peck-order ladder or just one rung down. I'm not sure if they climb the ladder intentionally or if we put them up there through body language mistakes. Once they're dominant, these dogs can become downright nasty and tough to handle. Whether they climb there or we put them there, it never ceases to amaze me how many Humans assume that if you have a Peke you have to put up with some nasty behavior. Peke owners seem to take in stride rules like "Don't go near Rover when he's eating" and "Leave Rover alone when he's in his favorite spot." I hear, "We can't seem to stop him from barking. He doesn't listen to a thing I say. Oh, I know he soils in the house but it's only in that one spot." "How do you discipline him?" I ask. "Judi, we tell him no but he doesn't pay any attention to us." Are you beginning to get the idea that many Humans are afraid of their Pekingese? If you have a Peke or you're planning on getting one, please insist from the beginning that you are the Head Honcho around here.

He's not going to respect you automatically; you're going to have to show strong leadership qualities. These dogs can be wonderfully loving, with really neat personalities, if you raise them right. If Rover becomes dominant, the playful and lighthearted part of him will be gone. He'll have far too many important things to worry about, like the house, your safety, and himself. All you have to do is show him that you can take care of him, against all odds. Just let him be a dog.

Rover is going to be suspicious of strangers, and even humans he knows, until he really gets to know them. Respect him. Suspicion of strangers is part of what he's all about. Pushing him will cause him to retreat when friends come over.

TRAINING. I do recommend training of some type with Pekes. They can get very bossy, and training automatically puts you in the lead position. If you decide there is really no reason to teach obedience commands, that's okay, but at least teach him the "Sit" command. Read Chapter 11, "Obedience," and you'll realize why "Sit" can be beneficial to both of you.

Pekes love to do a job, so teach Rover things that can apply around the house. Teach him the names of his toys, so that he can bring you one. Teach him how to put his toys away; definitely teach him "stand for a groom." You'll need a firm but kind hand with Rover, and expect some back talk. If you want to get Rover into high stress, you can carry him and achieve the same results.

BEST ENVIRONMENT: Jogger—Walker—**Teenagers**—Children 6 to 11— Children of any age—**Elderly**—Latchkey—**Active environment**— **Sedate environment**—**Multiple dogs okay**—**Apartment**—House with yard—Room to run—Needs daily exercise—Camping—Hiking

---

Pomeranian

BRED TO DO. Would you believe this tiny tyke was actually bred to herd? I don't know about you, but I'm having a hard time picturing exactly what this dog herded. Maybe it was geese. Poms were also used as watchdogs. Now, *that* I can understand.

HOUSETRAINING. Every once in a while I come across a personality trait I can't, for the life of me, figure out. One of those is in the female Pom. Male Poms are much easier to housetrain than females. Both, however, can easily become confused and find a favorite spot in the house. You're going to have to stick to the method to the letter. Keep verbal discipline low-key, or Rover will sit back on his heels and defy you for the hell of it.

PERSONALITY. *These dogs are barkers!* I yell this at you because barking can become a serious problem. Teach Rover the "Quiet" command so that you can stop at least some of it. Poms' bark isn't loud, but it's at a high pitch that can sound like fingernails on a blackboard. And when they do start barking, they seem to get on a roll and bark for barking's sake. Barking as a watchdog is one thing (and, I might add, Poms do that beautifully), but nuisance barking is another. Rover is going to be leery of strangers, and he will bark at them. Don't think in terms of Rover being shy; if you do that you're going to read all the wrong things into his actions, and you'll have a tendency to fall into the "It's okay, it's okay" trap. Read Chapter 6, "The Peck Order Factor," so that you can avoid Rover becoming dominant because of body language confusion. Poms are strong-willed dogs, and both males and females will become dominant if you hand power to them. Most are allowed on the furniture, which is fine, but keep Rover off the back of the couch or chair. That spot puts him in a physically dominant position, and even if it's unintentional, over a period of time he will become dominant, especially if you let him sleep on top of you when you lie down on the couch. But if he's on the back of the couch or chair when you're not sitting yourself, don't worry about it. Remember, he's an excellent watchdog, and the top of the furniture may give him a better vantage point.

Did you just bring home the cutest puppy you've ever seen in your life? I don't blame you. You think he's cute now, wait until you see him do the Pomeranian patter. It's like a little dance done with the front legs. You won't be able to resist a smile when he does it. Poms are lively, alert, and full of personality. They're not too comfortable around children, even if raised with them. If there's a toddler running around,

Rover will do everything he can to avoid him. The same goes for almost all children younger than ten or so.

TRAINING. Poms are proud dogs, and they love to strut their stuff. Use a kind hand and work with him to give him stuff to strut. As you know, I don't recommend obedience training with all dogs, and with this tiny tot structured obedience may not be necessary. I do, however, recommend teaching Rover how to walk on a leash correctly. During the cooler months Rover will love to go for walks, and he'll walk at your side as if he owns the sidewalk. Please shorten your stride, and slow your walking down a bit to accommodate Rover's tininess.

> BEST ENVIRONMENT: Jogger—**Walker—Teenagers**—Children 6 to 11— Children of any age—**Elderly—Latchkey (only if there's another dog)—Active environment—Sedate environment (Rover will fit in no matter your activity level)—Multiple dogs okay—Apartment—** House with yard—Room to run—Needs daily exercise—Camping—Hiking

Pug

BRED TO DO. Pugs have always been companion dogs, and they have always been very good at their job.

HOUSETRAINING. About the only time you'll see Rover with his nose down is when he's looking for a place to go. All you have to do is watch for his nose to go down and get him outside; you'll have him housetrained in no time. If you have children, Rover will want to be where they are, so, if possible, get the kids involved in the housetraining process.

PERSONALITY. *These dogs snore!* I yell this at you because I've seen too many of these sweethearts banished to the other side of the house, so the humans can sleep. If you can't stand snoring sounds, don't adopt a Pug.

I recommend Pugs for children of any age, especially kids with emotional disturbances or physical handicaps, and for the elderly, whether they are up and about or disabled in some way. Rover will love with all of his heart anyone who seems to need special attention. Winston was the best buddy of a twelve-year-old child with Down syndrome. It was amazing how many tricks that child taught Winston to do. I'm not sure how it happened but I was told that Winston's presence helped improve the child's learning. I was asked by a psychologist to recommend a dog for a child with anorexia. He was hoping she would understand the importance of the dog's nutritional and eating needs. The parents adopted the female Pug I recommended. The young girl was not impressed by the puppy; she wouldn't feed her and even refused to name her. Pugster (my name for her) insisted on interfering with everything the child did; she followed her everywhere, curled up in her lap every time she sat down, slept under the covers in her bed, and in every way became a major part of the girl's life whether she liked it or not. It took three or four months, but the little girl finally caved in and fell in love with her dog. She named her Fudge, and took on the responsibility of feeding her. It took quite some time, but there is no doubt in the parents' minds that Fudge was, and still is, a major factor in the child's return to health.

The two major disadvantages of Pugs are heavy shedding, and snoring. Otherwise, the Pug is an almost perfect pet. Because of their heavy coat and excess skin, they are very uncomfortable in the heat. You'll have to make a conscious effort to respect this. If you want him to take a walk at two in the afternoon in ninety-eight-degree weather, he'll do it because he loves you. If Pugs were human, they would be called insightful. They would know when you need a hug, when you need a stiff drink, and when you need a night out. Pugs are affectionate with their Humans; they'll give you more love than you've ever known, and all they ask in return is your love.

TRAINING. If you decide to work with Rover on obedience, do it because you want to, not because he needs it. I think Pugs are born knowing some obedience commands, and all you have to do is show Rover a few things to jog his memory. If you have two left feet and are all thumbs, this is the dog for you. Pugs are polite and patient, too. Winston's Child would always get Winston's leash out long before he was ready to take

Winston for a walk. Winston would contain his excitement while his child dressed himself. He waited patiently while his child tied his shoes, and sat quietly while his child put his collar and leash on. There was always the possibility that Winston would have to wait a half hour or more before actually going for the walk.

Pay attention to Rover's breathing. If it sounds like he's beginning to hyperventilate, end the walk or lesson.

> BEST ENVIRONMENT: Jogger—**Walker (as long as the walk's not too long)**—Teenagers—Children 6 to 11—**Children of any age**—**Elderly**—Latchkey—Active environment—**Sedate environment**—**Multiple dogs okay**—**Apartment**—House with yard—Room to run—Needs daily exercise—Camping—Hiking

Redbone Coonhound

BRED TO DO. Coons are his specialty, but he'll hunt cougars and wildcats as well. Can you imagine what went through this dog's mind the first time he came across a cougar? "Ahem . . . excuse me, sir. Did you happen to notice the size of the ram that cougar just had for lunch? Do you think he understands that I'm the chaser and he's the chasee? Okey-dokey, here I go. Here, kitty kitty. Get in the tree, kitty kitty." Hunting is a passion with this dog.

HOUSETRAINING. All the Redbones I've seen have been used as hunters. Housetraining goes quickly, because they seem to know from the outset that outside is the place to go. The hardest part of training is knowing the difference between nose down looking for a place to go, and nose down exploring.

PERSONALITY. Redbones are mellow, laid back, and sure of themselves. If you don't plan on using Rover to hunt, make sure he gets plenty of exercise. Also, don't be surprised if you hear a cat screaming, "Would you do something with your damn dog so I can get out of this tree?" Rover is going to be hurt if you don't praise him for treeing this animal.

In fact, he may wonder why you're not getting your trusty hunting rifle.

Redbones do not make good city pets. Their exercise requirements must be respected. If you're a slow jogger or walker, Rover will love being your buddy. If you're a runner or a fast jogger, the exercise would be great, but you must take into account Rover's terrific nose. You can be running along beautifully, then all of a sudden lose Rover to a scent. Your best bet is to backtrack and jog in place while Rover explores. If you don't plan on using your Redbone, at least get him into field trials. His ability as a hunter is too keen to let it go to waste.

You don't have to have children to make this Rover happy, but it would sure help. He'll will lie down and let kids climb all over him. Big Red would slow his pace to accommodate the stride of his five-year-old Human. He would also insist on being a part of the kids' fun when they put the tent up to camp out in the backyard. Swimming isn't his favorite thing, but he'll do it for the kids.

TRAINING. If you plan on using Rover to hunt, very little training will be necessary. He will do obedience for you but his heart won't be in it. If you plan on hunting with Rover, teach him the obedience that applies in the field. He'll become frustrated and ornery if you expect nothing more than "Sit" "Stay down," and "Heel." Use a gentle hand in any training.

BEST ENVIRONMENT: **Jogger (if you're slow)—Walker—**Teenagers—Children 6 to 11—**Children of any age—**Elderly—Latchkey—**Active environment—Sedate environment—Multiple dogs okay—**Apartment—House with yard—**Room to run—Needs daily exercise—Camping—**Hiking

---

Rhodesian Ridgeback

BRED TO DO. I can't wait to tell you what these dogs were used for. Rhodies are called safari dogs because they were used to hunt lion and puma. Can you imagine the courage? Lions show complete contempt for anyone thinking himself an adversary. Not so when they come up against a Rhodesian. Even the mighty lion will run. (Well, maybe not run exactly, but quicken his saunter.)

HOUSETRAINING. The hardest part of housetraining Rover is going to be getting him to come back in the house. He's going to love being outside, and won't mind whatever Mother Nature decides to do with the weather. Rhodies are very opinionated, and your puppy will have definite opinions about where he wants to go. If he doesn't like the spot you've chosen, he'll let you know. If the spot he chooses is okay, go along with him.

PERSONALITY. Rhodies are amazing dogs. They can cross the line between obedient pet and ferocious hunter in a heartbeat. I'm assuming your Rhodie is a companion and not being used for hunting. Safaris aren't common in the United States, and anyway the lions are in zoos. Rover is still going to be courageous, and he's still going to hunt. *Do not have livestock,* large or small, and a Ridgeback. If he can't hunt lion, he'll hunt cow. If you are a camper or hiker, please take Rover. He'll love the exercise, and he'll enjoy hunting rabbits.

This is not a breed I recommend with children. Rover doesn't have the patience necessary to make a good children's dog. He also has strong protective tendencies, and he may not tolerate the kids' friends. I've never known a Rhodie that wasn't dominant over the whole household. That is, until I'm called in. These are very strong-willed dogs, and will take over if given even the slightest encouragement. Read Chapter 6, "The Peck Order Factor," and Chapter 8, "The Head Honcho Human." You're going to have to know how to maintain your own dominant status if you plan on having a decent relationship with your Ridgeback. Rover needs strong leadership qualities in his Human.

The loyalty of Rhodesian Ridgeback owners is wonderful. I've never known any to have any other breed. And I've noticed they know this breed very well. They are aware of the Rhodie's strong will, and don't pretend he's mellow and passive. I don't think there's a passive bone in this dog's body.

As I've said, he's very opinionated and won't hesitate to let you know his likes and dislikes. If Rhodies were human, they'd be CEOs or public speakers. They'd never make good politicians, because they don't have the ability to double-talk. You will always know what's on Rover's mind. When you buy Rover toys or things to chew, keep your receipts. If he doesn't like what you got, you might as well take it back, because he's never going to like it. Don't think you can give it to him later. He won't like it any more later than he did the first time you gave it to him.

With most dogs, no matter the breed or mix, I recommend offering one diet and sticking to it. With your Rhodie you may have to try a couple of foods before he finds the one he likes. Try very, very hard not to give Rover human food. From the first potato chip you give him he will insist on human food from that point on. These dogs are terrible beggars. They have no shame or pride when it comes to your food.

TRAINING. You absolutely must train your Rhodesian Ridgeback! Training automatically puts you in the lead position and you're going to want to take advantage of anything that promotes you to the alpha position. You'll need a firm hand, but make sure it doesn't become harsh. If you become too harsh, Rover will balk at everything you try to teach. You're going to see some back talk, especially if a command doesn't make sense to Rover. Make sure you work hard on "Rover, let's go." Rhodies are powerful dogs, and won't hesitate to drag you along if there's something they want to see.

> BEST ENVIRONMENT: Jogger—**Walker—Teenagers (they must be strong enough to demand respect)**—Children 6 to 11—Children of any age—Elderly—**Latchkey—Active environment—Sedate environment (Rover will adjust to you)**—Multiple dogs okay—Apartment—**House with yard—Room to run**—Needs daily exercise—**Camping—Hiking (if he's trustworthy off leash)**

Rottweiler

BRED TO DO. Used to herd and guard. The Rottweiler would help with the herding; then, when the other herding dogs went of duty, Rover would guard the herd. This job means he has to do some serious independent thinking. He's also used in police work, but mostly in guarding and protection. He can be a hell of a tracker, as well.

HOUSETRAINING. You're going to get a lot of back talk no matter what the circumstances. If Rover were a child, the scenario would go something like this: "Rover, it's time to go outside." With his hands on his hips and a defiant look on his face, he'll reply, "I don't have to do what you say, you're not my mother!" Put your own hands on your own hips and say, "Rover, this is not a democracy. This is a monarchy, and I'm the monarch! Now, get outside!" Some of his back talk is bluff, and he really wants to please you. Stick to the method and as long as there's no confusion, he'll housetrain easily.

PERSONALITY. If you get a good one, Rotts are terrific. I say "if," because this dog has become popular. Unfortunately, that automatically means breeding goes on with no attention to temperament. Given the Rott's natural aggressive traits, bad breeding can easily produce some nasty-tempered dogs with uncontrolled aggressiveness. There are veterinarians who refuse to see Rottweilers even as puppies. I've seen three-month-old Rotts that would love a chunk of me, and of anybody else whom they perceive to be a challenge or a threat. The great power of these dogs mixes very badly with a poor disposition. Before adopting a Rott insist on seeing the bitch and, if possible, the stud. Good Rotts are mellow and self-assured. They know their power and won't hesitate to use it if the situation warrants.

I'm no longer surprised when someone says, "Judi, he doesn't even bark when the doorbell rings." Humans, listen up! An intruder is not going to ring your doorbell. You say, "Yeah, but I want people to know I have a Rottweiler." All you have to do is let Rover go to the door with you. If the person on the other side of the door is a potential burglar, he will see a very large, mean-looking dog at your side, and he'll go burgle on the next block. He'll probably even avoid the houses behind yours. Take my word for it, everyone is going to know you have a Rottweiler. Read Chapter 9, "Natural Protectiveness."

All Rotts are leaners. It comes to them naturally. If you could see

Rover herd, you'd notice he uses his body to get a stray back into the herd. Since he doesn't have cattle or sheep to lean on, you'll do. One aspect of his leaning can become very annoying. Because he's so big, when he leans on you his head is right under your hand. When he leaned on you for the first time, your hand was right there on top of his head, so you stroked him. I mean, he was right there. Right? Boy, you've gone and done it. He now expects you to pet him when he leans, and if you don't he'll use his island-sized head to throw your hand around so you'll notice him. He doesn't know that his 150-plus pounds leaning on you already clued you in that he was there.

Rotts are very much people dogs. They make terrible latchkey dogs! Most people are surprised when they realize how affectionate and loving—and needy—Rotts are. They need to be with you and they need your affection and love. Kinda shoots holes in the macho image, doesn't it?

If you have a good Rottweiler, he can easily be the best dog you've ever had. He'll take care of you and yours, as well as your property. Even when Rover's a pup, you'll notice that when you let him out he'll pause just outside the door. His chest will be out and his ears will be up and forward. He's letting the world know that he's taking care of his people and his territory. It's very possible that you will never see Rover totally in protective mode: You and/or your property may never need to be protected. What you must keep in mind at all times is that these gentle giants can top out at two hundred pounds.

TRAINING. I knew you'd be ahead of me on this one. Of course, I'm going to highly recommend training your Rott. The last thing you want is two hundred pounds of happy unruliness. As soon as you bring him home, start letting him know that you are the Head Honcho. Begin introducing Rover to the leash when he's about three months old. The biggest obedience problem I see with Rotts arises because their Humans have waited until the pup's about six months old before they put a leash on him. If you put an untrained Rover on a leash at six months and he decides he wants to check out a scent ten feet away, you're going to have absolutely no choice but to go along with him. He's not being willful or naughty, and he's not intentionally pulling you around, but unless your upper body strength is greater than his, whither he goes, you shall follow. Once he understands what this leash stuff is all about he'll love walking at your side and going whither you go. Serious, independent thinking is a part of what this dog is all about. Don't be surprised when you're confronted with his back talk. Once he learns something (and he'll learn quickly), he'll figure out a way around it. You will say, "Rover, sit," and he will say, "Now, Human, let's think about this for a minute. Can you honestly give me a good reason for sitting right now? After all, I'll stand immediately anyway, so why bother sitting in the first place?" You're going to need a firm—but loving—hand. Don't get so bogged down in training that you forget to let Rover play. Like Dobermans, Rotts can get far too serious, and totally wrapped up in their duties. They need light hearted play and affection.

BEST ENVIRONMENT: Jogger—**Walker—Teenagers**—Children 6 to 11—Children of any age—Elderly—Latchkey—Active environment—**Sedate environment—Multiple dogs okay**—Apartment—**House with yard**—Room to run—Needs daily exercise—**Camping—Hiking**

St. Bernard

BRED TO DO. Primarily used to rescue in the Alps. Often you hear stories of St. Bernards that knew in advance that there would be an avalanche. Most commonly, St. Bernards worked in pairs. One would stay with the person trapped in the snow, keeping him warm with his body, and the other would lead the rescuers to the site.

HOUSETRAINING. This is simple. If it's winter Rover will housetrain quickly. If it's summer, you'll have to talk him out from under the air-conditioning vent. If it's winter, you'll have a hard time getting him back in the house. If it's summer, you'll have a hard time getting him to stay out long enough to go. See? Told you it was simple. One of the advantages in housetraining a Saint is that he's going to want to be wherever you are.

PERSONALITY. *St. Bernards slobber and shed, heavily.* I hope you didn't adopt a Saint without knowing about the slobbering problem. If you did, it means you've used words like "gross" and "yuck," and you've called the breeder and possibly your veterinarian to ask if there's any way to do something about the slobbering. The shedding is easily controlled: Have Rover groomed regularly. You won't have to have him groomed as often as some other breeds but you should plan on doing it at least every four months or so. And you'll help him out a great deal if you have him groomed in April and again in June. Remember, he comes from the Alps, and he carries his coat with him wherever he goes. I've seen far too many Saints with "hot spots," skin infections due to hair matting, usually on the hips. Remember, God did not create this dog. Humans did, and it's up to Humans to take care of him. I'm hoping that if you have a Saint it's because you love the breed and you're aware of the drawbacks.

Unfortunately, Saints have become unpredictable, which means untrustworthy. Size and mask started winning shows, so breeders started breeding for size and facial colors and ignored disposition. If you get a good Saint, you've got a great dog. With a good Saint you'll have all the love, devotion, and companionship you could ever want. He'll let your children pull his ears and climb all over him, and then he'll help you tuck them into bed at night. If you live where the summers are really hot, you'll notice Rover will be like a piece of the furniture. You'll find you have to walk over him a lot. Go ahead; he won't mind. When it cools down in the evening he'll be up and ready for his required daily walk. Oops—did I forget to mention that Rover will need at least a daily walk? Saints don't require a lot of exercise, but they must have some. Remember, this dog is used to climbing mountains in the snow. If you're a hiker and you want a hiking buddy, this is the dog for you. He'll love every minute of being with you, and the challenge of the climb will be almost as rewarding for him as it is for you. When you reach the summit, the two of you will enjoy your achievement. Greg often hikes with his Saint, Brandy, and Brandy loves it. One day, Brandy refused to go. Every time Greg started out, Brandy would turn and go back to the car. Thinking there might be something wrong with Brandy, Greg drove him back to the house and went hiking alone. When Greg was about halfway up the trail, he was hit by a rock slide and his leg was broken in two places. Fortunately, he was hiking with two other people, who were able to get help and get him down the mountain. When he called to tell me about Brandy's refusal to go along that day, I reminded him that Saints are known to have the ability to predict an avalanche. Do you suppose Brandy was able to predict a rock slide? I can tell you, Greg is a believer. If Brandy ever again refuses to go hiking, I think it's a safe bet that Greg will stay home.

TRAINING. If you don't want to do the "Sit," "Stay," and "Down" stuff, don't worry about it. Your Saint already knows you're in control, and he respects the fact. You must, however, train Rover how to walk correctly on a leash. As I said, he needs a daily walk, and it should be pleasant for both of you. For some reason, Saints don't like smaller dogs, and you're not going to want all 120 pounds of him dragging you along while he chases a Cocker. Do not take Rover to a large obedience class. He's going to want to get at the smaller dogs, and he's not going to like the chaos. Saints are tranquil dogs, and they like the world around them to be tranquil as well.

BEST ENVIRONMENT: Jogger—**Walker (not in the heat)**—Teenagers—Children 6 to 11—**Children of any age (only if you have a good St. Bernard)—Elderly**—Latchkey—Active environment—**Sedate environment—Multiple dogs okay (if another Saint or of like size)**—Apartment—**House with yard**—Room to run—Needs daily exercise—**Camping—Hiking**

Saluki

BRED TO DO. Way back when, in the land of Persia, Salukis were used to hunt gazelles. Gazelles are speedy and very agile—at least the ones I've seen on the Discovery Channel are. This dog was fast enough to catch a gazelle, and strong enough to bring it down. Okay, now let's talk about the fact that this dog had to compete with lions, tigers, and cheetahs. If Rover began the chase and saw a tiger out of the corner of his eye, did he back off? Did the big cats and the Saluki share? I wonder if the cheetah and the Saluki ever raced. Did one of them say, "I'll bet I can beat you?" Salukis have also been—and still are—used as watchdogs. Salukis have an excellent sense of hearing and remarkable sight.

HOUSETRAINING. These beauties are clean dogs, and as long as it's not too cold they don't mind being outside. Salukis are also very sensitive, so keep the verbal discipline low-key. If you get too firm in verbal discipline Rover will fall apart before your very eyes. As long as there's no confusion, Rover will housetrain quickly.

PERSONALITY. As I said, Salukis are sensitive dogs. If you're sad, Rover will put his head on your lap and try to comfort you. If you're happy and laughing, Rover will bounce around you like a puppy. He will get moody and restless if there's arguing. He will be sensitive to the environment as well. If there's a sudden drop or rise in the barometric pressure Rover will become obviously agitated. He'll go outside and turn around and want right back in. He'll come in and in no time want back out. If you keep an eye on Rover, you won't have to watch the weather reports.

Picture yourself sitting with a flyswatter waiting for that pesky fly to land. Rover is at your side, watching the same fly. You were all set to get it—then you lost sight of it. You look everywhere for that fly; but company arrives and the phone rings. You've forgotten the fly by now, but if you look at Rover you'll notice he hasn't taken his eyes off it. With his amazing sight and concentration, he'll keep that fly in his sights until you swat it or he gets bored with it. With his sharp hearing he probably heard the fly tease, "Nonny nonny nonny, you can't catch me." The abilities of the Saluki are amazing. If Rover lifts his head suddenly, you can bet he heard something that he believes needs his attention. Of course you didn't hear it, but the amazing thing is that he probably heard it long before even the other dogs in the neighborhood. At the beginning of each new season, Rover is going to be a bit restless. He's going to have to filter through, and if possible, identify, the new sounds that come with rain, snow, and wind. Not to worry, he'll adjust soon.

If you're a jogger or runner, and you want a buddy, this is the dog for you. Just make sure you condition him as you did yourself.

TRAINING. If you praise Rover often, he will turn cartwheels for you. Salukis are affectionate dogs, and all you have to do is show love in return. Use a gentle hand. If you decide not to go the structured obedience route, make sure you work hard on coming when called. If you have Rover out in open fields, off leash, and he sees a rabbit, he's going to be off like a shot before you know what happened. Do me a favor and pause for a minute to watch the speed and grace of this beautiful dog. Okay, now you can try and get him back to you. Don't be surprised if he returns with the rabbit in his mouth.

BEST ENVIRONMENT: **Jogger**—Walker—Teenagers—**Children 6 to 11**—Children of any age—Elderly—Latchkey—**Active environment**—Sedate environment—**Multiple dogs okay**—Apartment—**House with yard**—**Room to run**—**Needs daily exercise**—**Camping**—Hiking

---

Samoyed

BRED TO DO. Samoyeds were mostly used as sled dogs, but they also make great watchdogs and have been known to hunt a walrus or two.

HOUSETRAINING. It takes time and patience to housetrain a Samy. My theory of this is based on the fact that all the Samys I've known and worked with are serious creatures of comfort. They did a very good job as sled dogs, not minding the cold and the long distances. But they were very happy when they became popular as companion dogs. They love sleeping in, they love carpets, and they love not having to live outside in the cold like their ancestors. Don't get me wrong, they're proud of their ancestors, but they prefer the life of luxury. I am going to make an exception to my rule of outside being off-limits except for eliminations until Rover's housetrained. With your Samy, make sure being outside is a positive experience, and go ahead and play with him outside. Compare the time it will take to housetrain Rover to the wonderful years ahead, and it won't seem that long.

PERSONALITY. *These dogs are barkers and can be diggers!* I yell this at you because I've found most owners aren't aware how bad the barking can be until they get complaints from neighbors. One of the problems with the barking is that when they're excited, Samys can hit a pitch that goes right through you and sets every nerve on edge. Work on the "Quiet" command.

Since Samys are a northern breed, digging is part of their behavior. Mother Nature tells the Samy to dig in the soil to get cool, and dig in snow to get warm. Of the northern breeds, Samoyeds seem to have fewer digging problems. Remember, the more emphasis you put on the digging, the longer it's going to go on.

Samys are also on the high-strung side, which adds to their tendency to bark at every sound and dig out of frustration. Read the chapter on Problem Solving.

Samoyeds are sensitive dogs. Rover will frolic when you're happy, put his head on your lap if you're sad, and become downright naughty if there's arguing. If there's too much discord in the household, he'll become depressed. And whenever there's a sudden change in the barometric pressure, you'll notice he walks with his head low and wants outside and then right back in. Samys are good with children if they're raised with them. If a child is plunked down in the middle of Rover's life, he may see it as an intruder. It wouldn't occur to him to hurt the child, but he will avoid it when possible.

Samoyeds do not make good latchkey dogs. They're used to working in teams and need your companionship or that of another dog.

Pay close attention to your Samoyed's grooming. Remember he's a northern breed and carries a heavy coat. To keep Rover comfortable you should have him groomed at least four times a year. When spring arrives, help him shed his winter coat. Have him groomed in April and then again in May. Believe me, he will thank you for your caring.

TRAINING. I do recommend training with Samys. They need strong leadership in their lives, and working with Rover will help to put you in the leader's role. Use a gentle hand at all times. If you become too harsh, Rover will fall apart before your very eyes, trying to go down into submission. He can't sit for you if he's trying to get on his back.

Rover will be in seventh heaven if you teach him to pull the kids in a wagon.

BEST ENVIRONMENT: Jogger—Walker—Teenagers—Children 6 to 11—**Children of any age—Elderly**—Latchkey—**Active environment (in the cooler months)—Sedate environment—Multiple dogs okay—**Apartment—**House with yard**—Room to run—Needs daily exercise—**Camping (he will take very good care of your campsite)**—Hiking

---

Schipperke

BRED TO DO. Bred mostly to be used on boats. This little dog could swim, guard, and hunt. I'm told Rover can put a cat to shame as a mouser and ratter.

HOUSETRAINING. Rover can put a cat to shame when it comes to curiosity as well. Don't give him run of the house until he's completely housetrained. Make sure you confine him when you can't watch him, and keep both eyes on him when you're around. The last thing you want is to find he's urinated in your favorite shoes because he found your closet too fascinating to leave. If you stick to the method and keep a close eye on him, he'll be housetrained before you know it.

PERSONALITY. Schippers are enthusiastic about everything they do and everything you do. It's easy to find yourself giving positive reinforcement for negative behavior with these little tykes. If you're on your hands and knees planting a rosebush, Rover is absolutely positive you're there for him. He will do everything possible to get you to play; he'll sit at your side and watch everything you do; then, after the rosebush is safely in the ground, he'll dig it up so that you guys can play that neat planting game again. I've known a few Schippers named Shadow because they wanted to be with their Human every minute possible. I wish I could tell you it's because he's so totally devoted to you that he can't bear a moment without you. Sorry, but he just wants to be involved in everything you do. If he's allowed on the furniture, he'll love every minute of helping you make your bed. With just a bit of encouragement, he'll take a bath with you, or at least watch you take a bath. He'll be under your feet constantly when you're cooking, not because he's waiting for food to drop, but because he really wants to know how you make spaghetti.

Rover can be a child's best friend, if the child is old enough to be gentle and respectful. Given Rover's curiosity, imagine how neat he'd find it to have a child of his own to lift up the rock and see what that was that went under it.

Rover is suspicious of strangers, so he's not going to get too involved with his child when friends come over. Don't confuse this suspicion with shyness; this dog doesn't have a shy bone in his body. He'll get to know strangers in his own time and in his own way. Don't push him, or from that point on he'll have a problem with the stranger you pushed him to meet.

TRAINING. Schippers are intelligent and don't mind learning. When you start working with Rover you'll notice he suddenly "clicks in" to the fact that he's learning something. Use a kind hand and Rover will learn whatever you want him to.

Schipperkes have a very faithful following; once someone owns a Schipperke he won't have any other dog. One of the reasons for this devotion is this dog's trainability. Don't let all that learning capacity go to waste.

Pay attention to the fact that Rover is black. He's very close to the ground, and his color absorbs heat. In the warmer months, use common sense about the times of day you pick to work with him outside.

> BEST ENVIRONMENT: Jogger—**Walker—Teenagers—Children 6 to 11**—Children of any age—**Elderly**—Latchkey—**Active environment— Sedate environment—Multiple dogs okay**—Apartment—**House with yard**—Room to run—Needs daily exercise—**Camping (as long as you understand that he'll make a beeline for any small wildlife)**—Hiking

Scottish Terrier

BRED TO DO. Bred to hunt animals in their den. Scotties will hunt fox, badger, otter and rabbit, but I'm told their favorite is the fox. Foxes are more of a challenge, and Scotties love a challenge.

HOUSETRAINING. It is very possible that the color of your Scottie will determine how easily he'll housetrain. If he's Black, he'll want to please you enough to make housetraining go smoothly. If he's Brindle, you're going to run into some defiance, so be prepared to try a little harder for a little longer.

PERSONALITY. "Independent" is the key word here. Of course, "proud" has to be another key word, and I must add "tenacious" as well. (I prefer "tenacious" to "stubborn." It's kinder, don't you think?) Boy, are you in for a lot of back talk. Scotties are very opinionated. If your Scottie were a person, he would sound something like this: "I'll sleep where *I* want to sleep! So get used to it! I appreciate the dog bed, but I can't stand wicker, I think it looks tacky! Why did you get me a plastic food bowl? Didn't you know that I could be allergic to plastic? Well, think about *me* next time, not what goes with the kitchen tile!" Think about it this way, Human. You will never have to guess what Rover wants and doesn't want. You will always know exactly where you stand. I have no doubt that Rover thinks himself to be a direct descendant of Scottish royalty, and he expects to be treated as such.

Scotties are plumb full of personality. Don't adopt a Scottie if you want a lapdog. He'll be happy to lie next to you on the couch, but it won't be because he wants to be close to you every minute, it'll be because he wants to take a nap, and the couch is comfortable.

"Courageous" should be added to the key words list. This dog will stand his ground, no matter what. He will fight any demons and dragons that threaten his family. Scotties are very much family dogs. Rover will love, and guard, every single member of your family with every fiber of his being, but he'll pay little or no attention to company unless they've spent a great deal of time with him. His devotion is to you, and he really doesn't want to be bothered with strangers. Make sure you read Chapter 8, "The Head Honcho Human." Given Rover's strong will and independence, he can become dominant very easily. What you'll notice is that, right out of the blue, Rover will snap at you. Scotties rarely warn with a growl. Brindles have stronger aggressive tendencies than Black Scotties do. The Blacks seem to want to please more, and they are a little more lighthearted than Brindles. Make sure you spend a lot of time playing with your Scottie. These dogs can take on too much responsibility and become far too serious. Read Chapter 5, "Playtime with Rover." I've never known a Scottie that enjoyed fetch, but I have known several that love "Go find . . ."

I'm always a little hesitant to recommend Scotties with children. If you do have small children and you're thinking about getting a Scottie, please make sure you see the bitch and, if possible, the stud. Black Scotties are likelier to be good with kids. No matter the age of a child, Rover won't hesitate to discipline him if he perceives him as naughty. The child must be old enough to be dominant with either the Black or Brindle. Remember, Rover's a family dog and may not take too kindly to your children's friends.

TRAINING. Use a gentle hand and a kind voice. Despite all his bravado, Rover is very sensitive to discipline and praise. You're going to see back talk with some commands and out-and-out defiance with others. Hang in there; Rover is a very proud dog, and once he learns something he wants to do it well.

If you work on nothing else, make sure Rover walks correctly on a leash. Most Scotties have nothing but contempt for other dogs. You don't want him going after every dog he sees.

If you take Rover any place that he can run free, make sure you bring your binoculars. If Rover sees a rabbit, you'll need them to keep track of where he is. I hate to say this, but I haven't been able to figure out a way to get a Scottie to come when called once he's gone into hunt mode. Work hard on the "Come" command, though, so that you can recall him when the hunt is over.

BEST ENVIRONMENT: Jogger—**Walker—Teenagers**—Children 6 to
11—Children of any age—Elderly—Latchkey—**Active environment**—
Sedate environment—Multiple dogs okay—Apartment—**House with
yard—Room to run—Needs daily exercise (a good long walk or
hard play will do it)—Camping**—Hiking

Shar-Pei

BRED TO DO. Long ago, when dogfighting was the in thing to do in
China, the Shar-Peis were serious fighters and very good at their job.
The Shar-Peis were praised because they were the protagonists.

HOUSETRAINING. When Shar-Peis are five to twelve weeks old they
are easy to housetrain. That is, if you follow the method and there's no
confusion. When they reach around fourteen to sixteen weeks, they seem
to wake up one morning with a defiant mind of their own. If you don't
have Rover housetrained by that age, or if you don't adopt him until that
age, you've got your work cut out for you. He will put his wrinkled little paws on his wrinkled little hips and say, "I prefer the carpet under
the dining room table!" You may have to spend a few days doing nothing but keeping an eye on Rover. Look forward to getting him housetrained, because once you have, accident will happen rarely if at all.

PERSONALITY. Before I even begin telling you about the Shar-Pei, you
have to promise me that you will get your Rover to the veterinarian the
moment you adopt him or her. This breed can have an eye problem
called antropion: The eyelids turn in, against the eyeball. Shar-Peis can
have ear cartilage so thick that it must be thinned out to enable them
to hear properly. They can have constant allergy problems, and in the
summer they can suffer from heat rashes between their wrinkles. If I'm
called about a Shar-Pei, whether there's a behavior problem, or the
owner wants to do obedience training, the first thing I do is ask about
the dog's health.

Also, I want you to get Rover used to being handled. Like Chows,

Shar-Peis don't like being held close. I think it causes anxiety, not anger. Work on being able to hold him in a relaxed manner, so that he doesn't struggle. I've seen far too many Shar-Peis that have to be sedated just to have a normal physical.

Now that I've gotten that over with, I can tell you about Shar-Peis. There are so many personality variations in this breed, it's hard to list across-the-board traits. I've worked with Shar-Peis that are terrific—loving, affectionate, and great with kids. I've also known some that have personality traits like those of black Chows.

Aggression toward both humans and other dogs is not unusual. Remember, Shar-Peis were bred as dogfighters, and they were the protagonists. This is a very ancient breed in China, but a very young breed in the United States. Breeders have been working hard to develop good temperament, but they still have a long way to go. All the Shar-Peis I know, without exception, have natural protective tendencies. For the most part they're very independent dogs, and some couldn't care less if they please you. They are also not big fans of other dogs. Any other dogs.

TRAINING. I give the same advice to Shar-Pei owners that I give to Chow Chow owners: You must teach Rover that pleasing you is neat. The best way to do that is through copious praise. Praise him for the slightest good deed. Read Chapter 9, "Natural Protectiveness," and give Rover a job to do. The tendency is already there, all you have to do is direct it.

Make sure you work with Rover on walking correctly on a leash. When you walk him, you're not going to want him lunging at every dog he sees. You're going to see quite a bit of back talk and blatant defiance. Use a firm but kind hand, and be prepared to be patient.

BEST ENVIRONMENT: Jogger—**Walker—Teenagers**—Children 6 to 11—Children of any age—Elderly—**Latchkey**—Active environment—**Sedate environment**—Multiple dogs okay—Apartment—**House with yard**—Room to run—Needs daily exercise—Camping—Hiking

---

Shetland Sheepdog (Sheltie)

BRED TO DO. Bred to herd. What sets Shelties apart from some of the other herding breeds is that fact that they are smart herders. They think through the way they herd. They can keep both sheep and cattle in line.

HOUSETRAINING. Shelties startle easily, so keep things calm and as low-key as possible. If you take Rover out and the wind is blowing, he's going to spook. Once he realizes that the wind is not a threat—this won't take him long—he'll relax. Make sure you don't fall into the "It's okay, it's okay" trap. Act as if nothing is wrong, and Rover will relax. A firm hand or voice in discipline will get you nowhere. Rover could very easily become a "shy eliminator": He won't want anybody to see him go, so he'll hide behind or under something, usually your couch or dining room table. If this starts, housetraining can become a nightmare for both of you. Have a clear understanding that Rover is shy. It's a part of who he is. Handle him gently without being solicitous.

PERSONALITY. *Shelties are barkers.* They are naturally shy, and for them barking is a survival mechanism, just as screaming is a survival mechanism in women and children. You can minimize the barking if you respect Rover's shyness and don't put him in uncomfortable situations. Don't insist that he join you in welcoming company. I can guarantee that if you push Rover to meet Friend John, he's going to have a problem with Friend John from that point on. When you see Rover back away from someone, he is being his natural shy self. Again I say, don't fall into the "It's okay, it's okay" comforting-tone-of-voice trap.

Shelties are lively and love to play. Read Chapter 5, "Playtime with Rover," because it's very unlikely that your Sheltie is going to enjoy straight fetch. He's going to be in seventh heaven if play involves chase. He might enjoy ball games if you use several balls.

I think one of the reasons Shelties get along so beautifully with children is that they see them as playmates. Obviously, I recommend Shelties with kids, especially ones old enough to play.

When you notice that Rover is restless and pacing, pay attention to where everyone in the household is. If the kids are in their rooms, Dad is watching TV, and Mom is in the kitchen, Rover will be restless until everyone is in the same room. When he's old enough to understand, say to him, "Rover, go get the kids. Dinner is ready." Don't scoff. He'll do it, and be happy to do it, because he can herd everyone into one room.

The herding instinct seems stronger in the Sheltie than in some of the other herding breeds. I have a client in Santa Fe, who moved herself and her Sheltie, Gopher, to the outskirts of town. She bought a place lock, stock, and barrel. The rain barrel was in the vegetable garden, and the stock included several hens, a couple of roosters, one pig, and one cow. Gopher was five years old and had been a city dog every minute of those five years. He wasn't at the new house for more than ten minutes before he started herding the hens and roosters. Donna tells me they weren't one bit happy about this strange dog telling them where to go. The pig wasn't in the least affected by having a barking dog at his heels. He seemed to know that pigs are not herded as a rule, and he wasn't going to be the first. The cow let herself be herded, but Gopher had no idea where he wanted her to go. Donna said the two of them just kind of went around near the barn, but without any real direction. So when you see Rover in the backyard running around the trees and barking, don't become concerned; he hasn't gone crazy, he's just trying to herd all the birds into one tree.

TRAINING. Use a gentle hand when working with Rover. Shelties have a stubborn streak in them, and it's going to be tempting to use a firmer hand. If you do, Rover will more than likely turn his back and act as if something else is much more important than you and your lesson. If you reach an impasse, give Rover a couple of commands so that you end in control, and stop the lesson. Please pay close attention to the fit and type of collar you use. With that mixed long and short coat, the wrong collar can tangle in the hair and tighten down.

BEST ENVIRONMENT: Jogger—**Walker**—Teenagers—Children 6 to 11—**Children of any age (preferably old enough to play)—Elderly**—Latchkey—**Active environment**—Sedate environment—**Multiple dogs okay**—Apartment—**House with yard—Room to run**—Needs daily exercise—Camping—Hiking

---

Shih Tzu

BRED TO DO. Not really a "sleeve dog," and not a working dog—though the heart and desire are there. Shih Tzus were "drawing-room dogs." A fancy way of saying companion dogs, for the wealthy.

HOUSETRAINING. As puppies these little sweeties are very active. You're really going to have to stay on your toes, trying to keep an eye on Rover. One advantage you'll have is that about the only time Rover will put his nose down is when he's looking for a place to go. If you take him out several times and he doesn't have an elimination, start looking for a favorite place in the house. I can bet you money he has one. If you find one, block it any way you can; more than likely you'll have to start housetraining from scratch. An advantage of housetraining your Shih Tzu is that he has the heart of a working dog, so he's not going to mind being outside.

PERSONALITY. I love working with Shih Tzus. They're full of personality and fun to be around. The first time Rover does something that makes you laugh, he'll do it over and over, to see you laugh again. Rover loves to play and entertain. Shih Tzus don't want any part of being dominant. You can do every possible thing wrong in establishing peck order, use all the wrong body language, and it still won't occur to Rover to become the alpha dog.

The main problem I see Shih Tzus about is nervous habits. I've seen at least three that chewed their tail until it was raw and bleeding. Veterinarians tell me there is a nerve problem in the tails of some Shih Tzus. I've seen a few that can't seem to stop whining. Nine times out of ten, that problem arises because of positive reinforcement for negative behavior. Bandit bonded very strongly with a stuffed cat. He would pull it under the couch or chair with him and suck on its tail. For the most part, though, Shih Tzus are well-adjusted.

I don't recommend this Rover with children younger than six or so. He loves to play with kids, especially any game that involves chase, but the kids have to be well-behaved. He won't hesitate to snap at or actually bite a child that is too rough or ill-mannered.

Rover is going to have times when he just wants to be left alone. He'll don his royal crown, jump up on the top of the couch or chair, and get a real attitude. Few dogs can get an attitude the way a Shih Tzu can. He'll look at you and say, "Leave me alone, I'm thinking. I don't find anything amusing right now, and if anybody is hungry, let 'em eat cake." Don't take this mood personally. He'll get over it.

TRAINING. Only if you want to. If you decide to work with him on some obedience commands, use a kind hand. There will be no doubt in your mind when the lesson is over: Rover will stop doing anything you say. I don't care how well he's followed commands for the last ten minutes, he's done. It's over! Finished!

BEST ENVIRONMENT: Jogger—Walker—**Teenagers—Children 6 to 11**—Children of any age—**Elderly (Shih Tzus are wonderful for the elderly)**—Latchkey—**Active environment—Sedate environment— Multiple dogs okay—Apartment**—House with yard—Room to run— Needs daily exercise—Camping—Hiking

---

Siberian Husky

BRED TO DO. Huskies are not your run-of-the-mill sled dogs. They don't have the muscle and size to pull sleds over long distances. Instead, they're sled racers. Sled racing is popular in Alaska and Canada.

HOUSETRAINING. Not the easiest dog to housetrain, but not the hardest either. Spend as little time as possible praising or disciplining. You'll notice that before you're done saying "Good dog," Rover will be off someplace else, saying "Yeah, yeah, I know. Get on with it, I have better things to do." Since this dog is a direct descendant of the Arctic Wolf, having eliminations outside is basic to him. In fact, you may have to do some coaxing just to get Rover back in the house.

PERSONALITY. *These dogs are diggers!* I yell this at you because I've seen far too many Huskies lose their happy homes because of digging. Ancestry and instinct come together and tell Rover to dig in the dirt to get cool, and dig in the snow to get warm. In other words, he can't help it, and he doesn't do it out of boredom or frustration (unless you make it that way). The more emphasis you put on the digging the longer it will go on. The first hole you fill in will be the next hole he digs. If you don't make a big deal out of it, he'll dig a few holes, keep a couple of favorites, and grow out of it. (You'll notice, by the way, that he doesn't dig down, he dens out.) You may have to decide what's more important, your landscaping for this year, or Rover.

As puppies and young adults, Huskies are hyper, loving, and affectionate. The way that plays out in your home is this: You come home from work and here gallops Rover saying, in his most excited voice, "Yippee yippee you're home! I want a hug and a kiss, and I want to show you how much I missed you and I want to tell you about the new, really neat, hole I dug, and I found this toy for you and I want to tell you how much I love you!" All at breakneck speed, on his hind legs. To avoid getting this kind of welcome every single time you come home, even when you've been gone ten minutes, you might want to establish homecoming as calm and cool.

Huskies don't know a stranger. Rover loves everybody, and assumes everybody loves him in the same way. Of course, all this love is shown physically, with every pound of his body. Huskies do everything with a passion, and when it comes to showing love, they do it with total abandon. Not to worry, he'll outgrow most of this and settle down to be a wonderful companion. Depending on his age, I've found that the first or second summer's heat settles some of the hyperactive behavior. He'll figure out in no time that the air-conditioning vent is a wonderful place to nap.

Even though he loves everyone, Rover's heart and loyalty will belong only to his master. These dogs really are sweethearts, and well worth your patience and understanding. When he's sixteen to eighteen months old, he'll begin to settle down and be the companion you've always wanted. Huskies are good with kids who are old enough to hold their own against his activity level.

TRAINING. Did I mention that Huskies aren't the easiest dogs to train? There I go again, getting in trouble with breeders. Remember, Humans, patience is a virtue. You'll need a firm but kind hand. Unless you're naturally a patient person, Rover is going to try every ounce of patience and understanding you have. From the moment you put a collar on him, *make sure you stay calm.* If Rover tries to paw you or go down while you're trying to put the collar on him, stand up, stop the effort, and wait until he calms down. If you buy into a struggle, that struggle will be repeated every single time you try to put the collar on him. The same goes for the leash. Once you get it on him, he's going to grab for it, try to bite it, bounce and jump around, and in general drive you nuts. All this happens before you even get out your front door. Understand that it may take you ten minutes just to get the collar and leash on and another ten to get out the front door. That may be the entire training session. Just say, "Okay, maybe we'll get farther tomorrow." He doesn't have to learn anything in a prescribed period of time. If your neighbor can't wait to tell you he had his German Shepherd trained in six weeks, just congratulate him and tell yourself that training time is not competitive. There is going to be some struggle with almost every command, if not with all of them. You must at all times be in the Head Honcho position. Huskies need strong leadership qualities in their Human.

If your Husky has blue eyes, he's going to be light-sensitive. Pay attention to where the sun is when you're working with him. If he keeps putting his head down, or tries to stand in your shadow, stop the session and wait until later in the day.

BEST ENVIRONMENT: **Jogger (in winter)**—Walker—**Teenagers**—
Children 6 to 11—Children of any age—Elderly—Latchkey—**Active
environment (in winter)**—**Sedate environment (in summer)**—
Multiple dogs okay—Apartment—**House with yard**—Room to run—
Needs daily exercise—Camping—Hiking

Silky

BRED TO DO. They are wonderful companion dogs, but will give your cat a run for his money as a mouser. Way back when, they were used to hunt den animals.

HOUSETRAINING. Absolutely do not give Rover run of the house until he's completely housetrained. Silkies are very curious, and as small as they are, there are very few corners they can't get themselves into. Rover will know every nook and cranny of your house and yard better than you do. If he has the run of the house too soon, he'll have favorite places to go, and housetraining is going to take quite some time. Usually Silkies are relatively easy to housetrain. I have, however, run across a few that never become totally housetrained. Stick close to the method, to avoid any confusion.

PERSONALITY. Silkies are out-and-out belligerent, and they are very caught up in who they are and what they want. If Silkies were humans, they'd be rebellious teenagers, starting about eleven years old. Anything you say would be filed under "They don't know what they're talking about. They don't understand me, and I don't care." But this little dog has so much personality that you can't help but love him. If your Silky isn't the number one dog in your life, you're going to hear about it. He won't jump on your lap and asked to be stroked, he will jump on your lap and *insist* on being stroked. When he has you in hand, he'll be bright and cheery, without a care in the world.

Silkies are also manipulators, but I admire the intelligence that goes with being a manipulator. It won't take long before you're living in his house, and not really minding. Don't get me wrong: He doesn't want to be dominant, in fact he'll insist that you be in control. He has no desire to take care of you or himself. But you'll find that in no time you're working around his schedule, and again not minding.

Your Silky will be good with kids if kids are good with him. If the children are old enough to play, Rover will be a happy camper. He will also welcome their friends and your friends. In fact, he'll be all over company if you don't stop him. When the doorbell rings, he's the first one to call out, "Get the door, somebody. There's company here to see me!"

TRAINING. Use a kind hand and Rover will learn anything you want him to, quicker then most. He really wants to be a necessary part of the family, so if you don't care about the obedience commands teach him to bring you one of his toys. And teach him to put his toys away. Make sure you incorporate play in with the training.

Missy showed all the signs of being a terrific mouser, but Carl and Jerry didn't have mice. In the attempt to make Missy happy they went to a toy store and bought a battery-operated mouse that scurried across the floor. Missy was in seventh heaven.

BEST ENVIRONMENT: Jogger—**Walker**—Teenagers—**Children 6 to 11**—Children of any age—**Elderly**—Latchkey—**Active environment**—**Sedate environment**—**Multiple dogs okay**—**Apartment**—House with yard—Room to run—Needs daily exercise—Camping—Hiking

---

Standard Poodle and Miniature Poodle

BRED TO DO. Poodles were used to retrieve game from marshland and water. Their coat gave them excellent buoyancy.

HOUSETRAINING. Poodles are one of the easiest breeds to housetrain. Over the years, I've been called only once about a housetraining problem with a Standard Poodle. The Humans thought if they left the sliding glass door open all the time, he would housetrain naturally. It didn't work. All you have to do is show Rover where he's to go, then follow the method; you'll be delighted at how quickly he'll housetrain.

PERSONALITY. Standards are the first breed I recommend if somebody wants a large dog that's good with kids. I mean kids of any age, shape, or size, in good health or bad health, troubled or doing fine. I adopted a Standard for my youngest son when he was really going through some tough times. The deep bond between them was instantaneous. My son still had rough times to go through, but when everyone around him failed him in some way, Java was always there, loving him with every fiber of her being.

All Poodles have the ability to understand the spoken word, but I see it most clearly in the Standards and Miniatures. You will be truly amazed at how easily Rover learns, and how he seems to understand everything you say to him. There's not a Standard owner I know who doesn't at some time say, "This dog is amazing. He seems to understand everything I say. I think he's part Human." Just between you and me, I think there *is* a little bit of Human in each Poodle. Java would sit up on the middle cushion of my couch, company would sit on the end of the couch, and I would sit kitty-corner from them on the love seat. Without fail, after the visitors had been talking for a while, they would begin to turn toward Java and include her in the conversation. After they had done that a few times, they would suddenly do a double take and realize it was a dog they were talking to.

The Standards can go through a tough displacement period, and you may see some serious destruction. Read Chapter 4, "Puppy Chewing and Destructive Chewing," so that you can understand what's going on and how you can help make it easier. Then, when a Standard gets to be about a year old, there's an almost overnight metamorphosis. Suddenly he's mature and settled. Miniatures do the same thing, but they settle down at about nine or ten months.

TRAINING. Poodles aren't happy if they're not a definite part of the family. They want to be involved in everything that goes on in the household. With a gentle hand, they're easy to train and they learn quickly. Don't let all that potential go to waste. Rover will learn almost anything you want to teach him. Go beyond obedience. You can teach him to bring your slippers, the newspaper, and his leash, and you can teach him how to help you bring in the groceries. If you want to teach him tricks, don't hesitate. He'll love doing anything you teach him.

BEST ENVIRONMENT: Jogger—**Walker**—Teenagers—Children 6 to 11— **Children of any age**—**Elderly**—Latchkey—**Active environment**— Sedate environment—**Multiple dogs okay**—Apartment—**House with yard**—Room to run—Needs daily exercise—**Camping**—Hiking

---

Standard Schnauzer

BRED TO DO. This dog has had many jobs and has done all of them well. He'll hunt rodents, guard your house (and stable, if you happen to have one), and be your bodyguard if the need arises.

HOUSETRAINING. If Rover doesn't like the spot you've chosen for him to have his eliminations, you might as well acquiesce, and work around where he wants to go. His activity level may be a problem in getting him housetrained. Keeping up with an adult Schnauzer is tough enough, but keeping up with a Schnauzer puppy is a real challenge. Stick to the method, and make outside easily accessible for both of you. There are going to be times when you have to scoop up the puppy and run outside.

PERSONALITY. The Standard Schnauzer's personality is similar to the Miniature's, but the Standard is more committed to his traits, and he's bolder. These little ones are born thinking they are the Number One Dog of the Western World. They have absolutely no self-image problems. And Rover will protect you and yours with every fiber of his being.

You have to be careful to keep barking under control, because Standards can become nuisance barkers. Teach Rover the "Quiet" command very early. This sweetie will also take total control of your front door, so that you'll have to pick him up at the door to stop him from charging people. Or you'll have to put him in the backyard or another room so that you can carry on a conversation. Rover will take responsibility for the front door, for the house when you're gone, for the house when you're not gone, for the yard, and eventually for himself. Standards don't seem to have as much of a desire to be Head Honcho as the Miniatures do, although they will take on the dominant role if you give it to them. Read Chapter 6, "The Peck Order Factor." These dogs are a little like the little girl with the curl: When they're good they're very very good, and when they're bad they're horrid.

I don't usually recommend Standard Schnauzers with small children. Rover won't hesitate to discipline a child he perceives as naughty, whether the child is two or fifteen. I've also seen this Rover get along beautifully with children in the family, while the children's friends can become a problem. And I've seen Standards that get along beautifully with all children, love company, and are totally devoted to their family. Growling and snapping never cross their minds.

You'll notice quickly that Rover has a tremendous amount of energy. He'll play almost any game you can think of at the drop of a hat, and he'll have as much energy when he's ten years old as he did when he was one. Give him a bit of time and you'll notice that he invents new games. Standards are very resourceful. They have an independent streak that allows them to entertain themselves and not mind their own company. They can be latchkey dogs as long as you don't abuse the "privilege."

The Standard Schnauzer's coordination and agility never cease to amaze me. I've seen these dogs climb ladders, walk around on a pitched roof (Scooter was helping his Human do repairs), and actually *run*, not walk, on a cinderblock wall. I hope you have the opportunity to take Rover to a wide-open space and let him go off leash. When Rover takes off at a dead run, it's truly a sight to see.

TRAINING. Schnauzers are very trainable. They love to learn, and they're proud when they can do something correctly. Given Rover's energy level, your best bet is to work with him no more than fifteen minutes at a time (except when you're taking him for a walk). If you try to stretch a lesson much past that, he'll become impatient and grouchy.

One of Rover's favorite things to do is go for a walk. He loves seeing and walking through the world around him. Once he learns how to behave on a leash, he'll beg and beg and beg to go for walks. Use a kind but no-nonsense hand. You're going to get some back talk, so be prepared for it. One way Rover will back talk is by following the command, but somewhere else and in his own time. For example, let's say you've told Rover to sit. He will first look at you and say, "@#*&#!" Then he will move four or five feet away from you and sit.

BEST ENVIRONMENT: Jogger—**Walker—Teenagers—Children 6 to 11**
(depending on you and the temperament of your Standard)—
Children of any age—Elderly—**Latchkey—Active environment**—Sedate
environment—**Multiple dogs okay**—Apartment—**House with yard**—
Room to run—**Needs daily exercise**—Camping—Hiking

Toy Poodle

BRED TO DO. The Toys have always been strictly companion dogs, but the way they enjoy fetch indicates to me that they'd retrieve in a heartbeat, given the opportunity.

HOUSETRAINING. Toys are a little harder to housetrain than other Poodles, and I'm not sure why. I've known them to housetrain in ten days, and I've known them to take five months. I have discovered over the years that Toys that are talked to a lot housetrain faster. Stick to the method, and talk to your Toy. Let him know that you're unhappy when he has an accident, and carry on every time he goes where he's supposed to.

PERSONALITY. I feel so bad for this sweetie. Breeders have tried to produce dogs so tiny that they can be put in a teacup, hence the name Teacup Poodle. I understand that in America we want what is already big to be bigger, and what is already small to be smaller. The Tiny Toys or Teacup Poodles (whatever the name is now) have health problems, and I've seen many that have very dull personalities. Maybe if all you Humans out there reading this refuse to adopt these tiny ones, the breeders will have no choice but to breed for the original standards.

Good Toy Poodles are full of personality; they're lively, smart, and affectionate. These dogs have an uncanny ability to understand the spoken word. Talk to your Rover a lot, and you will be amazed at how much he obviously understands.

The good ones are also great with kids of any age. The tiny ones have a hard time with kids less than ten or so. It's rare for a Poodle to growl or snap, and that's true of the tiny ones too, but they will avoid children whenever possible. What I've seen is that they'll glue themselves to your lap or arms; some will try to climb onto your shoulder and hide behind your head when kids are present. If you have a standard-size Toy Poodle, you can't ask for a better small dog. If you've read what I've had to say about some of the other breeds, you'll know that not all dogs give unconditional love. With Poodles of any size, the love they feel for their Human is definitely unconditional.

TRAINING. I don't see too many Toys that know obedience commands, or any commands for that matter. A part of me wants to say that that's a terrible waste of serious intelligence and trainability. The other part of me knows that very little training is necessary to make a Poodle a terrific companion. (Like the larger Poodles, the Toys aren't happy if they're not a major part of the family.) Just keep in mind that your Toy will learn almost anything you want to teach him.

BEST ENVIRONMENT: Jogger—**Walker**—Teenagers—Children 6 to 11— **Children of any age—Elderly**—Latchkey—**Active environment— Sedate environment—Multiple dogs okay—Apartment—House with yard**—Room to run—Needs daily exercise—Camping—Hiking

---

Vizsla

BRED TO DO. Vizslas are used for just about every type of hunting. They're from Hungary, but they're used as hunters everywhere that hunting is done.

HOUSETRAINING. Vizslas are smart dogs, and as long as there's no confusion they housetrain easily. If you're housetraining during the colder months, it may take a little longer. You'll notice that when you open the door and Rover gets a blast of cold air, he'll look at you as if you're crazy. You can't honestly expect him to go outside in this weather! The look will say, "You get to wear clothes and sweaters and coats. All I have is this one thin coat. How about if I just go in the corner for right now, and I promise I'll go out when it warms up a bit."

PERSONALITY. Vizslas are an odd mix of hardy hunter and nervous wreck. To say these dogs are high-strung and sensitive is a serious understatement. Rover will be constantly alert to *everything* around him. An odor that most dogs would ignore or take for granted will stir up this Rover. A sound that means nothing to the neighborhood dogs will set Rover's ears up and forward. He'll pace for no apparent reason. There is an apparent reason to him. Something is going on that he believes requires his attention, and since he can't face whatever it is directly, he paces. You can settle some of this down by *seeing to it that Rover gets the exercise he absolutely has to have!* I've seen several Vizslas over the years because of wall jumping and other forms of escape. One of them scaled an eight-foot wall, and another wasn't stopped by a ten-foot wall. Without exception, all these dogs needed was exercise. When I prescribed daily exercise, the jumping problem was solved. I cannot stress strongly enough that these dogs have to have daily exercise. If you're a jogger, and you want a jogging buddy, this is the dog for you. Just make sure you condition him as you did yourself.

You'll notice his sensitive nature when you realize he's very aware of your moods, good, bad, and ugly. He'll be upset if you're unhappy, he'll love it when you're happy, and he'll become grouchy if there's arguing in the household. If he wants to go outside, then turns around and wants right back in, then wants out again, you can bet the weather is going to change. I absolutely do not recommend Vizslas with children less than twelve to thirteen years of age. As high-strung as these dogs are, the last thing they need is a child that is still and quiet one second, and screaming and running the next. They are obviously uncomfortable around kids and won't hesitate to growl and snap.

When Vizslas are around two years old, you'll notice some settling, but exercise is still a must.

Don't ever make the mistake of taking Rover for granted. About the time you do, he'll be over a wall in a heartbeat. I also want you to make sure you play with Rover quite a bit. Vizslas can become depressed and serious if they don't have the opportunity to play.

If you don't use your Vizsla for hunting but you don't want his ability to go to waste, call around and see what you need to do to get him into field trials.

TRAINING. Vizslas are smart, and they don't mind training if it's done correctly. If you're going to train for hunting or field trials, take the advice of a good trainer in your area. If your Vizsla is strictly a pet, you must work with him on obedience. The "Sit" is important because there are going to be times you're going to want to get Rover in control of himself. A "Sit" can get him through any anxiety he may feel.

BEST ENVIRONMENT: **Jogger—Walker—Teenagers**—Children 6 to
11—Children of any age—Elderly—Latchkey—**Active environment**—
Sedate environment—**Multiple dogs okay**—Apartment—House with
yard—**Room to run—Needs daily exercise**—Camping—Hiking

Weimaraner

BRED TO DO. Just about any kind of hunting a hunter would want a dog for. These dogs are hardy and love to work.

HOUSETRAINING. You'll notice that no matter how many times you take Rover to the spot you've chosen, he'll find a spot of his own. This dog's scenting ability is more than likely going to determine where he wants to have his eliminations. And the hardest part of housetraining a Weimaraner is being able to tell the difference between his nose down looking for a place to go, and his nose down just checking stuff out. Stick to the method, and remember that you've committed yourself to housetraining this dog.

PERSONALITY. Weimaraners love to hunt and live to hunt. If your Weimaraner is strictly a pet, he'll still hunt. He'll hunt lizards, rodents, beetles, and anything else that moves. Nakita stalked a box turtle for most of an afternoon. It was something to watch. When the turtle stopped moving, Nakita stopped moving. She would stop and stand in a stalking position until she couldn't stand that way any longer; then she would lie down and just watch until the turtle moved again.

Daily exercise is an absolute must for these dogs. Don't get a Weimaraner if you can't meet his exercise needs. If you're a jogger and you want a jogging buddy, this is the dog for you. I don't say "If you're a runner," because Rover could pick up a scent, and you could be a quarter of a mile down the road before you realize Rover is off following it. Even when you're jogging, you should let Rover do some scenting, or he won't enjoy himself.

It's not a good idea to let Rover get bored. He'll use his energy to jump any wall in his way, or dig as if he's trying to tunnel out (we're talking a serious hole here), or become destructive.

Weimaraners do everything with a passion, and that includes loving and being loyal to you. This dog can be the best you've ever had or the worst. It all depends on your understanding exactly what Weimaraners are all about before you adopt one. Weimaraners don't have a lick of patience, and they are very moody. Because of this, I hesitate to recommend them with children. If Rover is in a bad mood for some reason, and little Johnny tries to take a rawhide chew away from him, he's going to growl and most likely snap. And there will be no doubt in Rover's mind that he's dominant; he won't hesitate to discipline what he perceives as a naughty child. If Rover is not your only dog, please read Chapter 10, "Living with Multiple Dogs."

TRAINING. You'll need a firm but kind hand when training this Rover. I don't usually use the word "stubborn" when talking about a dog, but Weimaraners are the exception. If you train for hunting, you'll have very little work to do. Training for obedience is a whole other show. You *will* get Rover trained, but you're going to have to forget about any six-week or eight-week time frame. Expect a few months to go by before you get Rover to the point that he'll follow several commands. When you're working with Rover on the "Sit", he'll act like he's just not getting it. *Wrong.* He knows exactly what he's supposed to do. The problem is, he just can't see any good reason for doing it. You may wonder at times if he's hard of hearing. His hearing is excellent. He just chooses not to pay attention to you right now.

BEST ENVIRONMENT: **Jogger—Walker—Teenagers**—Children 6 to 11—Children of any age—Elderly—Latchkey—**Active environment**—Sedate environment—**Multiple dogs okay (as long as you understand the dynamics)**—Apartment—House with yard—**Room to run—Needs daily exercise**—Camping—Hiking

---

Welsh Corgi

BRED TO DO. Corgis are still used as sheepdogs, mostly in the British Isles. They are also used to guard flocks. The Corgi is the Queen of England's chosen breed.

HOUSETRAINING. Corgis are easy to housetrain, because they're easy to train to do anything. These are very cooperative dogs and love to please. You may have a problem with Rover when he has to be confined. Corgis feel as if they're being punished when they're confined away from you. When you confine him, even if it's in a bright, cheery kitchen, with you in sight, you will see a look on his face that asks, "What did I do wrong? Why are you putting me in here? I'm sorry for whatever I did, and I promise I'll never do it again. So could I come be with you?" He may even go to a corner and pout. You may have to harden your heart a little until he's housetrained.

PERSONALITY. The best word I can come up with to describe the Corgi's personality is "vivacious." Corgis love to play, and they'll play any game you want them to. They are very energetic but not at all hyperactive. With almost all of my Corgi owners I recommend getting into a Therapy Dog program, especially in pediatrics. If you have a Corgi, and you want to do volunteer work of some kind, call around and find out how to get Rover into a Therapy Dog program. The favorite place for Queenie and her Human, Jerry, was a children's hospital. Jerry took advantage of how easy it is to train a Corgi; he taught Queenie some really neat tricks to entertain the kids. I went along with the two of them once, and every single child we saw totally forgot his or her illness, no matter how life-threatening, when Queenie came up and gave each and every one of them a kiss on the hand. When Jerry and Queenie started performing I got tears in my eyes watching those kids laugh and clap. Jerry now has Jeeves, a Cardigan Corgi (Queenie is a Pembroke), and the three of them work as a team.

Corgis are very loving dogs, and they're in seventh heaven whenever you pet and stroke them. Rover wants to be a part of the working family, and since he's so easy to train it's not difficult to include him in almost everything you do around the house. Needless to say, I recommend Corgis with kids of any age. They're great with the elderly as well.

TRAINING. Please don't stop at just basic obedience. Corgis are intelligent and want to learn. Use a gentle hand and Rover will do anything you ask of him. Don't think that teaching Rover tricks is somehow undignified. Rover doesn't know the difference between a trick and a command. All the things Seeing Eye, Hearing Ear, and Wheelchair Companion dogs do are sophisticated tricks.

> BEST ENVIRONMENT: Jogger—**Walker**—Teenagers—Children 6 to 11—
> **Children of any age—Elderly**—Latchkey—**Active environment**—
> **Sedate environment—Multiple dogs okay**—Apartment—**House with**
> **yard**—Room to run—Needs daily exercise—**Camping**—Hiking

Welsh Terrier

BRED TO DO. Bred to hunt animals in their lairs. Nowadays, the Welsh Terrier is strictly a companion dog.

HOUSETRAINING. Keeping up with this Rover is going to be the hardest part of housetraining. Make sure you don't give him the run of the house too soon. He'll go from room to room quickly, and he'll squat and go just as quickly. You may have a problem getting him back in the house after he's had his eliminations, because he's really going to want to stay out and play—and, of course, see if any animals are about that may require his hunting ability. Be strong, Human.

PERSONALITY. These are very strong-willed, opinionated dogs. They can take over a household in a New York minute, given just the slightest encouragement. They are also very independent thinkers; having one is a bit like having a spoiled teenager in the house. If you're not on the ball, Rover will have you trained in no time.

Picture a roomful of dogs. The Human says, "I need a volunteer for a dangerous mission." Before the Human is able to explain the mission, the Welsh Terrier raises his paw and shouts, "I will, sir! You can count on me." These truly are courageous dogs. They're quick on their feet, with intelligence to match. Their main disappointment in life is that they're not the size of an Airedale. Don't fall into the trap of calling Rover stubborn. Tenacious and single-minded, yes; stubborn, no. Rover will bond to you quickly, and the bond will be strong and lifelong. In spite of his independence and strong will, he wants to please. Make sure you play with Rover the way he wants to play. Read Chapter 5, "Playtime with Rover," so you'll understand what I mean. Keep in mind that this dog has the ability to become the dominant individual in the household. If that happens he'll become very serious and defensive. Play can help to keep him relaxed.

A Welsh Terrier will be good with children if they're good with him. He won't tolerate being pushed around by a child except in play.

These are good-hearted little dogs, with loads of personality and love. Rover is going to love you with all of his heart, but he's going to be a little shy with strangers. Let him meet people at his own rate.

TRAINING. You're going to get a lot of back talk and out-and-out contempt for obedience commands. To say he's a bit independent is like saying the sun is somewhat warm. You'll need to be firm but kind; at times you're going to be tempted to be harsh, but don't go with the temptation. If you do, Rover will dig in his heels and won't do even one more thing for you. Read, "Rover, let's go" in Chapter 11, "Obedience." Until you see it for yourself, you won't believe how headstrong and willful Rover will be on a leash. When he wants to see something, he wants to see it *now*. It's a good thing he's small and controllable. Rover loves to play, and I've found that if I interrupt training with recess, he doesn't mind the work as much. Don't be disheartened, once he learns something he does it with pride, and he's obedient. Be sure to teach him "Stand-stay," because he's going to need grooming.

Best Environment: **Jogger (short sprints)—Walker—Teenagers—**
Children 6 to 11—Children of any age—Elderly—Latchkey—**Active
environment**—Sedate environment—**Multiple dogs okay—
Apartment—House with yard**—Room to run—Needs daily exercise—
Camping—Hiking

West Highland White Terrier (Westie)

BRED TO DO. Like many Terriers, Westies were bred to hunt animals in their lairs. Even though they've been companion dogs for a very long time, they still have the makeup of a hunter.

HOUSETRAINING. I must tell you that I think that Westies, as pups, beat almost all other breeds in the cuteness category. I have no doubt that you just brought the "the cutest puppy I've ever seen." On to housetraining. One minute you'll have him in your sights; you look away for a split second and he's gone. You're going to have your work cut out for you housetraining this wee one. Rover will not be a happy camper when he's confined. He will sound something like this: "Come and get me now! I don't like it in the kitchen! I want out of the laundry room immediately! I don't like it in here, and I want out!" Westies usually housetrain fairly quickly; just stick to the method and make sure there's no confusion.

PERSONALITY. Westies are independent and confident. He'll sit gladly at your side or on your lap, but he'll also seek some freedom. Rover doesn't mind being alone, if you're not gone much more than six or seven hours. If he's alone much more than that, I recommend you get him a dog of his very own. I have several clients who have two Westies that get along quiet well. You don't have to worry about Rover One having bad habits and teaching them to Rover Two. Westies are very much individuals, and aren't easily influenced.

Westies are enthusiastic, to say the least, about everything they do. They love to play and they enjoy doing a job. As a mouser, Rover can put a cat to shame. Even though Westies haven't been used as hunters for quite some time, the ability and desire to do a job are still very strong, and very much part of who they are. Watch Rover the first time he spots something scurrying under a bush or a kitchen cabinet. You'll see, firsthand, Rover's tenacity and enthusiasm. I have a client with two Westies, Groucho and Harpo. They live on a small farm. Martha says

Groucho and Harpo keep the barn and stable free of rodents; when they spot one, they work as a team to get rid of it.

I don't usually recommend Westies with children. Their agitation level is too high. When confronted with a child they have a tendency to say, "Don't mess with me. Don't come any closer. I'm not going to play with you, and I want you to leave me alone." Their attitude toward children is a lot like W. C. Fields's. I can hear you now: "My Westie gets along great with my kids." I'm happy for you, but it's very possible that there will come a time when your Rover disciplines your child or one of his or her friends. These dogs are not known for their patience.

TRAINING. Westies, especially males, can take over the dominant position in your household very easily. Read Chapter 6, "The Peck Order Factor," and Chapter 8, "The Head Honcho Human," so that if you see him climb the ladder you'll know how to handle it. I do recommend training your Westie, because training automatically puts you in the lead position. Westies need strong leadership qualities in their pack. Rover is strong-willed and very sure of himself. You're going to get a lot of back talk, so you're going to have to be the one to say, "Rover, I am the Human, you are the dog. This is not a democracy, this is a monarchy, and I am the monarch. You *will* do as I say." You'll need a firm hand and a good grip on your patience. Don't let your hand become harsh.

BEST ENVIRONMENT: Jogger—**Walker—Teenagers**—Children 6 to 11—Children of any age—**Elderly (strong-willed)—Latchkey (don't take advantage)—Active environment**—Sedate environment—**Multiple dogs okay (especially another Westie)—Apartment—House with yard**—Room to run—Needs daily exercise—**Camping**—Hiking

---

Wolf Hybrid

HOUSETRAINING. Most Wolf Hybrids instinctively eliminate outside. *Do not crate train.* If you put a Hybrid in a crate, he's going to feel trapped, and there's no telling what he'll do when he gets out.

PERSONALITY. If Rover has a high percentage of Wolf his behavior will be wolflike. He will be *very* shy. Fear of humans goes so far back with wolves, that it's a part of who they are. I don't recommend adopting a Wolf Hybrid at all, but if you're getting one I warn you strongly not to have other dogs, cats, or any small animals. With a pure Wolf the pack etiquette is as it should be and would be in the wild. The admixture of Malamute, Husky, or German Shepherd changes that. One client of mine had a Hybrid and two other Mixed Breed dogs. They all seemed to get along—until one day Brenda came home to find one of her Mixed Breed dogs with its neck ripped open and its blood everywhere. Her Hybrid killed the other dog a couple of weeks later. When she called to ask what happened, I couldn't tell her. A pure Wolf wouldn't kill a pack member, because all members of the pack are needed for hunting. With the Wolf Hybrid there is no way to tell what the dogs did to warrant being killed.

I also don't recommend the Hybrids with children of any age. There is *nothing,* and I mean *nothing,* predictable about the Hybrid. I have several Hybrids in my practice; when I see them they seem docile and domesticated, but I can't say that they are. Don't own a Hybrid without arming yourself with as much education as you can get. Leave the dog books on the shelf and read the books about wolves.

When I first started seeing Hybrids, I must admit that I was thrilled to be so close to something so wild and beautiful. Hybrids were bred, with good intentions, in an attempt to reestablish pure wolves in what used to be their natural habitat. The original breeders didn't take into consideration that other people would breed these animals with no thought as to what they were doing. *You do not have a domestic dog, you have a wild dog. You can tame a wild animal, but you can't totally domesticate one.*

One of the most common "problems" I hear is that a Hybrid is killing small animals and birds and bringing them home. The Hybrid is trying to feed his pack. Don't discipline! Accept the kill, say thank you, and take it to where your Hybrid knows food is prepared. If you don't want it, wait until he's not looking and dispose of it. If you discipline him for killing a rabbit, he'll assume you don't like rabbit, so he'll bring you a quail. If you show him through discipline that you don't like quail, he'll bring you a chicken. If you show appreciation he may kill only once or twice a year. If you don't show appreciation he'll continue to bring you kills until he hits on something you like. I have heard the most horrendous ways to discipline this poor canine. One client was told to tie the kill—in this case a chicken—around the Hybrid's neck and leave it until it rotted. Another was told to put the animal in the Hybrid's mouth and tape it shut. Remember, all canines are carnivores, and hunting can be foremost in a Hybrid's mind. Having food in a bowl to which he always has access does not affect the hunting instinct.

I've seen Hybrids that get along beautifully in their domestic environment. (The problem is, I can't say what the future holds.) The lower the percentage of Wolf in the Hybrid, the better your chance of having a good "dog." (I use that term loosely.) The best way to stop the breeding of Wolf Hybrids is not to adopt one in the first place.

TRAINING. Most of the Hybrids I see can't relate to obedience commands. It's like teaching them a foreign language when there is no background in English. When you put the collar and leash on, you're not dealing with just counterpressure (explained in the Chapter 11, "Obedience"), you're also dealing with the Hybrid's instinct to break free of any trap. Unless it's introduced slowly, carefully, and gently, the Hybrid will always feel trapped when he's on a leash.

Yorkshire Terrier (Yorkie)

BRED TO DO. Yorkies have been strictly companion dogs for a very long time. Originally they were bred in Yorkshire, England, to rid mine shafts of rats. I once saw a rat in England, and it looked to weigh five or six pounds.

HOUSETRAINING. Rover will housetrain much more quickly in the warmer months. Yorkies can't tolerate too much cold weather, and need protection. You might want to invest in a small coat or sweater if you're housetraining in the colder months. The other thing I need to caution you about is the possibility of Rover finding a favorite spot in the house to go. If you take him out several times but he doesn't eliminate, you can bet he's got a place in the house he likes to go. When you find the spot, barricade it any way you can and start the housetraining process from scratch. Getting Rover completely housetrained could take a while, so muster your patience, and think of the years you have to look forward to.

PERSONALITY. Every Yorkie I know has more guts than brains. Now don't get insulted. I mean that in a loving way. My sister, Bobbie, has four of these wee ones. The smallest of the bunch is a little lady named Wicket. She weighs a walloping two and a half to three pounds. Wicket runs outside every morning and takes on the Rottweilers to her north and the Labradors to her south. If one of these large dogs were somehow to get into Bobbie's backyard, I have no doubt Wicket would stand her ground. With as much bravado as this dog has, I suspect the larger dog would back off. (Wicket doesn't have to know that the large dog would go away snickering.) Yorkies are very affectionate and love to be carried, but they also love rough-and-tumble outdoor play.

If you notice that Rover has alerted to a sound, pay attention: You may have mice. Before you call the exterminator, give Rover a chance to do his thing. He may rid your house of these pesky rodents without costing you a cent. Yorkies love to be a working part of the family, so let him do what he does best. If you don't have mice, that's okay; bugs will do. Rover will also take over your front door if you let him. He'll bark like mad when the doorbell rings, and really appreciates your opening the door for him. Believe me, Rover would give his eyeteeth if he could open the door himself. Occasionally, you'll notice he seems to be a little suspicious of a stranger. Let him meet this Human at his own pace and in his own way. If you push him or say "It's okay, it's okay," he'll never have anything to do with that person.

One of the neat personality traits of Yorkies is that they really, really, really don't want to be dominant. You can make every body language mistake and peck order mistake and your Yorkie will not take advantage. Even amongst themselves, they say, "You be dominant. I don't wanna be boss, you be boss. Go ahead, go through the door first, I don't wanna go through the door first."

Because of Yorkies' tiny size, I don't recommend them with young children, unless the children are very gentle and loving.

TRAINING. Whether you teach Rover structured obedience or not is entirely up to you. Remember, this dog loves to be a working part of the family. You might want to teach him things that apply around the house. Identify his toys and ask that he bring you one. Teach him to put his toys away. Her Highness helps Linda take the cloth diapers out of the dryer. She takes a diaper out of the dryer, runs down the hall and into the nursery, and puts it in the rocking chair.

BEST ENVIRONMENT: Jogger—**Walker**—Teenagers—**Children 6 to 11**—Children of any age—**Elderly**—Latchkey—**Active environment**—**Sedate environment**—**Multiple dogs okay**—**Apartment**—House with yard—Room to run—Needs daily exercise—Camping—Hiking

---

Index

English Setter *(continued)*
  personality, 175–76
  training, 176
entertainment and digging, 74
eye contact (significant) as power
    play, 37

face, position of as power play, 37
feces (pica), eating, 78–79
feeding, responsibility for, 9
fence jumping, 69–71
fighting
  and multiple dogs, 44–46
  when handled, 79–80
fleas and buttermilk, 88
food, guarding, 81–82
Fox Terrier, 176–78
  best environment, 178
  bred to do, 176
  housetraining, 176
  personality, 176–77
  training, 177–78
front door, in charge of, 75
frustration
  and barking, 67
  and digging, 74
furniture climbing as power play,
    37

German Shepherd, 178–81
  best environment, 181
  bred to do, 178
  housetraining, 178
  personality, 178–80
  and protectiveness, 40
  training, 180
German Shorthaired Pointer, 181–
    82
  best environment, 182
  bred to do, 181

housetraining, 181
personality, 181–82
and protectiveness, 39
training, 182
Giant Schnauzer, 182–84
  best environment, 184
  bred to do, 182
  housetraining, 182–83
  personality, 183
  training, 183–84
girlfriend, introducing dog to, 81
"Give it/Drop it," 11
"Go lie down," 53–55
Golden Retriever, 184–87
  best environment, 187
  bred to do, 184
  housetraining, 184
  personality, 184–86
  and playtime, 23
  training, 186–87
Golden Setter, 187–88
  best environment, 188
  bred to do, 187
  housetraining, 187
  personality, 187–88
  and playtime, 23
  training, 188
"Good"/"Bad," 2
Great Dane (black), 188–89, 191–
    92
  best environment, 192
  bred to do, 188
  housetraining, 191
  in general, 188–89
  personality, 191
  training, 192
Great Dane (blue), 188–89, 194
  best environment, 194
  bred to do, 188
  housetraining, 194

string bones, 24–25
submissiveness. *See* peck order
summer and dogs, 92
survival mechanism and barking, 66

tasting blood and killing, 89
terriers. *See* American Bull
      Terrier; American
      Staffordshire Terrier;
      Bedlington Terrier; Boston
      Terrier; Fox Terrier; Jack
      Russell Terrier; Scottish
      Terrier; Welsh Terrier; West
      Highland White Terrier;
      Yorkshire Terrier
territoriality and barking, 67
territory marking, 76–78
"Thank you," 11–12
things to keep in mind, 93–94
tone of voice, 31–33
   helpful hint, 91
Toy Poodle, 8, 261–62
   best environment, 262
   bred to do, 261
   housetraining, 261
   personality, 261–62
   training, 262
   See also Standard Poodle
toys
   chasing and being chased, 15–
      16, 23–24
   fetching a ball, 23
   objects held to the ground,
      24
   plastic milk containers, 24
   string bones, 24–25
   tieing to clotheslines, 25
   wadded newspaper balls,
      18

training. *See under* specific
      breed
training collar, choice of,
      49– 50

urine
   and lawns, 89
   rubbing nose in, 5

Vizsla, 262–64
   best environment, 264
   bred to do, 262
   housetraining, 262
   personality, 263
   training, 264

Weimaraner, 264–65
   best environment, 265
   bred to do, 264
   housetraining, 264
   personality, 264–65
   training, 265
Welsh Corgi, 266–67
   best environment, 267
   bred to do, 266
   housetraining, 266
   personality, 266–67
   training, 267
Welsh Terrier, 267–68
   best environment, 268
   bred to do, 267
   housetraining, 267
   personality, 267–68
   training, 268
West Highland White
      Terrier (Westie),
      269–70
   best environment, 270
   bred to do, 269
   housetraining, 269